EDUCATING IN FAITH

MAPS AND VISIONS

Mary C. Boys

1817

Harper & Row, Publishers, San Francisco

New York, Cambridge, Philadelphia, St. Louis
London, Singapore, Sydney, Tokyo

EDUCATING IN FAITH: *Maps and Visions.* Copyright © 1989 by Mary C. Boys. All rights reserved. Printed in the United States of America. No part of this book may be used or reproduced in any manner whatsoever without written permission except in the case of brief quotations embodied in critical articles and reviews. For information address Harper & Row, Publishers, Inc., 10 East 53rd Street, New York, NY 10022. Published simultaneously in Canada by Fitzhenry and Whiteside, Limited, Toronto.
FIRST EDITION

Library of Congress Cataloging-in-Publication Data

Boys, Mary C.
    Educating in faith.

    Includes bibliographies.
    1. Christian education.   I. Title.
BV1471.2.B68 1989   268   88-45667
ISBN 0-06-061037-9

89 90 91 92 93 HAD 10 9 8 7 6 5 4 3 2 1

To all women pioneers

Contents

Acknowledgments

Every mode of knowing is also a mode of waiting—of hoping and expectancy. . . . All who have tried their hand at creative writing, or the arts, or even speaking something other than the tired talk of gossip are aware of the importance, and the risk, of waiting. The pause is important in speech, the incubation period in creative work. A body full of jumbled and partial ideas, formless intuitions, and vague inarticulate feelings often requires changed focus, perhaps even sleep, before form emerges or takes over. Hard work and preparation are insufficient. Bringing previous structures and forms under question, stumbling around in the muck and mire of problems, filling the head with sensations and data are necessary. . . . If hope gives way to despair or is prohibited by time pressures, the formless is filled with premature form, accompanied by nagging doubt and dissatisfaction. The various modes of knowing are grounded in the possibility of a different future. . . . They are grounded in and depend upon hope.[1]

Writing, as Dwayne Huebner recognizes, is an act of hope and expectancy. It is also a solitary experience. Yet a writer depends on relationships for sustenance and encouragement. For those relationships I am grateful.

This book originated from an exchange during a graduate course six years ago. By way of constructing a synthesis for the final class, I had roughed out a primitive map of the field of religious education. One student commented that she found the map helpful and wondered why I hadn't used it from the beginning. "Because I hadn't thought of it yet," I replied. And so a book was born.

I am profoundly indebted to the graduate students whom I have taught at Boston College. Their comments, questions, and commitments have shaped my thinking. Their friendships have nurtured me personally and professionally.

I acknowledge with gratitude colleagues and friends who have read portions of the manuscript: Carol J. Allen, Ronald C. Chochol, Kathleen R. Fischer, Margaret Gorman, Thomas H. Groome, H. John McDargh, Padraic O'Hare, and Fayette Breaux Veverka. The members of the Association of Professors and Researchers in Religious Education (APRRE) have consistently helped to refine my ideas; in particular, I thank those APRRE colleagues who have commented on my papers and offered suggestions during our annual conventions.

Family and friends exercised much patience during my preoccupation with this project. I thank my family for help with my initial foray into the world of computer technology; this book was the first of many projects on that computer. The Archdiocese of Seattle, through the kindness of Edward Schau, provided an office for me during a six-month stint in 1984. Faculty grants from Boston College have offset some of the costs of this project.

Robert A. Dolci, whom I knew to be "master of the chart" from his graduate-student days at Boston College, drafted some of the charts. Maureen O'Brien, a doctoral candidate at Boston College, gave invaluable assistance in research and production.

Finally, I wish to single out three friends, members of my Congregation, the Sisters of the Holy Names: Linda Riggers, Director of Ministry in our Washington Province, whose interest in this project facilitated my research; Sheila McEvoy, whose generous and steady support energized my work; and Barbara O'Connor King, whose skill as editor and writing coach brought hope even when writing was difficult.

Mary C. Boys, S.N.J.M.
4 November 1987

NOTES

1. Dwayne E. Huebner, "Spirituality and Knowing," in Elliot Eisner, ed., *Learning and Teaching the Ways of Knowing* (Chicago: University of Chicago Press, 1985), 171–72.

Introduction

Once, while musing on my role as a teacher, I reflected on images related to the theme of journey. Numerous images came to my consciousness: guide, explorer, pilgrim—to name a few. None, however, seemed as fitting as *pioneer*.

Perusal of the *Oxford English Dictionary* confirmed my intuition: "pioneer" had its origins as a military term, referring to one of a contingent of foot soldiers who marched either with or ahead of an army or regiment so as to dig trenches, repair roads, and perform other labors necessary for the main body. Its figurative meaning—one who goes before to prepare or open up the way for others to follow—seemed to gain new depth when linked with its etymological ancestor: pioneering consists largely in the painstaking labor of breaking new ground so that others might have access. Teaching, then, is pioneering indeed.

It is as a teacher that I write this book. I write to give order and meaning to what I have learned while pioneering and to invite readers to frontiers of their own making by walking some freshly cleared paths. If, as one wag has suggested, "the best teacher is the one who gives an exhibition of an ignorant person thinking," then my role as teacher-pioneer is to make clear what I've seen on my preliminary forays and why I've chosen to break ground at particular junctures.

Pioneering, insofar as it also entails scouting, may well include *mapmaking*. In fact, in this book cartography dominates the pioneer's task. The initial section consists of a "map" of the field of religious education. The outlook provided by that map shapes the "vision" proposed in the second major section. Thus, a word on maps is appropriate.

A map is "a form of symbolization with a special utility for encoding and transmitting human knowledge of the environment," a graphic symbolization of one's milieu.[1] Though its origins are lost, historians find the earliest direct evidence of mapmaking in the third millennium B.C.E., where maps were drawn on clay tablets during the reign of Sargon of Akkad in what is now northern Iraq. From this sort of primitive outline to the highly sophisticated maps of our technological age, men and women have used maps to chart their knowledge.

Maps may be used both by natives of a given place and by newcomers to it. Since I write this book for any who are interested in religious education—including but not limited to professionals in the field—I hope that both those with extensive knowledge of the subject and those with lesser acquaintance will gain perspective. Presumably those with greater familiarity with the territory of religious education will wish to pore over the detail, while those making an initial foray may choose to situate themselves by simply taking note of the most important landmarks as indicated by categories, charts, and topical headings.

All theory, as Michael Polanyi reminds us, "is a kind of map extended over space and time."[2] Thus, I am using the metaphor of map to present a particular way of thinking about a fascinating and complex endeavor, educating religiously. I have sought to sketch this map in a way that is sufficiently *inclusive,* since religious education is an interplay of so many factors; properly *historical,* so as to provide an appropriate context for understanding; and simultaneously *analytical* and *imaginative,* so as to show relationships among theorists and movements in a way that stimulates fresh visions. Readers, therefore, can anticipate clarification, perspective, and coherence from the map—qualities all too often absent from discussion of religious education.

However useful maps are, they remain theoretical constructs, a means of conceptualizing the territory rather than the territory itself. Consequently, the map metaphor suggests that the way matters are construed herein is not necessarily the way things are. Reality is always socially constructed. Although we in North America are accustomed to seeing ourselves as front and center on most maps of the world, this is only one mode of charting the world. A favorite illustration of this is a map given to me by a student from New Zealand. His map puts Australia and New Zealand "on top" and relegates North Americans to "down under." Moreover, even a map's accuracy may be inadequate, as any who have taken a map in hand to make their way through Boston realize while wandering for miles on arterials "uncluttered" by any street signs. Descriptions may not always match realities.

In short, one's reading of a map is always shaped by standpoint, that is, by such factors as one's point of departure, mode of travel, and destination. Similarly, my map of the field is shaped by my particular standpoint: certain assumptions, experiences, limitations, convictions, and hopes undergird my study. My map is sketched by a post–Vatican II Catholic of middle-class origins who has lived virtually all of her life in the United States in large cities of both the Pacific Northwest and the Northeast. It is a map constructed by one who sees reality through the critical lens of feminism. It is a map designed by one whose profession has always involved teaching and who is by vocation explicitly committed to educating in faith for the full development of the person.

This identification of standpoint raises a crucial educational issue. How do I, the teacher-pioneer, lay out my map without imposing it on others, especially on those whose standpoints may differ sharply from mine? How do I develop analytical frameworks that function heuristically rather than as rigidly constructed categories? Such questions suggest that I attend to two interrelated tasks. The first demands that I be a cartographer, presenting with as much clarity as possible the field of religious education. Thus I propose a detailed map of the field, establishing its coordinates in the first chapter and detailing the layout in chapters 2 through 6. The second requires that I teach the art of cartography, presenting my own view in such a way that readers will see ways of making their own maps. While I attempt to do this throughout, I turn particularly to this teaching task in the final two chapters. In chapters 7 and 8, I take up explicitly the factors I believe are crucial for thinking about religious education.

A last word, before turning directly to the map. I initially had hopes of more extensive reference to the literature of other countries, but limitations of experience and point of reference have restricted my survey largely to the North American landscape. Yet I do sense that global awareness begins with the recognition of one's own roots. I also would have liked to study Jewish religious education, but was constrained by the relative newness of that subject as a distinct field and by the need to use space carefully, with a certain measure of homogeneity, in an already lengthy book. I hope, however, that this volume will enhance the depth of interreligious exchange in the field of religious education by clarifying Christian approaches.

NOTES

1. Cited in John Noble Wilford, *The Mapmakers* (New York: Knopf, 1981), 13.
2. Michael Polanyi, *Personal Knowledge: Towards a Post-Critical Philosophy* (New York: Harper & Row, Torchbooks, 1964), 4.

Part One

MAPMAKING

CHAPTER 1

Creating a Guidebook for Exploring: Foundational Questions and Classic Expressions

Wherever men and women have gathered to tell stories and enact rituals in response to the mystery of life, whenever they have searched for truth and sought to do what is good, religious education has been happening. Whether congregated around the fire in a cave, around the dinner table, or in the town square, people have passed on their traditions of faith.

On occasion, their handing on of these traditions has been systematic and didactic. More typically, their "instruction" has been evocative and informal, often mediated through music, poetry, dance, and drama. When people participated in medieval mystery plays or gazed around their magnificent cathedrals at statues and stained glass windows, they deepened their understanding of faith—albeit without an explicit awareness.

If, in our age, religious education is coming into its own as a distinct field, it is important not to lose sight that educating in ways of faith has always concerned humankind. If the twentieth century has accumulated an extensive body of literature about this "discipline in search of an identity," it is essential not to lose a sense of indebtedness to the contribution of our ancestors in faith.[1] Most of them were illiterate and certainly unschooled by the standards of our technological society. But with their keen sensitivity to paradox and mystery and with their profound awareness of finiteness, many possessed a sensitivity we might justly envy as a prerequisite for religious education.

Nonetheless, an awareness of this larger perspective does not alone suffice. Intensified efforts in recent years to clarify the dimensions of religious education indicate a healthy self-awareness. Particularly in the twentieth century, when knowledge has proliferated to an unprecedented degree and the disciplines have been subdivided into various fields, attentiveness to methodological issues is a significant vital sign. This means not just asking, "How shall we convey God's revelation?" but "What does it mean to educate in faith?" The former question invites reductionism—religious education as a means of transmission—but the latter, which is the generating inquiry of this book, educes exploration of profound issues.

DEVELOPING CATEGORIES FOR ANALYSIS

In the genesis of religious education as a distinct field (usually dated from the founding of the Religious Education Association in 1903), a number of important books by such leaders as George Albert Coe, Sophia Lyon Fahs, H. Shelton Smith, Josef Jungmann, and Johannes Hofinger established the agenda to which a later generation of theorists has contributed. In part, my task is to describe what these theorists have proposed and thereby to sketch the contours of the field.

My concern for methodology has spawned another sort of effort: developing analytical categories for surveying the field. I think of such efforts as the sixfold typology developed by Jack L. Seymour,[2] John Elias's ordering of current theorists according to their predominant audience (public, academy, or church);[3] and especially of Harold Burgess's 1975 compendium, *An Invitation to Religious Education,* an inclusive review of the literature.[4] Since his efforts most clearly parallel my attempt to provide a map of the field, a summary of his work is necessary.

Burgess compared and contrasted major schools of thought with respect to the fundamental constructs, definitions, and propositions in their respective theories of religious education. Accordingly, in his "descriptive analytical study," he generated six fundamental categories: the aim of religious education, including goals, purposes, and objectives; the content; the role of the teacher; the role of the student; the effect of the environment; and the means of evaluation. These categories were the lens through which he viewed four models that have dominated the twentieth century. Burgess names these as the "traditional theological," the "social-cultural," the "contemporary theological," and the "social science" models. Burgess has in effect constructed a matrix in which the four schools of thought are analyzed by graphing their position in each of the six categories.

In certain respects, Burgess's work is similar to what I hope to achieve in this first section. He provides readers with a way of making their way through the maze of disparate ideas by means of applying analytical categories. His work illustrates, as I intend mine to do, that "thinking is a struggle for order and at the same time for comprehensiveness."[5]

Yet my map will appear quite different from Burgess's typology because I have found other categories more illuminating and a different division of schools of thought more representative of the history of the field. My construct, also outlined in matrix form (figure 1), basically consists of the following:

- foundational questions
- classic expressions
- contemporary modifications of the classic expressions.

The remainder of this chapter will center on the foundational questions, chapters 2 through 5 on the classic expressions, and chapter 6 on their modifications. But perhaps a few brief comments here on the entire panorama—a sort of "fly-over" of the territory—will suggest to readers what view my logic affords.

My construct evolved from two thoughts that permeated my attempts to teach the literature of twentieth-century religious education. The first was the importance of history as the crucial context for interpretation. The first half of the twentieth century witnessed radically different rhythms in Protestantism and Catholicism. Thus, for instance, to include Catholics such as Josef Jungmann and Johannes Hofinger with Protestant evangelicals such as Frank Gaebelin and Lois LeBar under the rubric of "traditional theological approach," as does Burgess, seriously obscures the dynamic of history as a context for theology.[6] Therefore, my schools of thought—what I have termed "classic expressions"— needed to be historically situated. Moreover, I wanted to differentiate between their early development and the variations spawned in more recent years (especially from the late 1960s), hence, "contemporary modifications."

The second persistent notion revolved around certain questions that seemed to appear in differing guises and with varying degrees of explicitness and intensity but nonetheless surfaced (even if only implicitly) in all the major schools of thought. These "foundational questions," each of which encompasses numerous other questions, seemed to me to constitute the most appropriately inclusive categories for analysis of each classic expression. They are the telescope, so to speak, through which I have surveyed the territory. The foundational questions constitute a matrix for analysis of the history.

As I see it, there are two foundational questions: What does it mean to be religious? What does it mean to educate in faith, to educate persons to the religious dimensions of life? For the sake of symmetry, I have identified five component questions within the two larger questions.

WHAT DOES IT MEAN TO BE RELIGIOUS?

"Religion" is a notoriously difficult term to define and it is no less elusive in its adjectival form. Yet use of the latter at least takes note of Wilfred Cantwell Smith's important caution that one has fundamentally to deal not with *religions* themselves, but with *religious persons*.[7] Thus, the heart of this inquiry is discerning what the theorists in the various major approaches understood themselves to be doing when they sought to form persons as religious beings, that is, to lead people both to a deepened faith and to a more adequate comprehension of it.

Specifically, I have inferred five questions in pursuing the history of modern religious education. I list each below, amplifying it with specific questions illustrating the dimensions of the issue.

HOW IS GOD REVEALED?

Wherein lies the fundamental locus of God's revelation? In Scripture? In Tradition? In experience? What is the significance of worship and prayer? Who is the God who reveals? What is the anthropology underlying the image of God?

WHAT DOES IT MEAN TO BE CONVERTED?

Is one transformed for life at a given moment, or does conversion unfold gradually over one's lifetime? Is education to be directed toward conversion? To what extent does conversion have a psychological component, and how much importance is to be given to psychology? How central is conversion in a theory of religious education?

WHAT IS FAITH? BELIEF? HOW ARE FAITH AND BELIEF RELATED?

The distinction between faith, as one's primary apprehension of the sacred, and belief, as one's secondary articulation of it, is frequently made today. But whether or not they have made explicit this distinction, how have religious educators seemed to understand their work of forming people in faith and of developing cognitive understandings? How important is assent to a creed? How important is cognition? How significant is the affective dimension of one's faith?

WHAT IS THE ROLE OF THEOLOGY?

Just as faith and belief may be separated for the sake of analysis, so too may religion and theology. How is theology understood in each theory of religious education, and how important is it in the theory? What importance is given to the intellectual life?

WHAT IS THE RELATION OF RELIGION TO CULTURE?

Here the categories of H. Richard Niebuhr's classic, *Christ and Culture*, are extremely useful.[8] Does one's commitment of faith lead to any of the following positions: An uncompromising countercultural stance? An acquiescent position, receptive to the categories and claims of one's milieu and desirous of making one's faith "relevant" above all else? A dualistic position, in which one acknowledges the essentially corrupt nature of humankind, yet recognizes both one's "caughtness" in it and God's sustaining grace? A synthetic position, in which one sees God's rule established in the nature of things and so attempts to reconcile divine and human into one system? A transformist position, in which one seeks to change the world in accord with the values of one's faith?

The complexity of these questions obviously precludes simple solutions; each could well lead to a lifetime of study. Their value lies in their heuristic quality: they function as leading questions so that we might discern in each of the classic expressions different ways of understanding what it means to be religious.

WHAT DOES IT MEAN TO EDUCATE IN FAITH?

Education, not unlike religion, is a widely used term that varies in meaning. Again, by listing some of the questions contained within the larger question, the analytical framework becomes clearer.

TO WHAT PURPOSES DOES ONE EDUCATE ANOTHER (OR ONESELF)?

What constitutes an educated person? Why does one educate in (or for) faith—why not simply be with another person in faith? What is encompassed by the term "education"?

WHAT DOES IT MEAN TO KNOW? TO LEARN?

How is knowing more than comprehending information? What is the role of ritual, story, and symbol? Can one always articulate or measure what has been learned? What is the relation between knowledge and know-how?

WHAT IS THE ROLE OF THE SOCIAL SCIENCES IN RELIGIOUS EDUCATION?

How much emphasis should be given to psychology, anthropology, and sociology in developing a theory of religious education? Within each, which field is stressed (e.g., developmental [either structural or psycho-social] psychology, psychoanalytic psychology, social psychology, psychology of learning) and which theorists are adhered to? How important is social science in relation to theology?

HOW SHALL WE THINK OF CURRICULUM AND TEACHING?

What might a curriculum developed from one of the classic expressions look like? What is the teacher's role, and how significant is teaching for religious education? What theories of curriculum and teaching undergird a particular theory?

IN WHAT WAY IS EDUCATION A POLITICAL ACTIVITY?

Toward what view of society is a theory of religious education oriented, either explicitly or implicitly? Can one find a "hidden" curriculum—those values conveyed by structures and procedures? Can one identify the components of a "null" curriculum—what is taught by virtue of not being taught?[9]

These ten questions (and their subquestions) constitute the analytical categories for the classic expressions. The matrix in figure 1 provides a guide.

At this juncture, the framework is abstract; its usefulness will be revealed in the following chapters. Not all of the questions are equally applicable to each classic expression, but they serve to delineate the basic thrust of the inquiry. Also, I must stress that these are questions I have *inferred* from the material, not the questions every theorist or movement confronted directly nor the questions readers might necessarily deduce from the history. They function "below the surface" of the historical narrative and will become most apparent in the summary of each of the classic expressions. The classic expressions might be thought of as the surface topography and the foundational questions a means of in-depth stratigraphy.

THE CLASSIC EXPRESSIONS

Having clarified my understanding of "foundational questions," I turn now to my definition of "classic expression." Simply put, by "classic expression" I mean *a specific, historical manifestation of educating in faith that has resulted from the intersection of a particular theological perspective with a particular educational outlook.* In other words, my interest lies in identifying varying standpoints that have developed out of a combination of theological and educational understandings.

As I have struggled to provide some order to various ways Christians of the twentieth century (particularly in North America) have educated in faith, I have delineated four "classic" ways—four quite different approaches that not only originated in a given historical context but that continue today in modified form. Indeed, I see them as ways continuing to set the agenda for the present. That is not to say, however, that new dimensions and directions have not emerged. It is to claim that much of what our ancestors in the field have wrestled with still makes a claim on us today.

One difficult decision centered on the most appropriate name for each classic expression. There is as yet no unanimity in the field as to terminology. Thus, I was left with the task of specifying as clearly as possible what I meant while at the same time warning that the categories are not carved in stone. The attempt for precision may be misleading, since actual usage is far more muddled.

An especially troublesome dilemma in regard to clarity in terminology revolves around the term "religious education." As I develop in detail in chapter 3, *religious education* names a classic expression that represents the wedding of liberal theology and progressive education. Yet, only

Figure 1

A Matrix for Analysis of the
Classic Expressions of Religious Education

THE FOUNDATIONAL QUESTIONS	THE CLASSIC EXPRESSIONS			
What Does It Mean to Be Religious?	EVANGELISM	RELIGIOUS EDUCATION	CHRISTIAN EDUCATION	CATHOLIC EDUCATION
REVELATION How is God revealed? Significance of worship?				
CONVERSION What constitutes the experience of conversion? Role of psychology?				
FAITH & BELIEF What is faith? How important is assent to a creed?				
THEOLOGY Significance in religious education?				
FAITH & CULTURE How does faith situate the person in the world?				
What Does It Mean to Educate in Faith?				
GOAL OF EDUCATION Why educate in faith? What constitutes an educated person?				

THE FOUNDATIONAL QUESTIONS	THE CLASSIC EXPRESSIONS			
What Does It Mean to Educate in Faith?	EVANGELISM	RELIGIOUS EDUCATION	CHRISTIAN EDUCATION	CATHOLIC EDUCATION
KNOWLEDGE What does it mean to know? What is the relation between knowing & doing?				
SOCIAL SCIENCES How formative a role should the social sciences play? Which ones are most influential?				
CURRICULUM & TEACHING What does the curriculum look like? How is teaching understood?				
EDUCATION AS A POLITICAL TERM Toward what view of society is one educating?				

partly related to its historical referent, it also denotes a synonym for "educating in faith." To keep the two usages distinct, I have chosen to italicize *religious education* whenever I refer to it as a classic expression; otherwise, it simply reflects a term I find an especially appropriate way of talking about educating in faith. For the sake of consistency, I have italicized each of the other three classic expressions: *evangelism, Christian education,* and *Catholic education—catechetics (catechesis).*

CLARIFICATIONS

Two other methodological clarifications are important. The first concerns my commitment to inclusive language, that is, language that includes both male and female. To decide to write inclusively is a relatively easy decision for oneself; the difficulty comes in citing the words of others, most especially those who wrote or spoke in an era when such an awareness had not yet dawned. Anachronism is not scholarly. Yet I am acutely conscious of how alienating it is to read continually about "men," "he," and "his" when the writer is not referring simply to one gender. Thus, I have inserted in brackets the "partner" term, e.g., "God's revelation is made known to all men [women]." While this is occasionally distracting, particularly in citations with numerous exclusive nouns and pronouns, its very awkwardness serves to highlight the way women have remained invisible.

Since few of these quotations will be read aloud, I do not think that the resulting awkwardness will prove troublesome. More difficult, however, is the problem of whether or not the author truly intended to use "man," for instance, generically. As Susan Moller Okin has demonstrated in her study *Women in Western Political Thought,* certain philosophers have used what we would term a "generic" referent (e.g., the Greek *anthropos,* which can be translated "human being") when in reality they have simply meant males. Even words such as "person," "human," and "rational being" do not necessarily include women:

This phenomenon, made possible by the ambiguity of our language, is not confined to political philosophy. The grand statements of our political culture, too, such as the Declaration of Independence and the Constitution, are phrased in universal terms, but . . . they have frequently been interpreted in such a way as to exclude women. Thus, when the Founding Fathers declared it to be a self-evident truth that "all men are created equal," not only did they intend the substantial slave population to be excluded from the scope of their statement, but they would have been amused and skeptical (as indeed John Adams was to his wife's appeal that they should not forget the ladies) at the suggestion that women were, and should be considered, equal too.[10]

Thus, one should not always presume that the author was in fact speaking inclusively even when employing "generic" terms. Perhaps my insertions will serve to remind us all of women's invisibility when "reality" is being described.

A second methodological note concerns the appropriate format for a particular audience. I wrote my first book *Biblical Interpretation in Religious Education* for a more specialized audience, largely graduate students and professors. While I believe such writing contributes to the development of a field, I am mindful of its limited readership and, hence, relatively limited impact. In this book I have consciously attempted to write for a more general readership and have resisted the temptation to document every idea or trace every circuitous detail—though undoubtedly many will find herein more than they had in mind. Accordingly, I have made notations only of direct quotations or heavy dependence on a source and have not written the sort of discursive footnotes the academic in me favors. But since mine is a discipline full of such lively controversies, I have attempted also to write for my colleagues by appending a bibliographic essay to each chapter, so that they will be able to follow more closely the works and people that have shaped my thinking.

NOTES

1. See Berard Marthaler, "A Discipline in Quest of an Identity: Religious Education," *Horizons* 3 (1976):203–15.
2. Jack L. Seymour, "Contemporary Approaches to Christian Education," *Chicago Theological Seminary Bulletin* 69 (1979):1–10.
3. John Elias, "The Three Publics of Religious Education," *Religious Education* 77 (1983):615–27.
4. Harold Burgess, *An Invitation to Religious Education* (Mishawaka, IN: Religious Education Press, 1975).
5. Charles Wright Mills, *The Sociological Imagination* (New York: Oxford University Press, 1959), 223.
6. Burgess, *Invitation to Religious Education,* 21–58.
7. Wilfred Cantwell Smith, *The Meaning and End of Religion* (San Francisco: Harper & Row, 1978), 153.
8. H. Richard Niebuhr, *Christ and Culture* (New York: Harper & Row, 1951).
9. See Elliot W. Eisner, *The Educational Imagination: On the Design and Evaluation of School Programs* (New York: Macmillan, 1979 [2d rev. ed., 1985]), 97–107.
10. Susan Moller Okin, *Women in Western Political Thought* (Princeton, NJ: Princeton University Press, 1979), 6.

CHAPTER 2

Surveying the Territory: Evangelism

Of the classic approaches that have shaped contemporary religious education, *evangelism* stands out as the most difficult to define with precision. Moreover, the task of tracing its paths with any degree of accuracy requires a point of departure earlier than that for the other expressions—a consideration suggesting both its formative power and the reason for its placement as the first of the four classic expressions.

EVANGELISM DEFINED AND SUBDIVIDED

Perhaps a broad, working definition will best reveal the full range of *evangelism:* preaching or teaching the Scriptures in such a way as to arouse conversion. More specifically, revivalism and evangelicalism constitute the two closely linked manifestations of *evangelism.* In a way, of course, mention of those manifestations only compounds the problem of definition, since revivalism by its nature defies discursive analysis and evangelicalism remains a notoriously imprecise referent. But even if exactness is elusive, the umbrella term *evangelism* deserves close attention because its dynamics have established much of the agenda of religious education in the twentieth century. And that careful scrutiny must proceed from its historical context, since *evangelism* is deeply rooted in the American experience and cannot be understood apart from its connection with this "redeemer nation."[1]

REVIVALISM

Historian Jay Dolan describes a revival as an event gathering "into one powerful showing all the warning of Divine Justice," an experience intended to "startle, to terrify, and to rouse the consciences of the people."[2] Such a means of moving sinners to repentance appears to have been a quintessential part of the American landscape from colonial days.

Indeed, revivals appear to have been the leading edge of larger cultural "awakenings," periods of revitalization developing out of crises of beliefs and values.

The revivals accompanying the First Great Awakening (1730–1760) heralded the development of evangelism. With the revivals came a new definition of the religious person, a definition placing less stress on orthodoxy and more on the affections. Jonathan Edwards expressed this well: "Our people do not so much need to have their heads stored as to have their hearts touched."[3] Thus itinerant preachers—among whom Edwards, Gilbert Tennent, George Whitefield, and Theodore Freylinghuysen stand as giants—exhorted their hearers to a conversion of the affections. Aiming to preach a "felt Christ," they sought a change of heart rather than a change of opinion. Their sermons contrasted sharply with the smooth words of "velvet-mouthed and downy D.D.'s"; instead, they made detailed drawings of the vicissitudes of the sinner and of the terrors of hell. As "pulpit artists," the revivalists worked over their words in order to change the hearts of their hearers; these revivalists were a vivid contrast to those whom George Whitefield accused of preaching about "an unknown, unfelt Christ. The reason why congregations have been so dead is because they had dead men [women] preaching to them."[4]

The theology of Edwards's famous sermon of 1741, "Sinners in the Hands of an Angry God," now seems unbelievably harsh, but few since Edwards have so eloquently painted word pictures.[5] God's word, as mediated by these powerful preachers, broke, crushed, stormed, shattered, and cracked stony hearts. When Tennent preached, members of the congregation wept, sobbed, cried out in terror, sank to their knees, and called out for salvation. Apparently Tennent's younger brothers William and John sank into comas as a result of his preaching. William was even pronounced dead by a physician and prepared for burial before he awakened and reported on the indescribable beauty of his experience of conversion.[6] Clearly, the new style of preaching fostered a religion of the heart.

Among this generation of preachers for whom a revival was a "surprising work of God," no systematic theory of religious education was clearly outlined. Nevertheless, in probing further by means of the foundational questions, an implicit understanding of religious education develops.

THE CENTRALITY OF CONVERSION IN THE REVIVALS

Conversion served as a leitmotif of the revivalists' ministry, and its centrality suggests the importance of clarifying its usage in the revivalist experience. There is a glimpse in the diary of Isaac Backus, who, after his conversion in 1741, became one of the leading Baptists of New England. Backus recounted that several weeks earlier, a revival had swept through his town, but he had not been moved to conversion. This lack of response greatly troubled him. Backus continued:

On August 24, 1741, . . . I was mowing the field alone. . . . It appeared clear to me that I had tried every way that possibly I could [for salvation] and if I perished forever I could do no more—and the justice of God shined so clear before my eyes in condemning such a guilty Rebel that I could say no more—but fell at his feet. I saw that I was in his hands and he had a right to do with me just as he pleased. And I lay like a dead, vile creature before him. . . . And just in that critical moment, God, who caused the light to shine out of darkness—shined into my heart with such a discovery of that glorious righteousness which fully satisfied the law that I had broke, and of the infinite fullness that there is in Christ to satisfie the wants of such a helpless creature as I was that my whole heart was attracted and drawn after God and swallowed up in admiration in view of his divine glories.[7]

Backus's account, with its imagery of darkness and light, death and glory, misery and joy, evokes the affectional and intensely personal conversion engendered by revivalist preaching. Whereas before he had been weighed down with guilt, overcome with the "plague of my heart and the fountain of corruption that was there," God's grace in Christ had now liberated Backus: "And now my Burden (that was so dreadful heavey before) was gone: that tormenting fear that I had was taken away, and I felt a sweet peace and rejoicing in my soul."[8]

Remarkably similar imagery was used a century later by Amanda Berry Smith (1837–1915) to describe her conversion. Smith, who ultimately became the most famous black female evangelist of the nineteenth century and who evangelized in Britain, Africa, and India as well as in the "holiness" camp meetings of the South, wrote in her autobiography about her conversion at the age of nineteen:

O, what a conflict. How the darkness seemed to gather around me, and in my desperation I looked up and said, "O Lord, I have come down here to die, and I must have salvation this afternoon or death. If you send me to hell I will go but convert my soul." Then I looked up and said, "O Lord, if thou wilt only please to help me if ever I backslide don't ever let me see thy face in peace." And I waited. . . . Then in my desperation I looked up and said, "O Lord, if Thou wilt help me I will believe Thee," and in the act of telling God I would, I did. O, the peace and joy that flooded my soul! The burden rolled away; I felt it when it left me, and a flood of light and joy swept through my soul such as I had never known before. I said, "Why, Lord, I do believe this is just what I have been asking for," and down came another flood of light and peace. And I said again, "Why, Lord, I do believe this is what I have asked Thee for." Then I sprang to my feet, all around was light, I was new. I looked at my hands, they looked new. I clapped my hands; I ran up out of the cellar, I walked up and down the kitchen floor. Praise the Lord! There seemed to be a halo of light all over me. . . . I went into the dining room; we had a large mirror that went from the floor to the ceiling, and I went and looked in it to see if anything had transpired in my color, because there was something wonderful had taken place inside of me, and it really seemed to me it was outside too.[9]

JONATHAN EDWARDS ON CONVERSION

No more eloquent explanation for the revivalist notion of conversion exists than Jonathan Edwards's *Treatise Concerning Religious Affections* (1746), a volume that anticipated by more than two hundred years the insight that "holiness is wholeness,"[10] and the emphasis now placed on so-called holistic understandings of the person. In arguing that, to a significant extent, true religion consisted in the affections and their power in the inward exercises of the heart, Edwards established the theoretical underpinnings of his itinerant preaching. He asserted that "there never was any considerable change wrought in the mind or conversation of any person by anything of a religious nature, that ever he [she] read, heard or saw, that had not his [her] affections moved":

Never was a natural man [woman] engaged earnestly to seek his [her] salvation; never were any such brought to cry after wisdom, and lift up their voice for understanding, and to wrestle with God in prayer for mercy; and never was one humbled, and brought to the foot of God, from any thing that ever he [she] heard or imagined of his [her] own unworthiness and deserving of God's displeasure; nor was ever one induced to fly for refuge unto Christ, while his [her] heart remained *unaffected*. Nor was there ever a saint awakened out of a cold, lifeless frame, or recovered from a declining state in religion, and brought back from a lamentable departure from God, without having his [her] heart *affected*. And in a word, there never was any thing *considerable* brought to pass in the heart or life of any man [woman] living, by the things of religion, that had not his [her] heart *deeply affected* by those things.[11]

JONATHAN EDWARDS AND EPISTEMOLOGY

Edwards was not unaware that revivalist preaching had been criticized for its enthusiastic spirit. Foremost among the critics was the Boston pastor Charles Chauncy, who scathingly observed in 1743 that "religion, of late, has been *more a Commotion in the Passions,* than a *Change* in the *Temper* of the *Mind.*"[12] In contrast to Chauncy, for whom "the plain Truth is, an *Enlightened Mind,* and not *raised Affections,* ought always to be the Guide,"[13] Edwards refused to foster a dichotomy between cognition and affection. For Edwards, God's grace engendered a new kind of perception, a "spiritual sensation" to be impressed upon the mind, thereby enabling "enlightened understanding": "Holy affections are not heat without light; but evermore arise from some information of the understanding, some spiritual instruction that the mind receives, some light or actual knowledge."[14] Of course, Edwards realized that not all affections arose from "light in the understanding"; affections that had nothing of knowledge or instruction in them were not genuinely spiritual and, therefore, not the basis of true religion.

Edwards's phrase "information of the understanding" offers a clue about his theory of knowing. He distinguished a *notional understanding*—"wherein the mind only beholds things in the exercise of a speculative faculty"—and a spiritual knowledge, a *sense of the heart*—"wherein the mind not only *speculates* and *beholds,* but *relishes* and *feels.*"[15] The former "remains only in the head" and is gained by the natural exercise of human faculties, whereas the latter, revealed by God, embraces the whole person. For Edwards, no speech could be a means of grace unless it conveyed knowledge. When he preached, therefore, Edwards sought to bring knowledge that was spiritual and thereby salvific. His concern was not simply to create a unity of thinking and feeling, but to identify the roots of action as well. As the *Treatise Concerning Religious Affections* makes clear, spiritual understanding not only transcends the rational, it encompasses practice: religious affection is the "spring" of human motives and action. In contrast, "passing affections easily produce words; and words are cheap; and godliness is more easily feigned in words than in actions."[16] Learning the ways of God demands more than correct doctrine: "Hypocrites may much more easily be brought to *talk* like saints, than to *act* like saints."[17] According to Edwards, a person sought knowledge so as to live differently.

JONATHAN EDWARDS ON FAITH AND BELIEF

Clearly, for Edwards, faith was experiential and oriented toward changing a person's entire outlook on life. Beliefs, such as creedal formulas, were relatively unimportant. Theology, however, possessed great significance; as Edwards remarked in his sermon "Christian Knowledge," human nature is such that "no object can come at the heart but through the door of the understanding: and there can be no spiritual knowledge of that of which there is not first a rational knowledge."[18] Moreover, Edwards urged that all people should be concerned with matters of divinity. The "common people" ought not to say, "Let us leave these matters to ministers and divines; let them dispute them out among themselves as they can; they concern not us."[19] Edwards regarded matters of divinity of "infinite importance" to everyone, urging his hearers: "Consider yourselves as scholars or disciples, put into the school of Christ; and therefore be diligent to make proficiency in Christian knowledge."[20] Edwards's exhortation was a way of giving all people access to knowledge of God. As Alan Heimert remarks, in the First Great Awakening God was democratized.[21]

EPISTEMOLOGY AND A DEBATE ABOUT QUALIFICATIONS FOR THE MINISTRY

But not every preacher could work out a theory of knowledge as insightful and as unified as Edwards's. The First Great Awakening witnessed a debate over ministerial qualifications that has yet to be satisfactorily resolved. A 1740 sermon, "The Danger of an Unconverted

Ministry," by Gilbert Tennent catapulted the controversy into public consideration. In excoriating "Pharisee-Teachers, having no experience of a special work of the Holy Ghost," Tennent railed against the ministry of "natural men [women]."[22] They were, in his purview, "blind as moles, and as dead as stones, without any spiritual taste and relish."[23] Tennent's conviction was that experience of God constituted one's primary qualification for ministry. Erudition was of no avail without this prerequisite. Tennent's confrere Solomon Stoddard expressed this belief as follows:

[Ministers must] get the Experience of this Work in their own Hearts. If they have not Experience, they will be but blind Guides, they will be in Great Danger to entertain false Notions concerning a Work of Conversion. . . . Whatever Books men [women] have read, there is a great need of experimental knowledge in a Minister. . . . It is a great calamity to wounded Consciences to be under the Direction of an unexperienced Minister.[24]

In Edwards's holistic theory of knowledge, in his recognition of the power of the affections, and in the learned ministry controversy, one can detect the roots of many concerns central to religious educators in the late twentieth century. No one has more insightfully discerned the heritage bequeathed by the revivalists of the First Great Awakening than historian Douglas Sloan, who calls attention to five tensions that have persisted in the educational realm to the present day.[25]

· The first involves the purpose of education; specifically, the relation between continuity and change: how does one preserve and honor the traditions of knowledge that have accumulated over generations while at the same time remaining open to creative innovation and spontaneous inspiration?
· The second and third questions suggested by Sloan lead to reflection on what it means to know. How does one safeguard the frail hold culture has on ordered and rational knowledge while simultaneously empowering it with vital emotional and aesthetic experience?
· How does one link objective "knowledge about" with personal, subjective "knowledge of?"
· Sloan's fourth and fifth questions involve a person's understanding of education as a political activity. How does one relate and mediate the frequently conflicting claims of immediate, pragmatic social problems and the long-range strategies and goals of a larger social vision?
· How does one uphold standards of excellence and at the same time remain responsive to popular needs, tastes, and demands?

REVIVALS IN THE NINETEENTH CENTURY

The dimensions of these questions became even sharper in the revivals of the nineteenth century, both in the Second and Third Great Awakenings (1800–1830 and 1890–1920, respectively) and in the parish missions of the American Catholic church (1830–1900). Particularly significant were issues revolving around understandings of knowledge, and views concerning the relationship between religion and culture and its correlate, education as a political activity. Before exploring these issues, a preliminary word about theological developments is in order, since revivalism witnessed changing conceptions of God and human nature.

In the classical Calvinist view, a revival directed toward conversion from sin is anomalous: though all people, by virtue of their innate depravity, deserve hell, God has mysteriously predestined some for salvation. Thus, one's pledge of repentance has little meaning because God's will cannot be changed by human action. At best, one's pious living—obedience to God's laws, hard work, self-control, and faithful prayer—manifested God's grace at work in a sinful, evil world.

Because the emphasis placed on God's absolute omnipotence effectively negated human freedom, arguments over determinism dominated the Calvinist theological agenda from its earliest days. Most prominent among its critics was Jacobus Arminius (1560–1609), whose antipredestination arguments, though condemned by the synod of Dort (1618–1619), reappeared with new meaning in nineteenth-century American revivalism, most notably in the preaching of Charles Grandison Finney (1792–1875) and John Wesley (1703–1791).

These "Arminian" tendencies had not been as pronounced among the early generation of revivalists. Edwards's "New Light" or "Consistent Calvinism," for instance, was essentially a revitalization movement stressing spiritual rebirth through the crises of conversion. Edwards's God, though merciful and gracious, was demanding and harsh as befit the depraved creatures whose woefully fallen state deserved condemnation. Yet Edwards and his colleagues, especially Samuel Hopkins, since their preaching suggested that repentance somehow "won" God's mercy, had inadvertently weakened the classical notion of predestination. Proceeding from this already tenuous foundation, certain revivalists in the Second Great Awakening cleared away the remnants of strict Calvinism in their appreciation for human free will, denial of the depravity of children, and less harsh images of God.

CHARLES FINNEY: NINETEENTH-CENTURY REVIVALIST PAR EXCELLENCE

In the Northeast, well-educated preachers such as Timothy Dwight, Lyman Beecher, and Nathaniel Taylor most capably articulated the changing conceptions of Calvinism.

But it was the colorful Finney whose revivals throughout the midwestern United States most graphically testified to the modifications in Calvinist thought. Like Edwards, Finney considered the human heart desperately wicked. Consequently, the minister was called to subdue sinners, stripping them of their excuses, answering their cavils, humbling their pride, and breaking their hearts. Then the revivalist's task was to "pour in the truth, put in the probe, break up the old foundation and

. . . use the word of God like a fire and a hammer."[26] In contrast to his predecessor Edwards, for whom a revival was a "surprising act of God," Finney claimed a more scientific outlook: it was "not a miracle, or dependent on a miracle in any sense." Rather, a revival was "purely a philosophical result of the right use of the constituted means," just as a connection existed between the right use of the means to raise grain and a crop of wheat. Moreover, conversions had to be actively sought. Humankind ought not merely wait upon God: "No doubt more than five thousand millions have gone down to hell, while the Church has been dreaming, and waiting for God to save them without the use of means. It has been the devil's most successful means of destroying souls." In faithfulness, however, to his Calvinist heritage, Finney at least admitted that the "constituted means" alone could not engender a true revival "without the blessing of God."[27]

Finney's famous *Lectures on Revivals* carefully delineated the means and measures for promoting revivals and constituted a kind of professional handbook on revival techniques. Claiming that his work was as soundly based upon scientific laws as any text of physics or engineering, he expostulated on the concrete means of arousing attention and the specific techniques leading to conversions. He objected, for example, to written sermons, because they impeded the natural flow of thought, hindered the emotions, and minimized the use of gestures. If, in an earlier era, ministers had looked to teachers as their models, now Finney—who had been admitted to the New York state bar—proposed that the lawyer and the actor should serve as models. Ministers ought to preach in a "colloquial, lawyer-like style," so that they could be understood by the congregation. Furthermore, in order that the congregation could be moved to repentance, ministers should aim to imitate actors, who gave themselves so entirely to the spirit and meaning of the author that they presented the spirit and meaning to the audience as a "living reality."[28]

Yet Finney was no advocate of emotionalism for its own sake. He considered it permissible to excite individuals to "awaken" them, to employ an "anxious seat" in the front pew so that sinners might squirm in discomfort, and to "push matters to an issue." But preachers, in his view, ultimately had to use a different approach to lead hearers from awakening to deepened conviction. Indeed, Finney warned, fanaticism was incompatible with genuine revivalism; decency and order must always prevail.

Quite clearly for Finney, "subjective knowledge *of*" took precedence over less transformative notions of knowledge, a rank order that engendered tensions reminiscent of the learned ministry controversy. Like many of his revivalist colleagues in both awakenings, Finney considered education of the utmost importance. He regarded schools as highest priority, particularly because he believed that they had the potential of deepening the convictions initiated by conversion. In 1827 he assisted George Gale in founding Oneida Academy for the purpose of educating a new set of revival preachers to replace the "inefficient and lukewarm graduates of eastern seminaries." He helped establish Gilbert Morgan's Rochester Institute for Practical Education in 1831 and was instrumental in the founding of the Troy and Albany School of Theology in 1833. Most significantly, Finney went to Oberlin College in 1835 to become a professor of theology and later served as its president. The college, he declared, "should make the conversion of sinners and the sanctification of Christians the paramount work and subordinate to this all the educational operations."[29]

The increasingly Arminianized Calvinism of Finney and others of his generation gave rise to a new vision of Christianity and the social order. Having rejected notions of a world totally depraved and without hope of change short of God's intervention, Finney was among those who saw the world gradually moving toward perfection by means of the spread of Christianity. And especially during the Second Great Awakening millennialist hopes were wedded to nationalistic sentiments: within the not-too-distant future, a thousand years of universal peace and plenty would begin in the United States. Moreover, this new era would be brought about by the conversion of sinners rather than by reform of political and economic structures—even though a transformed social order would characterize the millennium.

FINNEY ON THE RELATION OF FAITH TO CULTURE

Finney saw, with a clarity shared by few others of his generation, that conversion from sin required one to work toward the creation of a righteous society. Yet because his understanding of sin was framed almost exclusively in individualist categories, he retained an ambivalence about social reform. On the one hand, he rejected the social and class divisions fostered by rental of pews during services; he and his followers constructed "free churches" in which all had equal access to seating. He condemned "war, slavery, and licentiousness and such like evils and abominations" as "great and sore evils" for which the saint longed for a "complete and final overthrow." On the other hand, his attitude toward slavery was less than consistent. Though convinced by the arguments of friends that Christianity ought to judge slaveholding as immoral, in the face of crisis Finney's conviction wavered. When confronted in 1834 with rioting mobs protesting abolitionism, Finney kept silent. He refused to integrate the seating in his Chatham Street Chapel on the grounds that there was a difference between freeing slaves and treating them as social equals. By 1835 Finney had become less active in antislavery activities, refusing to pray or preach on the divisive topic. Finally, in 1836 he openly broke with the abolitionist movement, angered that some of his students at Oberlin College seemed to be far more concerned with the liberation of slaves than with the liberation from sin resulting from conversion. Social reform was always subordinate to revivalism in Finney's world. Faith was countercultural insofar as it challenged people to repent from the evils of drink, lust, dishonesty, and other such sins, but not insofar as it confronted what a later generation of theologians has termed "social sin," structures that oppress human beings, violate human dignity, stifle freedom, and impose gross inequality.

Admittedly, Finney's blindness to reconstruction of the social order is more obvious in hindsight. In fact, revivals were typically directed toward personal reform; this stress on personal morality combined with a dualistic outlook on the world resulted in a vigorous moral code that also encompassed the "success ethic." Revivals powerfully formed individuals in an outlook that condemned impurity and intemperance but embraced the myth of the self-made person, the one who achieved by dint of thrift, hard work, and rugged individualism.

REVIVALISM IN AMERICAN CATHOLICISM

Though the myth of the self-made person reflected an Arminianized Calvinism, it prevailed as well in Catholic revivalism, a phenomenon less well known than its Protestant counterpart but just as formative. Revivals served as vital means of educating an immigrant people; they came at a point of unprecedented growth in the U.S. Catholic church. Between 1830 and 1860, for instance, the Catholic population, nearly 70 percent of which was immigrant, expanded by 876 percent. The number of clergy increased by 863 percent, the number of dioceses quadrupled to 43, and the value of church properties tripled between 1850 and 1860.[30] Most of the immigrants were poor and unlettered, and their need for education in faith was desperate.

The parish mission revitalized these people. Usually about a week long, the mission aimed to move sinners to repent and reform. Though distinguished from Protestant revivals by their audience of already professed believers in need of a second conversion and by their sacramental character, which included daily Eucharist, evening devotions of the rosary and benediction, and stress on the sacrament of Reconciliation, the parish mission also emphasized a conversion of the affections. As Paulus Scharpff expresses it, "The evangelistic message is a persistent, pleading invitation to seize the proffered hour for repentance from sin and for surrender to Christ."[31] Or, as Alexander Doyle put it more directly, "Convict them of sin, Infuse the fear of the Lord in their hearts by the terrors of judgment."[32] Charismatic preachers, particularly those drawn from among Jesuit, Redemptorist, and Paulist priests, instilled a fear of eternal damnation to move people to a change of heart. Dolan claims that the preachers on the parish mission circuit could paint a scene of the crucifixion as vividly as could the Baroque masters. Words were the medium of these "pulpit artists," and the scenes they portrayed created a formidable impression on the congregation. The conversion thus fostered a return to the sacraments and a commitment to reform erring ways. Much attention was devoted to the drunken sinner's repentance; Catholic revivalism contributed mightily, as did Protestant, to the growth of temperance societies. The Paulist mission band took fifteen thousand pledges of temperance in just nine years (1888–1897). Such pledges were a manifestation of a personal decision for Jesus. Temperance, of course, was not without societal ramifications but, nonetheless, it was individualistically oriented.

COMMON CHARACTERISTICS OF REVIVALISM IN PROTESTANTISM AND CATHOLICISM

Indeed, regeneration of the individual epitomized revivalism, whether in the context of the Catholic parish mission or in Protestant revivals. Five common characteristics highlight the "ecumenical" aspect of revivalism: development of a new mode of ministry, itinerant preaching; emphasis on technique, particularly on "sensational preaching" intended forcibly to impress the hearers' senses; overwhelming stress on conversion as a heartfelt decision; championing of a rigorous moral code on the personal level rather than for the social order; and organization of parish and denominational life that followed in the wake of the revivals.[33]

FUNDAMENTALISM: A MILITANT MODE OF REVIVALISM

One further piece completes this sketch of revivalism: its emergence in a more militant form, fundamentalism. Fundamentalism might be regarded as one trajectory of revivalist thought. Many of its characteristics were evident in the ministry of two revivalist preachers of the late nineteenth century, Dwight Moody (1837–1899) and Billy Sunday (William Ashley Sunday, 1863–1935).

Moody shared in many of the revivalist assumptions about personal morality, but his anti-intellectual tendencies set him apart from his predecessors. Unlike the pulpit artists who preceded him, he resisted creating hellfire sermons aimed at producing fear. Convinced that terror never made a convert, he concentrated instead on what he called the "Christian fundamentals," the "three R's": "Ruin by sin, Redemption by Christ, and Regeneration by the Holy Ghost."[34] Yet Moody was no less convinced of the pervasiveness of sin. Though his view of God might have inspired less fear than Edwards's, his worldview was profoundly pessimistic: "I look upon this world as a wrecked vessel. God has given me a lifeboat, and said to me, 'Moody, save all you can.'"[35] Thus, he too exhorted his hearers to make a decision to change their lives and to repent of the vices of "worldly pleasures": "Whatever the sin is, make up your mind that you will gain victory over it."[36] His view of the church's relation to culture was plain in his denunciation of the theater, people's disregard for the Sabbath, Sunday newspapers, and atheistic teachings (including evolution) as the four great temptations of the era.

Despite the dualism at work in Moody's outlook ("A line should be drawn between the church and the world, and every Christian should get both feet out of the world"),[37] he preached a gospel of success: "It is a wonderful fact that men and women saved by the blood of Jesus rarely remain the subjects of charity, but rise at once to comfort and respectability."[38] Such inconsistency was not new in the history of revivalism, but Moody was particularly prone to it because of his ignorance of matters theological. Charles Finney had written a book of nearly one thousand pages to explain how his theology departed from classical Calvinism, but books other than the Bible held no interest for Moody: "I have one rule about books. I do not read any book, unless it will help me to understand *the* book. . . . I would rather have zeal without knowledge; and there is a good deal of knowledge without zeal."[39] Apparently, a woman once confronted him with the comment that she did not believe in his theology. Moody replied: "My theology! I didn't know I had any. I wish you would tell me what my theology is."[40]

Moody's anti-intellectualism was more than matched in the man who championed "old-time religion" and whose revival crusades from 1896 to 1920 made him a national prophet. Billy Sunday was a baseball player who had never gone beyond eighth grade, but his conversion in 1886 led him to the revival circuit. He converted so many that when he appeared before a Presbyterian board in 1908 to be examined for ordination, his presbytery had no choice but to ordain him despite his lack of preparation. After all, Sunday had single-handedly won more souls for Christ than had all the board members combined. His remark, "I don't know any more about theology than a jack rabbit knows about ping pong, but I'm on my way to glory," provides a fairly succinct indication of the value he placed on theological study.[41]

To conclude, however, that fundamentalism as a sub-species of revivalism was essentially anti-intellectual would be unwarranted, even if Moody and Sunday represented cases in point. Rather, fundamentalism, a militantly antimodernist Protestant evangelicalism that developed in the late nineteenth and early twentieth centuries, paradoxically embraced both a strong respect for the intellect and a deep suspicion of it. Though much else might be said about the development of fundamentalism, this particular ambivalence toward knowing has important ramifications for the development of religious education and thus deserves special mention.

Fundamentalism is best understood as a reaction to modernity, both in modernity's broad cultural manifestations and in its more specific appearance in the guise of progressive theology. Two intellectual movements in the mid-nineteenth century promulgated theories against which a "return to the fundamentals" would serve as a rallying cry. The first, new theories in geology regarding the antiquity of the earth and in biology regarding evolution, seemed to pit science against revelation, since these theories clashed with the biblical accounts of creation. The second, developments in biblical study—the so-called historical-critical method or "higher" criticism—seemed to set in opposition a more technical, demanding way of interpreting Scripture and its plain sense.

Undergirding the fundamentalist reaction to these perceived evil tenets was a worldview shaped by the philosophy of an earlier era, "Scottish commonsense realism."[42] At its base were two assumptions: God's truth is a single, unified, order and all persons of common sense are capable of knowing the truth. These assumptions, a legacy from the Deistic notion that the universe is governed according to a rational system of laws by an all-wise and benevolent creator, gave rise to the conviction that the human mind can know the real world directly. Indebted especially to the inductive, scientific method of seventeenth-century thinker Francis Bacon, in which knowledge was attained by painstaking and objective observation of facts, Scottish commonsense realism resisted speculative hypotheses. As appropriated by fundamentalists, this meant that knowing came to be equated with comprehending facts. Scripture, for instance, was an "encyclopedic puzzle," a "dictionary of facts that had been progressively revealed in various historical circumstances."[43] The interpreter's task, therefore, was to classify carefully, generalize logically, and thereby reach conclusions. This fundamentalist perspective contrasted sharply with the hypothetical character of theories of the higher critics or of the evolutionists. As Billy Sunday put it in his inimitable way, he gave no credence to a "bastard theory that men [women] came from protoplasm by the fortuitous concurrence of atoms."[44]

Fundamentalism is a phenomenon of great complexity that has been described as a "mosaic of divergent and sometimes contradictory tendencies."[45] But at its heart is the conviction that truth is unchanging and knowable by *true* science and common sense. Though many who preached in the fundamentalist tradition certainly were anti-intellectuals—among whom Moody and Sunday were outstanding exemplars—theirs was not the only or even necessarily the prevailing attitude toward knowledge. Perhaps more characteristic was, on the one hand, an enthusiastic embrace of what was regarded as observable, objective data (since truth was perspicacious and immutable) and, on the other, an extreme wariness toward theoretical schemas, since they could not be proven with absolute assurance. The fundamentalist's passion for *plain* truth sparked militant opposition to those whose idea of truth seemed excessively abstract, ambiguous, and often agnostic or atheistic.

Despite the heightened militancy flowing from its conception of knowledge, fundamentalism nevertheless belongs squarely in the revivalist tradition, primarily because of the centrality of the conversion experience—revivalism's most singular characteristic. And, though fundamentalism is certainly deserving of a fuller analysis than has been done here, it is most important for present purposes to highlight the link between revivalism and fundamentalism as modes of religious education.

REVIVALISM: A SUMMARY

Perhaps at this juncture a summary is in order, lest one become lost in the details of the history of revivalism. The foundational questions offer a way of charting the review.

To ask what it means to be religious involves first and foremost recognition of the overwhelming importance of conversion, understood as a moment of decision to give oneself to Christ (which in the Catholic tradition entailed a return to the sacraments). The God whom the Scriptures revealed—and in the Catholic tradition about whom the Church taught authoritatively—demanded the renunciation of one's sinful, evil ways. The threat of hell was all too real if one did not heed God's commands. This understanding of revelation, moreover, depended to a large degree on an anthropology rooted in the Calvinist conviction of the innate depravity of humankind or, often in the Catholic tradition, on an anthropology influenced by the rigorism and harshness of Jansenism. Faith was, as so many of the first generation of revivalists described it, experimental insofar as it was derived from sense experience. Faith was a product of one's affections, one's experiential knowledge. Belief, embodied in creeds and dogmas, played a secondary role. Theology was not without significance, particularly to Edwards and Finney, but the controversy over the learned ministry pointed to the ever-present tensions exacerbated by the study of theology.

Yet even Gilbert Tennent, whose sermon on the unconverted minister sparked that controversy, had a high regard for education. He, like nearly all the revivalists (excluding Moody and Sunday, for example) saw in education a means of deepening one's conversion. Tennent once concluded a sermon with a reading list designed to guide hearers toward conversion. Essential to the early revivalists' purposes was the creation of "alternative education": "The public academies being so much corrupted and abused generally" that "private schools, or seminaries of learning which are under the care of skillful and experienced Christians" ought to be founded.[46] Jonathan Edwards served as president of the College of New Jersey (later Princeton University), Timothy Dwight as president of Yale, and Charles Finney as president of Oberlin.

Educating religiously was inextricably linked to a view of knowledge as transformative; mere rationality had no power to lead to conversion. A person learned in order to be changed from depravity to grace. Even though the fundamentalist trajectory prized objective knowledge *about* more than did revivalism in general, the linkage of knowledge and conversion remained key. In reaction to ways of teaching and preaching that had previously been tediously formalistic—"What have we had lately but a dry formality?" asked Samuel Finley in 1741—revivalism spawned a more vivid style of presentation.[47] As historian Lawrence Cremin notes, revivalists did not downplay religious education, previously understood as memorization of Scripture, prayers, and catechism, but, significantly, changed its pedagogy. Prophecy replaced edification as the central technique.[48]

The arsenal of institutions that formed an adjunct to the church for the "war on Satan" had a profound effect. The classical curriculum of the academies and colleges, with its emphasis on the liberal arts, "resolutely humanized religious life in general and religious enthusiasm in particular." Thus the curriculum of the schools, albeit unintentionally, had to some degree a "taming" effect on American Protestantism.[49]

Revivalism rested on a sharp distinction between natural and supernatural, between secular and sacred. Yet its preachers most often could not recognize ways in which they, too, were caught into certain cultural norms and beliefs, especially the "success ethic." Thus they generally failed to recognize the political nature of educational activity, how their exhortations formed a people in the American mythology of the self-made person—a strange irony for a movement rooted in awareness of God's surprising grace.

EVANGELICALISM

As the enthusiasm of revivalism was tamed by educational institutions and as Calvinism became more Arminianized, the evangelistic impulse was furthered in ways that extended beyond the confines of revivalism. Evangelicalism here denotes this extension of the revivalistic spirit. Conversion remained central, but another dimension emerged as characteristic: mission, a sense of the urgency of converting others to Christ. The primacy of the scriptural revelation remained a constant in revivalism and evangelicalism, though of course in fundamentalism the emphasis was quite clearly on the inerrant nature of the Bible, that is, that the autographs of Scripture contain no error.

Evangelicalism is a useful umbrella term for evangelistic enterprises in the nineteenth century that in effect created an "ecology" of supporting institutions that extended and deepened the conversions engendered by revivalism.[50] Evangelicalism is best seen in the work of the benevolent societies formed between 1800 and 1865; these constituted a "united front" for the "conversion of every American and ultimately every non-Evangelical in the world."[51]

THE BENEVOLENT SOCIETIES

Two benevolent societies emerged in 1815. The American Education Society was founded to "provide a ministerial phalanx against heresy";

it subsidized poor students in the academies, colleges, and seminaries. The American Bible Society (still in existence) drew together over one hundred Bible societies in the United States, becoming a national organization in 1816. Its influence in making Bibles available to the ever-increasing population ought not to be overlooked, especially in view of the profound influence the Scriptures had in American education. The work of the American Bible Society was energized in part by a concern over the influx of Catholic immigrants. The society warned in 1830: "His Holiness, the Pope, has with eager grasp, already fixed upon this fair portion of our nation, and he knows well how to keep his hold."[52] In 1855 the legislature of Massachusetts ruled that schools must use and read the Scriptures.

Closely allied with the American Bible Society was the American Tract Society, constituted in 1825, since "too long have men [women] stood still, in criminal supineness or silent despondence while a flood of licentiousness has been sweeping away the institution of Christianity."[53] By 1840 its principal works were embodied in a series of forty-five volumes; the series, together with its bookcase, sold for twenty dollars. The publications were carried by colporteurs, itinerant booksellers; in 1856–1857 some 580 colporteurs worked the region of Pennsylvania, Virginia, New York, Ohio, and Illinois. The Home Missionary Society, formed in 1826, provided for the education of ministers, based on the conviction that "the Gospel is the most economical police on earth."[54]

The formation of numerous women's missionary societies greatly enhanced mission work in the nineteenth century. From 1861 until 1894, foreign missionary societies organized by and for women originated in thirty-three denominations, and home missionary societies in seventeen. Growing out of a profound sense of the imperative of making the gospel known to many who had not heard the "good news," the members of these missionary societies dedicated themselves to a "woman's work for woman."[55] "More than ever before,", said Christian Golder in 1903, "are we in need today of female power."[56] Leaders of the various societies urged church members to support the work of the missions at home and abroad. An article in the *Heathen Woman's Friend* in 1869 expressed the need for support as follows:

The foundation principle of our Society is the command to give the gospel to every creature. Heathen women are without Christ. This includes everything else; social, mental, and physical degradation. Women without Christ! What is it? We can never take in all that it means of suffering, of sorrow, of social degradation, of mental darkness, and worse than all these, of soul pollution. Women without Christ! because there *are* such, our Society is in existence and will continue to be, just as long as we remember this. We send her help, not because she is a servant to her husband, and suffers untold cruelties from him, not because she is poor, and wretched and miserable, even when she don't know it, but because she is without Christ.[57]

Other societies also had significance. The American Peace Society (1828) and the American Anti-Slavery Society (1833) were the most controversial and had, consequently, the fewest members—a fact not surprising in view of the privatized morality inculcated by revivalist preaching. The American Society for the Promotion of Temperance (1826) served a cause more popular with church people, but it needs to be understood as more than a condemnation of "demon rum" that distracted its critics from larger social agendas. A larger perspective on the work of temperance societies comes into view when one understands the work of its women members in particular.

Excessive drinking led in many cases to abusive behavior by husbands toward their wives and neglect of their children. Thus women, who often had not played a role in the public forum, became prominent in temperance work. For many women, this entry into social reform did not come easily. Eliza Daniel "Mother" Stewart (1816–1908) described this in her memoirs:

It had been with many, a fearful struggle to yield up their preconceived ideas of what was a lady's place, and what the world might think and say. Not a few carried the subject to their closets, and there on their knees fought the battle with self and pride before the Lord, till He gave them strength and they came forth anointed for the war.[58]

But once embarked upon their campaign against drunkenness, women discovered that they needed the power of the vote. During her twenty-year (1879–1899) tenure as president of the Women's Christian Temperance Union, Frances Willard spoke out forcefully for women's suffrage, since their present circumstances dictated that "His militant army [the WCTU] must ever be powerless to win those legislative battles, which, more than any others, affect the happiness of aggregate humanity."[59] Willard, whose commitment to the work of temperance was "to help forward the coming of Christ," tirelessly promulgated women's role in the reform of society.[60]

The role of women was also at issue in the American Anti-Slavery Society. Its founders had solicited the help of women by encouraging the development of women's auxiliaries, but their attitudes toward women's roles was best revealed in their decision neither to list the women present at the first national antislavery convention nor to permit them to sign its "Declaration of Sentiments." Yet abolition was a cause to which numerous women were drawn, not in the least because slavery destroyed family life. Their increasing participation in the abolitionist cause led to conflict both over women's right to speak in public and over women's suffrage, a cause to which a "radical" faction of the abolitionists was devoted. This eventually became such a source of controversy that the organization split into two factions in 1840, one contending that women's rights should not be part of the abolitionist agenda and the other main-

taining that equality between the sexes was indissolubly linked to abolition.[61] The latter point of view was perhaps most eloquently articulated
by Angelina Grimké (1805–1879):

Anti-Slavery men are trying very hard to separate what God hath joined together. I fully believe that so far from keeping different moral reformations entirely
distinct that no such attempt can ever be successful. They are bound together
in a circle like the sciences; they blend with each other like the colors of the
rainbow; they are the parts only of our glorious whole and that whole is Christianity, pure *practical* Christianity. The fact is *I* believe—but don't be alarmed,
for it is only *I*—that Men and Women will have to go out on their own responsibility, just like the prophets of old and declare the *whole* counsel of God to the
people. The whole Church Government must come down, the clergy stand right
in the way of reform, and I do not know but this stumbling block must be
removed *before* Slavery can be abolished, for the system is supported by *them;* it
could not exist without the Church as it is called.[62]

THE BENEVOLENT SOCIETIES AND FAITH IN RELATION TO CULTURE

The work of the benevolent societies has been criticized for its conformity with a particular Protestant interpretation of the gospel and for
its preaching of a "morality by persuasion and compulsion." As Clifford
S. Griffin points out, the societies frequently exercised a stewardship of
the prosperous and a righteousness preoccupied with the deeds of others.[63] Yet, as Lois W. Banner argues, the benevolent societies must be
appraised in a different spirit. Given all their shortcomings—their limited vision, their moralism—they provided a "signal service" in excoriating materialism and questioning the direction of American life.[64]
Moreover, the involvement of women in the work of social reform
through the various societies, including those of their own creation,
offered an impetus to women of the twentieth century. Indeed, evangelicalism, by virtue of its strong sense of mission, served as an imperative
for women. It was largely the evangelical spirit that sparked the movement for women's suffrage.

THE SUNDAY SCHOOL

One other benevolent society is especially significant: the American
Sunday School Union, formed in 1824. This society became the major
vehicle in the evangelical drive for "conquest" of the United States; in
1830 it pledged that within two years and "in reliance upon divine aid,"
a Sunday school would be established "in every destitute place where it
is practicable, throughout the Valley of the Mississippi."[65] Its conquest,
however, was a joint endeavor. For instance, the Sunday school worker
sent by the union distributed Bibles and tracts furnished by the Bible
and tract societies. Any Sunday school had the potential of becoming a
nucleus of a congregation that would be supported by the Home Missionary Society. Missionaries themselves were urged to walk from village

to village with "a good satchel well stored with specimens of library books, and catalogues to show, and miscellaneous books to sell, and tracts and papers to give away."[66]

The missionaries evangelized not only while actually in their territories; wherever they went, they left libraries in their wake. The library became the mark of a bona fide Sunday school. Statistics in an 1859 *Manual of Public Libraries* document that 30,000 of the 50,000 libraries in the nation were Sunday school collections. As late as 1858 the American Sunday School Union was selling hundreds of thousands of spelling books. Wherever agents went, schools and libraries followed; without the Sunday school, the entire educational landscape of the nineteenth century would have had a very different shape.

The Sunday school also was linked with the revival. Reading and writing were important by-products, but the Sunday school's true business was incubating the young for conversion. Its stories and songs were directed toward a religion of the heart, thereby preparing its students for the revivalist experience they would encounter during adolescence. But many of its songs served another task as well: to reinforce family education about death. An 1835 hymnal contained hymns such as "Death of a Pious Child," "Death of a Scholar," "Triumph in Death," "For a Dying Child," and "The Fear of Death Removed."[67]

Linked with the benevolent societies, the revival, and the home, the Sunday school wielded enormous power. In 1852, an English investigator discovered that in New York City the average weekly Sunday school attendance of 30,000 children equalled 75 percent of that in public, ward, and corporate schools; in Philadelphia and Boston it equalled 80 percent, in Cleveland, 67 percent. Simply by existing, the Sunday school helped to prepare for the development of the public school. It was a model of an organized school with buildings, books, teachers, pupils, and the broad support of people and publications. It was both "precursor and pioneer" of common schooling,[68] what Lynn and Wright have called the "big little school": "compared to public education, Sunday school is marginal to American society, yet it is an important *little* school in the rearing of the whole nation. The Sunday school is the big little school of the United States."[69]

EVANGELICALISM: A SUMMARY

Evangelicalism embraced a number of institutions that served to deepen and extend the conversionist thrust of revivalism. Insofar as it served as an extension of revivalism, no notable differences appear in the way the foundational questions were addressed. Yet evangelicalism contributed a particular stress on education as a central means of making the gospel known. Education was viewed as strictly didactic and transmissive, with biblical literacy through memorization and song its chief goal. Also noteworthy is the role of the benevolent societies in providing women with a public forum by which to infuse the culture with their convictions born of faith. Clearly, the educational outreach of evangelicalism was politically oriented toward a reform of society, albeit somewhat more along individualistic lines than one would hope for today.

The two modes of *evangelism*—revivalism and evangelicalism—were crucial in establishing the basic contours of religious education before its "official" existence as a distinct field in 1903. *Evangelism* is the classic expression that provides the context out of which religious education and Christian education develop.

Figure 2

Evangelism

FOUNDATIONAL QUESTIONS	THE CLASSIC EXPRESSION *EVANGELISM*
REVELATION	· Primacy of revelation accorded to Scripture. · God's word meant to "crush" and "crack" the stony heart through the preached word. · Fundamentalists emphasized the inerrant character of the Scriptures.
CONVERSION	· Conversion of the affections stressed: "A change of heart, not of opinion." · Preaching engendered personal decisions to reform, to give oneself to Christ. · Catholic parish missions aimed at drawing people back to the sacraments. · Mission—leading others to Christ—seen as urgent.
FAITH & BELIEF	· "Experimental" religion dominated over creedal formulas. · Faith developed from one's experiential knowledge. · Fundamentalists emphasized truth as propositional.
THEOLOGY	· Importance varied; more integral to Edwards and Finney than to Moody or Sunday. · Revivalists modified Calvinism with Arminian emphases. · Debate over the "learned ministry" reflected tensions about significance of theology.
FAITH & CULTURE	· Distinction made between supernatural and natural. · Benevolent societies excoriated materialism and questioned direction of American life. · Ambivalance about social reform seen in nearly exclusive stress on the individual. · Benevolent societies offered women a public forum.
GOAL OF EDUCATION	· To deepen one's personal conversion. · Schools established to maintain and deepen conversion. · Schools helped to humanize religious life.
KNOWLEDGE	· Knowledge linked to conversion. · Edwards distinguished "notional" and "spiritual" knowledge. · Spiritual knowledge unified thinking, feeling, and action. · Fundamentalists stressed "Common Sense."
SOCIAL SCIENCES	· Though social sciences not yet "of age," Finney systematized revivals, thereby anticipating later behavioral systems.

FOUNDATIONAL QUESTIONS	THE CLASSIC EXPRESSION *EVANGELISM*
CURRICULUM & TEACHING	· Teaching essentially transmissive. · Curriculum largely oriented to biblical literacy. · Sunday schools helped to prepare for public school system.
EDUCATION AS POLITICAL	· Education vital for reform of society. · Provided an impetus for women's suffrage.

NOTES

1. See Ernest Lee Tuveson, *Redeemer Nation: The Idea of America's Millennial Role* (Chicago: University of Chicago Press, 1968).
2. Jay P. Dolan, *Catholic Revivalism: The American Experience 1830–1900* (Notre Dame, IN: University of Notre Dame Press, 1978), 58, 61.
3. Cited in William McLoughlin, *Revivals, Awakenings, and Reform* (Chicago: University of Chicago Press, 1978), 74.
4. Ibid., 63.
5. See Perry Miller, *Jonathan Edwards* (New York: Sloane, 1949), 144–48.
6. See Lawrence Cremin, *American Education: The Colonial Experience 1607–1783* (New York: Harper & Row, 1970), 317.
7. William G. McLoughlin, ed., *The Diary of Isaac Backus*, 3 vols. (Providence, RI: Brown University Press, 1979), 3:1525.
8. Ibid., 3:1525–26.
9. Amanda Berry Smith, *An Autobiography. The Story of the Lord's Dealings with Mrs. Amanda Smith, the Colored Evangelist Containing an Account of Her Life Work of Faith, and Her Travels in America, England, Ireland, Scotland, India and Africa, as an Independent Missionary*, intro. Bishop Thoburn of India (El Segundo, CA: Micro Publications Systems, for the American Theological Library Association Board of Microtext, 1980), 47. Originally published in 1893.
10. See Josef Goldbrunner, *Holiness Is Wholeness* (New York: Pantheon, 1955).
11. Jonathan Edwards, *The Works of President Edwards*, 10 vols. (New York: Burt Franklin, 1968), 4:16.
12. Charles Chauncy, *Seasonable Thoughts on the State of Religion in New England* (Boston: Rogers & Fowle [for Eliot in Cornhill], 1743), 109.
13. Ibid., 326–27.
14. Edwards, *The Works of President Edwards*, 4:163.
15. Ibid., 4:168.
16. Ibid., 4:302.
17. Ibid., 4:303.
18. Ibid., 5:380.
19. Ibid., 5:384.
20. Ibid., 5:389.
21. See Alan Heimert, *Religion and the American Mind: From the Great Awakening to the Revolution* (Cambridge, MA: Harvard University Press, 1966).
22. Gilbert Tennent, *The Danger of an Unconverted Ministry* (Philadelphia: Benjamin Franklin, 1740), 7ff.
23. Ibid., 18.
24. Cited in James W. Jones, *The Shattered Synthesis: New England Puritanism Before the Great Awakening* (New Haven, CT: Yale University Press, 1973), 116–17.
25. Douglas Sloan, ed., *The Great Awakening and American Education: A Documentary History* (New York: Teachers College Press, 1973), 52.

26. Charles Grandison Finney, *Lectures on Revivals of Religion* (Cambridge, MA: Harvard University Press, Belknap Press, 1960), 377.

27. Ibid., 14–15, 13.

28. Ibid., 219–20.

29. Robert Samuel Fletcher, *A History of Oberlin College: From Its Foundations Through the Civil War,* 2 vols. (Oberlin, OH: Oberlin College, 1943), 1:209.

30. See Dolan, *Catholic Revivalism,* 26–28.

31. Paulus Scharpff, *History of Evangelism,* trans. Helga Bender Henry (Grand Rapids, MI: Eerdmans, 1966), 3.

32. Cited in Dolan, *Catholic Revivalism,* 112.

33. Ibid., 188–191.

34. This scheme is attributed to Moody in William Haven Daniels, ed., *Moody: His Words, Work, and Workers* (Beltsville, MD: Reproduced by the NCR Corporation for the American Theological Library Association Board of Microtext, 1977), 256. Originally published in 1877.

35. D. L. Moody, "The Second Coming of Christ," in Wilbur M. Smith, ed., *The Best of D. L. Moody,* (Chicago: Moody, 1971), 193–95. Cited in George M. Marsden, *Fundamentalism and American Culture: The Shaping of Twentieth Century Evangelicalism 1870–1925* (New York: Oxford University Press, 1980), 38.

36. D. L. Moody, *Sowing and Reaping* (Chicago: Moody, 1896), 83. Cited in Marsden, *Fundamentalism and American Culture,* 36.

37. D. L. Moody, *Moody's Latest Sermons* (Chicago: BICA, 1900), 27–28. Cited in Marsden, *Fundamentalism and American Culture,* 36.

38. Cited in McLoughlin, *Revivals, Awakenings, and Reform,* 144.

39. Cited in McLoughlin, *Modern Revivalism* (New York: Ronald Press, 1959), 273.

40. Gamaliel Bradford, *D. L. Moody: A Worker in Souls* (Garden City, NY: Doubleday, Doran, 1928), 61.

41. William G. McLoughlin, *Billy Sunday Was His Real Name* (Chicago: University of Chicago Press, 1955), 123.

42. See Marsden, *Fundamentalism and American Culture,* 11–21.

43. Ibid., 58.

44. Cited in Sidney E. Ahlstrom, *A Religious History of the American People* (New Haven, CT: Yale University Press, 1972), 769.

45. Marsden, *Fundamentalism and American Culture,* 43.

46. Tennent, *Danger of an Unconverted Ministry,* 16.

47. Cited in Sloan, *The Great Awakening and American Education,* 51.

48. Cremin, *American Education,* 321.

49. Ibid., 331–32.

50. See Robert Wood Lynn, "Sometimes on Sunday: Reflections on Images of the Future in American Education," *Andover Newton Quarterly* 12 (1972):130–39.

51. See Charles I. Foster, *An Errand of Mercy: The Evangelical United Front, 1790–1837* (Chapel Hill, NC: University of North Carolina Press, 1960).

52. Cited in Clifford S. Griffin, *Their Brothers' Keepers: Moral Stewardship in the United States, 1800–1865* (New Brunswick, NJ: Rutgers University Press, 1960), 140.

53. *Proceedings of the First Ten Years of the American Tract Society* (Boston: Flagg and Gould, 1824), 9.

54. Cited in Griffin, *Their Brothers' Keepers,* 111.

55. See Rosemary Skinner Keller, "Lay Women in the Protestant Tradition," in Rosemary Radford Ruether and Rosemary Skinner Keller, eds., *Women and Religion in America, Vol. 1. The Nineteenth Century: A Documentary History* (San Francisco: Harper & Row, 1981), 242–53.

56. Rev. Christian Golder, *History of the Deaconess Movement in the Christian Church* (El Segundo, CA: Micro Publications Systems, for the American Theological Library Association Board of Microtext, 1981), 488. Originally published in 1903.

57. Mrs. E. E. Baldwin, "The Great Motive," *Heathen Woman's Friend* 2 (1871):135.

58. Cited in Ruether and Keller, *Women and Religion in America*, Vol. 1, 325. See also Carolyn De Swarte Gifford, "Women in Social Reform Movements," in Ruether and Keller, eds., *Women and Religion in America*, Vol. 1, 294–303.
59. Ibid., 326.
60. Ibid.
61. See Dorothy C. Bass, "'Their Prodigious Influence': Women, Religion and Reform in Antebellum America," in Rosemary Radford Ruether and Eleanor McLaughlin, eds., *Women of Spirit: Female Leadership in the Jewish and Christian Traditions* (New York: Simon and Schuster, 1979), 289–97.
62. Edith H. Barnes and Dwight L. Dumond, eds., *Letters of Theodore Dwight Weld, Angelina Grimké Weld and Sarah Grimké [1822–1844]* (Gloucester, MA: Peter Smith, 1965) 431.
63. See Griffin, *Their Brothers' Keepers*.
64. Lois W. Banner, *"Religious Benevolence as Social Control,"* The Journal of American History 60 (1973–74): 23–41.
65. American Sunday School Union, *Sixth Annual Report* (Philadelphia, 1830), 3.
66. American Sunday School Union, *Thirteenth Annual Report* (Philadelphia, 1854), 77.
67. Robert Wood Lynn and Elliott Wright, *The Big Little School* (New York: Harper & Row, 1971), 41–44.
68. William Bean Kennedy, *The Shaping of Protestant Education* (New York: Association Press, 1966), 23.
69. Lynn and Wright, *The Big Little School*, xi.

Bibliographic Essay

Evangelism

Whenever possible, primary sources have been cited in this chapter. I encourage readers, however, to consult the secondary sources in the following for commentary on the historical figures discussed and quoted in this chapter.

I owe my recognition of the educational character of evangelism to Lawrence Cremin. Particularly significant have been his two richly detailed volumes *American Education: The Colonial Experience 1607–1783* (New York: Harper & Row, 1970) and *American Education: The National Experience 1783–1876* (New York: Harper & Row, 1980). Another historical volume of great usefulness has been Douglas Sloan, ed., *The Great Awakening and American Education: A Documentary History* (New York: Teachers College Press, 1973). Essential background material was found also in Robert T. Handy, *A History of the Churches in the United States and Canada* (New York: Oxford University Press, 1979); Sydney E. Ahlstrom, *A Religious History of the American People* (New Haven, CT: Yale University Press, 1972); Sidney E. Mead, *The Nation with the Soul of a Church* (New York: Harper & Row, 1975); and Martin E. Marty, *Righteous Empire: The Protestant Experience in America* (New York: Dial, 1970). Also pertinent are the documentary histories edited by Rosemary Radford Ruether and Rosemary Skinner Keller, *Women and Religion in America*, 3 vols. (San Francisco: Harper & Row, 1981–1986).

The literature about revivalism makes for fascinating reading. The work of William McLoughlin is foundational: *Modern Revivalism: Charles Grandison Finney to Billy Graham* (New York: Ronald Press, 1959) and *Revivals, Awakenings and Reform* (Chicago: University of Chicago Press, 1978). See also Charles G. Finney's *Lectures on Revivals*, 12th ed. (London: John Johnson, 1849). Also Perry Miller, *The Life of the Mind in America* (New York: Harcourt and Brace, 1965); Timothy L. Smith, *Revivalism and Social Reform in Mid-Nineteenth Century America* (New York: Abingdon, 1957); and Ernest Lee Tuveson, *Redeemer Nation: The Idea of America's Millennial Role* (Chicago: University of Chicago Press, 1968). A Catholic perspective is provided by Jay P. Dolan, *Catholic Revivalism: The American Experience 1830–1900* (Notre Dame, IN: University of Notre Dame Press, 1978) and Christian Duquoc and Casiano Floristan, *Spiritual Revivals* (New York: Herder and Herder, 1973).

George M. Marsden's *Fundamentalism and American Culture: The Shaping of Twentieth Century Evangelicalism: 1870–1925* (New York: Oxford University Press, 1980) provides a superb interpretation of American fundamentalism. His work represents a somewhat different interpretation from the earlier work of Ernest R. Sandeen, *The Roots of Fundamentalism: British and American Millenarianism, 1800–1930* (Chicago: University of Chicago Press, 1970). C. Allyn Russell offers some biographical notes in his *Voices of American Fundamentalism* (Philadelphia: Westminster, 1976). See especially Timothy P. Weber's essay, "The Two-Edged Sword: The Fundamentalist Use of the Bible," in the fascinating volume of Nathan O. Hatch and Mark A. Noll, eds., *The Bible in America: Essays in*

Cultural History (New York: Oxford University Press, 1982), 101–120. Relevant also is Hatch, Noll, and John D. Woodbridge, *The Gospel in America: Themes in the Story of America's Evangelicals* (Grand Rapids, MI: Zondervan, 1979). James Barr's *Fundamentalism* (Philadelphia: Westminster, 1977) offers a theological interpretation from a British standpoint, and his collected essays in *The Scope and Authority of the Bible* (Philadelphia: Westminster, 1980), esp. 65–90, develop his earlier views.

The work of the benevolent societies is scrutinized in Charles I. Foster, *An Errand of Mercy: The Evangelical United Front, 1790–1837* (Chapel Hill, NC: University of North Carolina Press, 1960) and Clifford S. Griffin, *Their Brothers' Keepers: Moral Stewardship in the United States, 1800–1865* (New Brunswick, NJ: Rutgers University Press, 1960). Their work needs to be read in light of Lois Banner, "Religious Benevolence as Social Control: A Critique of an Interpretation," *Journal of American History* 60 (1973–1974):23–41.

In addition to the above-mentioned documentary history *Women and Religion in America,* several other works contribute to a fuller understanding of women in the evangelical cause: Nancy A. Hardesty, *Women Called to Witness: Evangelical Feminism in the 19th Century* (Nashville, TN: Abingdon, 1984); Barbara Leslie Epstein, *The Politics of Domesticity: Women, Evangelism, and Temperance in Nineteenth Century America* (Middletown, CT: Wesleyan University Press, 1981): and Dorothy C. Bass, "'Their Prodigious Influence': Women, Religion and Reform in Antebellum America," in Rosemary Radford Ruether and Eleanor McLaughlin, eds., *Women of Spirit: Female Leadership in the Jewish and Christian Traditions* (New York: Simon and Schuster, 1979), 289–97. Also of interest is Carl Degler, "What the Women's Movement Has Done to American History," in Elizabeth Langland and Walter Grove, eds., *A Feminist Perspective in the Academy* (Chicago: University of Chicago Press, 1983), 67–85. For a fascinating story of "women missionaries from Chicago," see Debra Campbell, "Part-Time Female Evangelists of the Thirties and Forties: The Rosary College Catholic Evidence Guild," *U.S. Catholic Historian* 5 (1986): 371–84; a brief summary appears in *Commonweal* 123 (June 1986): 334.

A rather extensive literature on the Sunday school has accumulated in recent years. Among the most perceptive of these works is that of Robert Wood Lynn and Elliott Wright, *The Big Little School* (New York: Harper & Row, 1971). Also valuable are Edwin Wilbur Rice, *The Sunday-School Movement and the American Sunday School Union* (New York: Arno Press and the New York Times, 1971 [original, 1917]); William Bean Kennedy, *The Shaping of Protestant Education* (New York: Association Press, 1966); and Jack Seymour, *From Sunday School to Church School: Continuities in Protestant Church Education, 1860–1929* (Washington, DC: University Press of America, 1982).

CHAPTER 3

Surveying the Territory: Religious Education

Revivalism provides an important backdrop against which to view the contours of *religious education,* since to a significant degree the latter must be understood as a movement sparked by a reaction to the enthusiastic spirit of the former. *Religious education* is a classic expression that weds classic liberal theology and progressivist educational thought. Its boundaries, therefore, are easier to trace and its theories more explicitly linked to the foundational questions. Yet it is more than a successor to the evangelistic impulse: *religious education* is both its alternative and its counterpoint. Just as *evangelism* developed in reaction to the formalism and rationalism bequeathed to the churches by the Enlightenment, so did *religious education* evolve in opposition to many of the emphases of the revivalist preachers and of the benevolent societies.

THE LIBERAL MOVEMENT

From the period of the First Great Awakening, the liberal cause had been gaining momentum, particularly in Massachusetts, where Unitarianism became the dominant ethos at Harvard College. Enlightenment religion in general and the Unitarian voice in particular had no more eloquent spokesman in its early days than William Ellery Channing (1780–1842), whose sermon at the tenth annual meeting of the Unitarian Sunday School Society in 1837 reflected a quite different opinion about the work of Sunday schools than that of their evangelical patrons. Channing's fear was that Sunday schools would become vehicles of mechanical teaching, thus passing on religion as a "lifeless tradition and not as a quickening reality": "I do not think that so much harm is done by giving error to a child as by giving truth in a lifeless form. [The trouble with some Christians is] not that they hold great errors, but that truth lies dead within them."[1] Of course, one hears in this commentary echoes of George Whitefield's denunciation of "dead men preaching," but Channing grounded his critique in a distinctly liberal view. His conviction about the goals of religious education is worth quoting at length:

The great end in religious instruction, whether in the Sunday school or family, is not to stamp *our* minds irresistibly on the young, but to stir up their own; not to make them see with our eyes, but to look inquiringly and steadily with their own; not to give a definite amount of knowledge, but to inspire a fervent love of truth; not to form an outward regularity, but to touch inward springs; not to burden the memory, but to quicken and strengthen the power of thought; not to bind them by ineradicable prejudices to our particular sect or particular notions, but to prepare them for impartial, conscientious judging of whatever subjects may, in the course of Providence, be offered to their decision; not to impose religion upon them in the form of arbitrary rules, which rest on no foundation but our own word and will, but to awaken the conscience, the moral discernment, so that they may discern and approve for themselves what is everlastingly good and right; not to *tell* them that God is good, but to help them see and feel him live in all that he does within and around them; not to tell them of the dignity of Christ, but to open their inward eye to the beauty and greatness of his character, and to enkindle aspirations after a kindred virtue.[2]

HORACE BUSHNELL: NURTURE, NOT CONVERSION

Unitarians did not stand alone in articulating liberal thoughts; in Congregationalist minister Horace Bushnell (1802–1876) liberalism had one of its most profound thinkers. In many respects, *religious education* as a classic expression begins with Bushnell, because in his immensely influential work *Christian Nurture* (1847), as well as in his later theological studies (especially on religious language), he established positions that later generations of theorists would refine and extend.

Bushnell, like Jonathan Edwards, rooted his theory in experience. Yet the difference in theological perspective—Bushnell was a "post-Calvinist" insofar as his theology was distinctly Arminian—and of his own life history gave rise to a new understanding of "experimental" religion. Perhaps the itinerant character of the work of the revivalist preachers, combined with their Calvinist strictness, had prevented family life from shaping their outlook. For Bushnell, however, the family was central. In particular, the death of his only son in 1842 at the age of four exercised a formative power: "I have learned more of experimental religion since my little boy died than in all my life before."[3]

Much of his 1847 classic centered around the contrast between two types of nurture. Ostrich nurture, so called because the ostrich—"nature's type of unmotherhood"—simply hatches her eggs without incubation and then allows the young to go forth untended, imaged what Bushnell saw happening among parents shaped by the prevailing orthodoxy (evangelism). These parents were, for all practical purposes, deserting their children until they came of age for conversion.[4] Because Calvinism so emphasized human depravity, the conventional wisdom assumed that children were in the devil's hands until they underwent a conversion experience in adolescence. Consequently, argued Bushnell, parents were drilling their children into "all the constraints, separated from all the hopes and liberties of religion; turning all their little misdoings and bad tempers into evidences of the need of regeneration," thus unintentionally offering a "nurture of despair," making "even the loving gospel of Jesus a most galling chain upon the neck of childhood!"[5] Instead, he proposed, children should be brought up *in* conversion and begotten anew "in the spirit of a loving obedience to God," which made grace an element in the home.[6] Bushnell's argument was epitomized in his famous dictum "that the child is to grow up a Christian, and never know himself [herself] as being otherwise."[7]

The Yale-educated minister made clear that he did not subscribe to the theories that asserted the radical goodness of human nature; rather, he believed that the development of Christian values and virtues was no "vegetable process, no mere onward development. It involves a struggle with evil, a fall and a rescue."[8] For Bushnell, the logic of the conversionist thrust was seriously distorted because it rested on the need to foster in the young a sort of enmity toward God so that they could experience regeneration. Bushnell's solution differed radically. Parents should nurture their children with a kind of teaching compatible with the child's age:

First of all, they should rather seek to teach a feeling than a doctrine; to bathe the child in their own feeling of love of God and dependence on him, and contrition of wrong before him, bearing up their child's heart in their own, not fearing to encourage every good motion they can call into exercise; to make what is good, happy and attractive; what is wrong, odious and hateful; then as the understanding advances, to give it food suited to its capacity, opening upon it gradually the more difficult views of Christian doctrine and experience.[9]

Bushnell's conviction that education properly began with nurture seems to be grounded upon a heightened awareness of the social character of Christianity. On numerous occasions in *Christian Nurture,* he comments critically on the "extreme individualism" of the culture and suggests that Baptism counters this. The linkage of the sacrament of Baptism to his theory of education is made explicit in his remark that it was his "settled conviction" that no one ever objected to infant baptism who had not at the basis of his or her objections "false views of Christian education—who did not hold a notion of individualism in regard to Christian character in childhood, which is justified neither by observation nor by Scripture.[10] The baptism of infants symbolized for Bushnell the organic unity of the family and served to recognize that the child's growth in the matrix of parental care was a deeply religious matter.

Not only did he believe that infants should be baptized, but Bushnell argued that children should have membership in the church, including the opportunity to partake of the Lord's Supper. Theirs is a membership standing on the faith and promise of their parents; as they mature ("for there is a maturity of grace, as well as a grace of conversion")[11] they will come forward into faith and assume their role as fully partici- pating congregants. Bushnell's stance may seem unremarkable to twen- tieth-century Christians, particularly those from denominations that practice infant baptism; but in the nineteenth century it was more con- troversial because of the stress on late adolescent conversion. In fact, the radical character of Bushnell's advocacy can be clearly seen in his critique of revivalism under Edwards and Whitefield.

PARENTAL EDUCATION: ALTERNATIVE TO REVIVALISM

What Bushnell termed the "Great Revival," that is, "a distinct era introduced by Edwards and extended and caricatured by his contem- poraries," had in his view one great merit: it displaced an era of "dead formality, and brought in the demand of a truly supernatural experi- ence."[12] But its great defect was serious indeed: by casting a type of religious individualism, it made nothing of the family or the church— or even of the "organic powers God has constituted as vehicles of grace."[13] Revivalism took each person as if he or she existed *alone* and presumed the action of God's Spirit to be isolated and individualized so that it had no connection with any other of God's means or causes. Thus, in effect, revivalism rested on a sort of *deus ex machina,*

—an epiphany, in which God leaps from the stars, or some place above, to do a work apart from all system, or connection with his other works. Religion is thus a kind of transcendental matter, which belongs on the outside of life, and has no part in the laws by which life is organized—a miraculous epidemic, a fireball shot from the moon, something holy, because it is from God, but so extraordi- nary, so out of place, that it cannot suffer any vital connection with the ties, and causes, and forms, and habits, which constitute the frame of our history.[14]

Thus Bushnell argued forcefully for a parental education that would not press children into "some crises of high experience, called conver- sion," but would be a teaching stimulating growth rather than stirring revolution.[15] Because growth, not conversion, was the aim of Christian education, home life was of the utmost importance. Thus parents should always temper their rule with love, for their authority depended on the reality of their own living of Christian life and on their mutual relation- ship. Overbearing absolutism, an excessively exacting manner, hasty judgments, harshness, and overemphasis on prohibition: all of these Bushnell advised parents to avoid because they discouraged piety in their children. Moreover, religion was to be the "friend" of play. Parents should delight in the play of their children: "any sort of piety or sup- posed piety that is jealous of the plays and bounding activities of childish life, is a character of hardness and severity that has . . . a very question- able agreement with God's more genial and fatherly feeling."[16] In addition, Bushnell warned parents against exerting pressure upon their children to have religious experiences, thus inadvertently fostering undue anxiety. Parents, moreover, ought to respect their children's development even if they were to go through a period of doubt. "Never be in a hurry to believe," he advised, and "never try to conquer doubts against time. . . . If you cannot open a doubt today, keep it til tomorrow; do not be afraid to keep it whole years."[17]

Bushnell's theory of Christian nurture sparked fierce controversy but was so at odds with prevailing modes of church education that it had little immediate impact; instead, his ideas were developed by a later generation of theorists, even though their theological perspective was considerably more liberal. Yet to the extent Bushnell influenced his own era, his views on family life were part of a new perspective on religion and culture. This was particularly evident in childhood education, wherein a new stress on the mother's role in moral education reflected both the social emergence of the mother as a free and responsible individual and the recognition of children as persons in their own right rather than merely as little adults.

EDUCATING IN FAITH BECOMES A WOMAN'S WORK

Unlike Bushnell's healthy realism about familial relationships, much of the prevailing rhetoric concerning the family was sentimental. Said one pastor, "This world's redeeming influence must come from a mother's lap," since "the brightest rays of the millennial morn must come from the cradle."[18] Mothers were urged to reflect in their behavior what they wished their children to become. In particular they were urged to work at cheerfulness, because "Christians ought to be happy, and being so, should make it visible,"[19] Moreover, mothers were instructed by passages such as the following: "Children should always hear death spoken of as a blessed change; and if the selfishness of our nature will wring some tears from us . . . they should be such tears as we shed for a brief absence, not . . . utter separation."[20] The mother was instructed to seize every small opportunity to deepen the child's faith; because the father now generally worked outside the home, instruction in prayer became the mother's task.

Ann Douglas, in her social history of the period from 1820 to 1875, argues that underlying such sentimental views of motherhood was a shift in the role of women and of clergy. The nineteenth-century woman was generally far less involved in household labor than was her eighteenth-century predecessor; consequently, she tended to live in relative comfort tending her husband's house or, in the case of the poorer woman, to work in a low-paying factory job. Women of the former group were perceived as a sort of leisure class, since they no longer had to work at so many backbreaking labors. As Bushnell somewhat unkindly put it, the "Age of Homespun," with its transition from "mother and

daughter power to water and steam power" had passed: women no longer married to help their husbands earn a living, but to help them spend
their income.[21] The clergy, too, were in the throes of change after the
disestablishment of the churches in 1833; lacking stability and increasingly marginal to society as a whole, they were viewed as powerless and
ill-informed. The business class, claimed one report, regarded clergy as
"people halfway between men and women."[22] No furious exchange of
opinion on what constituted a "learned ministry" seemed to concern
church people. Too many divinity school students were apparently
preoccupied with themselves and with what Douglas terms the "cult of
self-nurture," and too many preachers were concerned with creating a
favorable impression. Women became the "consumers" of a sentimental-
ized religiosity and sought to gain power by exploiting what nineteenth-
century society defined as "feminine": piety, timidity, self-preoccupation,
and vulnerability.

Ann Douglas names this phenomenon the "feminization" of American
culture: an anti-intellectual sentimentalizing of life that ultimately gave
rise to the consumer society and mass culture. Religion was increasingly
relegated to the periphery of the culture, since it was the domain of
women and clergy, neither of whom dealt with serious matters in their
preoccupation with superficial literature. Not surprisingly, educating
others in the faith became a woman's work, since the men (except for
the clergy) were preoccupied with obligations in the "real" world. Woman was "God's appointed agent of *morality,* the teacher and inspirer of
those feelings and sentiments which are termed the virtues of humanity."[23]

But other currents moved in the stream of American culture, and two
related developments bear special significance for twentieth-century religious education: liberal theology and progressive education. A brief
look at each will establish the immediate backdrop for the emergence of
the classic expression *religious education.*

LIBERAL THEOLOGY

The emergence of liberal theology in the nineteenth century represented the confluence of several streams of thought. Perhaps the prime
notion was progress, particularly as this was imaged in the evolutionary
line of ascent in Darwin's *Origin of the Species.* The development of historiography contributed a sense of the relativity of all things, which
Einstein's theory of relativity would later enhance in the popular imagination, and gave scholars a set of tools by which they could, for instance, identify the pluralism of voices in the biblical texts. The
Enlightenment bequeathed a supreme confidence in human ability and
in the potential of science to discover the laws of nature; it asserted the
ascendancy of the ethical dimensions of religion over the dogmatic. The
Romantic Movement further deemphasized the doctrinal character of

Christianity in its stress on religion as feeling. The Arminian "takeover" of Calvinism emphasized human freedom and one's natural capacity for altruism; in certain circles, sin came to be thought of as an error that could be mitigated by moral education and by following the example of Jesus.

Perhaps liberal theology can be described most simply as a reconciliation of the scientific spirit of the late nineteenth and early twentieth centuries with traditional Christianity; it is a rethinking of Christianity in light of science. Characteristically, it regards modernity as entirely compatible with the essence of religion and the realms of the sacred and secular as harmonious. Energized by the metaphor of evolution, liberals looked on the world optimistically; they saw themselves as moving slowly but surely away from more primitive religion. When this outlook was joined to the American triumphalism of the New Zion, its arrogance now seems very naive. But in 1912, Walter Rauschenbusch thought differently: "The largest and hardest part of the work of Christianizing the social order has been done. [Americans need] only to complete the task of redemption."[24]

Liberalism established a new agenda for theology. Now the normative criteria for theological thought were derived from the dominant philosophical, scientific, and historical movements rather than from ancient texts. This meant, of course, that certain well-established concepts underwent considerable change, if not elimination, since supernatural intervention and miracles were clearly outmoded in a scientific era. In addition, a new perspective on the value of Christian life emerged. Its relevance lay in its potential to transform the social order.

Theologian Langdon Gilkey has identified four principal ways in which liberalism accommodated itself to the modern world. First, it proffered a different understanding of religious truth. Truth was no longer to be considered as divinely bestowed propositions but rather as a system of human symbols elucidating the mystery and depth of existence. Therefore, religious truth need not be seen in competition with science or history. Second, liberalism advanced a notion of Christian doctrine that acknowledged the historicity of all pronouncements; doctrine was not so much a statement of unchanging validity as an articulation of the community's understanding for a particular time and place. Third, a changed view on Christian life emerged from liberal circles. Holiness was not removing oneself from the cares and concerns of this world in preparation for the world to come, but a commitment to a more just world order. Fourth, liberalism counseled tolerance for divergent views and accepted the situation of religious pluralism. Christians were to love their neighbors above all else; proselytizing was discouraged— true evangelism happened by participation in the building of a more just society. These four modes of accommodation to modernity are essential to liberalism. As Gilkey points out, "every creative form of modern Christian life, Protestant or Catholic . . . assumes these basic liberal contributions, however much they may or may not agree with other aspects of liberal theology."[25]

LIBERAL THEOLOGY'S CONTRIBUTION TO RELIGIOUS EDUCATION

To dwell on the profound influence of liberalism on the present scene is to jump ahead of the story, since here the task is merely to establish the context for the theorists of *religious education*. To assess the liberal contribution is to identify five essential components of *religious education:* a receptivity to "secular" culture, particularly an openness in curricular planning to insights from the arts and sciences; an emphasis upon growth and continuity in the religious life rather than upon conversion and regeneration; a conviction that religious experience bears far more importance than dogma and creeds; a view of the divine inspiring the person from within rather than compelling a person from external authority to obey or be punished; and, finally, a willingness to employ the principles of modern biblical criticism.[26]

Liberal theology's *rapprochement* with modernity animated the *religious education* movement, but progressivism also lent vitality to this classic expression.

PROGRESSIVISM

Progressivism describes a late nineteenth-century movement that sought to extend the myth of the American dream to a nation of immigrants struggling with industrialization. Its humanitarian impulse quickened by democratic ideals, progressivism charted a way of reconstructing American society through education. Progressives viewed education as first and foremost among ways of transforming society. Accordingly, a progressive education movement, including the formation of the Progressive Education Association in 1919, functioned as a centerpiece of progressivism, since, as Lawrence Cremin summarizes, its motif was threefold: social reform, reform through education, and reform of education.

The constellation of images and values surrounding evolutionary theory seemed to enlighten progressive educators in many of the same ways they influenced liberal theologians. Social Darwinists, particularly as interpreted by Herbert Spencer, taught a notion of history as the progressive adaptation of the human character to life's circumstances, thereby giving rise to a view of education as preparation for life—a notion that sparked new views of administration, of teaching, and of curriculum. Under the leadership of theorists such as G. Stanley Hall (whose famous phrase "ontogeny recapitulates phylogeny" reflected his Darwinist leanings), William James, and Edward L. Thorndike, psychology came of age. Hall stressed the scientific study of feelings and attitudes for learning; James instructed teachers on ways of incorporating psychological insights; Thorndike, with unbounded faith in quantitative methods, proffered a way of measuring intelligence. Harold Rugg's work *The Child-Centered School* typified the attention given to the student, and Franklin Bobbitt's *How to Make a Curriculum* classified and detailed the full range of human experience upon which schools could draw as they prepared pupils for life. In 1925, William H. Kilpatrick proposed his "project method" of purposeful activity. But no other theorist so captured the imagination of his and succeeding generations as did John Dewey (1859–1952). His importance for this study, underscored by his role in founding the Religious Education Association in 1903, Dewey's work is crucial for the emergence of *religious education*.

JOHN DEWEY

Dewey, a prolific author whose writings spanned many years, does not readily yield to summary. Yet in possibly his best known work, *The School and Society*, three lectures delivered in 1899, one can see a reflection, a criticism, and a synthesis of American educational thought at the turn of the century. Dewey's thinking evidences the democratic faith in common schools as the instrument of reform. According to Dewey, what the best and wisest parents want for their children is what the community must want for all of its children: "Any other ideal for our schools is narrow and unlovely; acted upon, it destroys our democracy."[27] He envisioned schools as the lever of society wherein students were saturated with a spirit of service and provided with instruments of effective self-direction. Thus he was critical of the standard way of educating, since schools were isolated from the struggle for a better life and dominated by a medieval conception of learning. Instead, he argued, schools should be a genuine form of active community life, not a place set apart for the learning of lessons. To teach merely for the acquisition of information fostered individualism; Dewey passionately believed that schools must be social in orientation so as to teach students the processes necessary for the workings of democracy. Schools should not merely reflect society, but improve it. As embryonic forms of community life, they should be permeated with the spirit of art, of history, and of science. If the school were related to life, all of its studies would necessarily be correlated.[28]

Dewey devoted himself to fashioning an alternative form of schooling, one in which passivity, mechanical massing of children, and uniformity of curriculum and method were replaced by activity, group participation, and adaptation to the needs of the student. He acknowledged that his cause was revolutionary—not unlike the case of Copernicus. Only, as Dewey saw it, "the child becomes the sun about which the appliances of education revolve; he [she] is the center about which they are organized."[29] Yet Dewey's methodology also simply recognized what already existed in the child—interest in conversation, inquiry, construction, and artistic expression:

If we seek the kingdom of heaven, educationally, all other things shall be added unto us—which, being interpreted, is that if we identify ourselves with the real instincts and needs of childhood, and ask only after its fullest assertion and growth, the discipline and information and culture of adult life shall all come in their due season.[30]

"My Pedagogic Creed," written in 1897, encapsulates the principles to which Dewey devoted his educational vocation; its very title suggests the religious character education held for Dewey. Education, conceived of as a "continuing reconstruction of experience," was religious insofar as it provided the "fundamental method of social progress and reform," the "most perfect and intimate union of science and art conceivable in human experience." Because it shaped human powers and adapted them to social service, education was the "supreme art."[31]

Education was the supreme art because Dewey believed that the potential of societal reconstruction made the teacher the "prophet of the true God and usherer in of the true kingdom of God."[32] His view of the exalted vocation of the teacher rested upon a perspective shared with certain other liberals of his time, a naturalistic philosophy that regarded belief in the supernatural as a remnant of a more primitive outlook. His objections to supernaturalism rested on numerous grounds. It ruined religion, since it made religion an absolute in which people settled for security in fixed doctrines rather than risked discovery of truth by way of experimental methods. It distracted people from the realities of life, since it focused on ideal existence; it led to the false dualism of sacred and secular and was all too often grounded in crass ignorance. Moreover, supernaturalism was incompatible with democracy, because it too often legitimized the authoritarian rule of an elite.

Whether or not Dewey was a theist himself is debated. Certainly his 1934 Terry Lectures at Yale, published as *A Common Faith,* do not reflect traditional theism. Here Dewey used the term "God" to denote "the unity of all ideal ends arousing us to desire and actions" and ultimately defined God as "this *active* relation between ideal and actual."[33] Enamored as he was of scientific method, Dewey could not assent to a transcendent God who could not be empirically verified. Though he continued to use the term and to make frequent reference to the "divine," his usage evoked images not of a personal Creator, but of the point at which the ideal became present. His profound commitment to education was a religious act, though not in the theistic sense.

PROGRESSIVISM'S CONTRIBUTION TO RELIGIOUS EDUCATION

Perhaps the contribution of Dewey and other progressives to *religious education* can be summarized in three points. First, their insistence upon the interrelatedness of doing and knowing engendered a new enthusiasm for "learning by doing," what a later age has termed "hands-on" education. This recognition of the power of experiential learning was formalized in Dewey's laboratory school at the University of Chicago and has continued to challenge succeeding generations of educators. Second, their articulation of a child-centered curriculum considerably influenced religious educators who accordingly reworked creed-centered curricula. The assumption that teaching begins with the situation and needs of the learner rather than with content is rooted in the progressive outlook. Third, the progressivist emphasis on the "whole child" and on formation rather than conversion harmonized with Bushnell's notion of nurture. It provided religious educators with an impetus to use the social sciences and to incorporate psychology into their considerations; it legitimized their awakening sense of the dual character of education as both a political activity and a religious act.[34]

RELIGIOUS EDUCATION: LIBERAL THEOLOGY AND PROGRESSIVISM WEDDED

The union of progressive education and liberal theology bore fruit in the classic expression *religious education*. Particularly in the work of George Albert Coe (1862–1951) were these complementary emphases articulated and developed; in his theories the liberal-progressive standpoint is transparent and the distinctive posture of the classic expression most clearly manifest. Thus any exposition of *religious education* necessarily examines the corpus of Coe's writings, though other theorists— William Clayton Bower, Ernest J. Chave, Sophia Lyon Fahs, and Harrison S. Elliott—also deserve attention.

GEORGE ALBERT COE

Coe exemplified, in William James's words, the "once-born" person gifted with the religion of "healthy-mindedness."[35] Raised in a Methodist parsonage in an atmosphere of evangelical pietism in which adherence to doctrine and attainment of salvation by means of an experience of conversion played a significant role, Coe ventured on the "road not taken." Despite his adolescent efforts to seek a conversion in the conventional manner, Coe's revival "showers" failed to dispel his mounting anxieties about his failure to be reborn. Finally, while still a college student, he resolved his dilemma, as he later reported, by a "rational and ethical act" of will.[36] Shortly thereafter, his encounter with Darwin in *The Origin of the Species* and *The Descent of Man* set off another crisis of faith, since Coe recognized the conflict between traditional religion and evolutionary theory. His subsequent resolution reveals his departure from the path taken by evangelicals: "I settled the question, as far as I was concerned, on a Sunday morning by solemnly espousing the scientific method, including it within my religion, and resolving to follow it wherever it should lead."[37] Coe himself acknowledged the critical nature of this experience in an essay written late in his life: "I judge that the most significant turning point in my life, religiously considered, was this early turning away from dogmatic method to scientific method."[38]

Coe's "conversion" to scientific method shaped his movement away from what he perceived as theology's "congenital defect," dogma, and energized his commitment to philosophy and psychology of religion. His first book, *The Spiritual Life: Studies in the Science of Religion* (1900), centered on an empirical study of seventy-seven people in the conversion experience; he concluded that the personalities of those who underwent more pronounced and striking changes, i.e., those "twice born," showed greater emotional sensibility, more susceptibility to "automatisms" (religious dreams, hallucinations, odd impulses).[39] In a later study, Coe's empirical research on 1,784 cases showed the average age of conversion to be 16.4 years, a finding that further strengthened his reservations about revivalism and spurred his efforts to elucidate "the religion of a mature mind."[40] He argued that revivalism, since it failed to attend to the natural laws discovered by empiricism and governing religious development, "wasted" efforts by its preoccupation with the extraordinary. Instead of nurturing and forming persons, revivalism directed its energies at "salvaging." Coe believed that the church's emphasis on dramatic transformations ultimately meant the surrender of the care of souls to a process over which it had no control. Nurture, in contrast, was a process the church might beneficially direct. Hence, Coe's interest in religious education, what William Hutchison has termed a "massive institutionalization of the Bushnellian theories of Christian nurture."[41]

Despite his disillusionment with the established church and his rejection of dogma as unscientific, Coe argued for the inclusion of the religious dimension of education. Without religion, Coe contended, education could never properly fulfill its aim of developing the "whole child." Even if a particular religious tradition were not especially well-founded, the person's desire for adjustment to the larger world and for "unity with the ultimate ground of our being" was fundamental to education, "the end that presides over the beginning and gives unity to all stages of the process."[42] Thus he argued against Dewey, in the formative days of the Religious Education Association, that the association's primary purpose should be directed to religious, rather than secular, education. His point of view triumphed, as can be detected in the statement of the association's aims: "To inspire the religious forces of our country with the educational ideal; to inspire the educational forces of our country with the religious ideal; and to keep before the public mind the ideal of moral and religious education and the sense of its need and value."[43]

EDUCATION AS REDEMPTIVE

But Coe's differences with his colleague Dewey were relatively few. (Coe joined Dewey as a professor at Teachers College, Columbia University in 1922, after thirteen years on the faculty at neighboring Union Theological Seminary.) Coe had a similarly exalted view of education, perhaps most eloquently expressed in this telling phrase: "The process of redemption is at root all one with the process of education."[44] Thus he redefined certain key concepts of Christianity, removing their supernatural layer of meaning and casting them in characteristically progressive terms. He understood incarnation as the supreme instance of sharing life, the way by which an incomplete life unfolded or attained education. In a similar vein, Coe considered atonement as the achievement of education. For Coe, atonement translated to a oneness with the human race. A clue to his "low" Christology, typical of the liberal outlook, lies in his reference to Jesus as the "supreme Educator" rather than as the Redeemer.[45]

EVANGELISM AS "UNEDUCATIONAL"

A book written relatively early in his career (1917), *A Social Theory of Religious Education,* plainly attests to Coe's liberal-progressivist roots.[46] He boldly articulated his differences with revivalism: "The constant aim of elementary religious education should be to make conversion unnecessary"; one should never give over an adolescent to "uneducational evangelism," a phrase reminiscent of Bushnell. Coe believed evangelism was "uneducational" for several reasons: it separated surrender to God from devotion to humankind; it induced a decision either so general or so indeterminate in content as to separate it from specific decisions in a young person's education; it awakened aspirations without providing immediate outlets in social living; it separated conversion from either (or both) habit formation or intelligent analysis; and it depended upon the power of suggestion and emotional enticements, thereby reducing one's self-control.[47] Coe maintained that the aim of Christian education was misdirected when it centered on instructing children in things Christians ought to know, on preparing children for full membership in the church, on unfolding their religious capacities, or on producing Christian character. Its aim should be the facilitation of "growth of the young toward and into mature and efficient devotion to the democracy of God, and happy self-realization therein."[48]

Coe's use of the expression "democracy of God" reveals both his progressivist devotion to democratic ideals and his revulsion for the authoritarian connotation of the more common translation (of the New Testament's *basilea tou Theou*), "kingdom of God." It also suggests the relentlessly social orientation of Coe's work, since, like Dewey, he regarded society as the prime educator and education as the means of the reconstruction of society. In contrast to the individualistic emphases of the revivalists, Coe stressed the importance of social interaction. As far as he was concerned, the primary content of the curriculum was to be found in "present relations and interactions between persons." Otherwise, "as long as one keeps one's attention upon inner and private qualities . . . one can escape the sense of responsibility for the social order of which one is a member."[49] Here the Bible had a certain (if limited) usefulness; its value for social interaction lay to a large degree in the "sharpness with which it presents issues without abstracting them from persons and events."[50]

THE RELATION OF FAITH TO CULTURE: CREATIVE EDUCATION

Coe's commitment to the social order permeates his 1929 work, *What Is Christian Education?*[51] In many respects, the heart of the book lies in his distinction between transmissive and creative education: "Shall the primary purpose of Christian education be to hand on a religion, or to create a new world?"[52] Convinced that "we cannot maintain vital continuity with Jesus unless we take his road of discovery and creation," Coe invited church people to be creators with Jesus, "evoking the unprecedented by our own thinking, experimenting, daring and suffering. Reconstruction, continuous reconstruction, is of the essence of the divine work in and through the human."[53] Moreover, Coe reminded Christians, "there can be no purely private relation to God, for our very selfhood is conjunct. We are made selves by a give-and-take with others—and we are made in his image."[54]

But the church too often failed to incorporate a social vision into its education. The transmissive mode of education prevailed, even though its premises were incompatible with true Christianity. Its policies and practices perpetuated an existing culture; it employed either force or evasion in the interest of effectiveness. Further, the church, in Coe's judgment, ignored the need for rigorous analysis of changing conditions. Its obedience to God resulted in some persons being subject to certain church officials. Creative education, in contrast, sought to improve or reconstruct the culture; even when it employed transmissive processes, they were directed toward transformation. Creative education (not to be confused with self-expression) oriented its adherents to the unfinished tasks of the democracy of God. It contained the potential to reform and revitalize the church. Creative education, in fact, might save the church from institutionalism by developing a system of continuous self-criticism. It might counteract denominational introversion, make the church a base of social radicalism, and reduce the membership and wealth of the church. It might also bring in a true revival for which so many longed. In short, Coe saw education not simply as a way of transforming society, but also as a powerful means of ecclesial renewal and as a creative, life-giving force.

RELIGIOUS EDUCATION DEFINED

Coe viewed his commitment to transformation of the social order as entirely compatible with his devotion to human growth and wholeness. As a personalist who believed that ultimate reality was personal, he understood God at work in persons in ways that did not violate their uniqueness or interfere with the natural laws of human development. As a psychologist of religion, he defined religion functionally as that which enabled individuals and communities to transform their values. As a liberal, he optimistically believed in the advent of progress; as a progressive he fervently upheld democracy as the ultimate enhancement of personal selfhood.[55] All of these threads formed the tapestry of his definition of religious education: "It is the systematic, critical examination and reconstruction of relations between persons, guided by Jesus' assumption that persons are of infinite worth, and by the hypothesis of the existence of God, the Great Valuer of Persons."[56]

Obviously, Coe's definition only makes sense when understood in context. His emphasis on "systematic" and "critical" derived from his embrace of the scientific method, since "every scientific mind submits its processes and its products to other minds for their critical appraisal."[57] The phrase "reconstruction of relations between persons" incorporates both his progressivist and personalist leanings. Furthermore, Coe's appraisal of Jesus' ministry primarily as affirmation of the "infinite worth of persons" quite typically expresses liberal Christology: the Christ's divine character is deemphasized while Jesus' ethical actions are emphasized. Finally, though Coe's theism was certainly more explicit than Dewey's, his image of God as the "Great Valuer of Persons" reveals his reluctance to give credence to a transcendent God. In this he was once more in league with other liberals, for whom divine immanence was a key concept. Here it is noteworthy that the existence of this God is a "hypothesis," a term necessitated by Coe's scientism.

Coe's later career unfolded quite consistently with his liberal-progressivist roots. As did certain other progressivist educators, most notably George S. Counts, who challenged the Progressive Education Association in 1932 to recognize its class bias and to challenge the social order,[58] Coe became increasingly concerned by the "inversion of values" industrial capitalism had brought. The title of his final book, *What Is Religion Doing to Our Consciences?* (1943), indicates his preoccupation with social ethics. The book is a gloomy assessment of what Coe saw as increasing alienation, of estrangements arising from "disagreement with respect to power over material things."[59] He therefore argued for commitment to a classless society, criticized liberals for fleeing from life's actualities, and utilized the categories of Marxist analysis. His "road not taken" took him from Methodist pietism to Marxist messianism.[60]

Though Coe's reconstruction of piety provided the most extended articulation of *religious education,* other theorists likewise exercised influence. William Clayton Bower took up the notion that experience is the source of personality development and echoed Coe's predilection for creative education. Education, he proposed, should not be understood as what adults determined and imposed upon passive learners, but as the "initiation of the young into a creative personal and social experience."[61]

SOPHIA LYON FAHS

Perhaps the religious educator who most brilliantly embodied "creative personal and social experience" for the young was Sophia Lyon Fahs (1876–1978). Fahs was the China-born daughter of Presbyterian missionary parents, an ardent champion of John Dewey and progressive education from her year (1903–1904) of graduate study at Teachers College, a Sunday school teacher and author, the principal (1926) of Union Theological Seminary's Union School of Religion (an experimental Sunday school), a lecturer (1927–1944) in Religious Education on the seminary faculty, and staff member (1933–1942) at New York's Riverside Church. All of this served as a prelude to the work that would make her the "principal figure in the remaking of liberal religious education" in the American Unitarian Association,[62] where she served as editor of its curriculum materials from 1937 to 1951, was ordained to the Unitarian ministry at the age of eighty-two, and completed her final book, *Worshipping Together with Questioning Minds,* at the age of eighty-eight.

Fahs' most singular characteristic was her commitment to listen to children's inquiries and to provide a rich variety of resources by which teachers and students could together educe answers. For instance, in the first publication of the American Unitarian Association's New Beacon Series, she juxtaposed creation myths from various cultures with modern scientific conclusions about the world's beginnings so that children could realize that all peoples in history had been asking the same questions. Thus might children discover a communion with the rest of humankind, a oneness with the "great company who have struggled, have been curious, have wondered and have sought for understanding."[63]

Fahs articulated the philosophy undergirding her teaching and writing in a 1952 work, *Today's Children and Yesterday's Heritage.*[64] There she laid out twelve dimensions of the curriculum of those who have "changed the conception of the educational process from one of indoctrination and acceptance of authority to one of creative discovery, intelligent examination and free decision."[65] Following is a summary of these dimensions:

There is no special religious knowledge that belongs properly to the sphere of the church or synagogue rather than to the public school. Any subject, phenomenon, or thing may be the starting point of religious education.

The focus belongs in the present and future rather than in the past.

The Bible ought to be left to study until that point when children are mature enough to profit from knowledge of the past; the Bible should be studied not as an authority for certain ideals or beliefs but as a means of understanding a way of life that has shaped the West.

Children need breadth in their exposure to history, not simply knowledge of the Judeo-Christian heritage, but of the world religions.

Schools of religion should become laboratories for experiments in human relations so that children can learn to cooperate maturely.

As children mature, they should be given the opportunity to understand the broader conflicts of the age, e.g., the dynamics of war and peace.

Children need not merely to learn about human relationships, but also to explore the world of nature; religious education needs to be linked with all things, living and nonliving.

Self-understanding is a goal for a child's religious education so that his or her emotional autonomy might be developed.

Especially can very young children be taught about mysticism through experience with plant seeds, animals, and babies.

Schools of religion most appropriately deal with sex education.

Schools of religion most appropriately deal also with death education.

To learn to participate wisely in the religious development of children is to learn a profession demanding scholarship of high quality in a wide range of fields.[66]

HARRISON S. ELLIOTT

The classic expression *religious education* is also elucidated in the work of Harrison S. Elliott, Coe's successor at Union Theological Seminary. Over the years, critics had assembled a number of negative judgments about the theological and educational premises of Coe and his cohorts (see the next chapter for a detailed exposition of the criticisms), and Elliott's *Can Religious Education Be Christian?* (1940) offered not only a rejoinder to the critics but also an insightful summary of the religious education movement.[67]

Progressive religious educators, Elliott maintained, gave an important place to continuous manifestations of God in nature and in human life. In their perspective, revelation did not cease merely with the first century of the Christian era—nor was it confined to Christianity. True, God was supremely manifest in Jesus Christ, as their critics emphasized, but "nature and history are also manifestations of God who becomes known only through the experience and relevant search" of men and women.[68] If that view of revelation is true, then the educational process—with a stress on process—is essential to the Christian faith, and scientific knowledge furnishes important data for attaining knowledge of God. To claim that one learns in and through experience is not a mere pedagogical slogan but a claim about the way humankind has discovered everything it knows. Nurture and growth are not faddish terms, but the fundamental way Christian faith develops in individuals. Elliott accused the critics of endeavoring to establish a "single, authoritative interpretation of the Christian religion" and challenged them with the judgment that such attempts have never succeeded.[69] In contrast, the educational process allowed for varied and rich interpretations of the faith and fostered appreciation for God's diverse ways of revelation.

Like Coe and Fahs, Elliott believed fervently in the social orientation of religious education. In response to critics who accused the liberals of naively overlooking the powerful reality of sin, he made this argument:

There should be more sense of social responsibility and a larger consciousness of social sin. This gives the basis for a realistic religious education which recognizes fully the limitations of human beings and the seriousness of the human problem, but, at the same time, renders it possible to make a positive attack upon the problem through the educative process.[70]

Elliott was not opposed to utilizing the Bible in Sunday schools or to worship that sought "direct experience of God," but he felt both Bible study and worship had to be brought to bear on present experience and reinterpreted in light of contemporary problems, lest they were merely interesting or consoling rather than pertinent to modern life:

Bible study and prayer and worship will not of themselves produce vital religious experience. It is only when these are utilized because of a concern for human life and because of a sense of need for resources beyond those which seem available in human endeavor that they lead to the vitalizing of religious experience. The experience of God is integrally related to a social process of religious education.[71]

A key concern of Elliott's book was revelation, obviously a response to his critics, who considered the proponents of *religious education* insufficiently appreciative of the distinctiveness of Christian revelation. Reading Elliott, one may be surprised at his frequent use of the term "revelation." Yet this frequency only points up the extent to which the progressive religious educators had largely ignored any explicit exposition of revelation; their inattention is a clue to their turning away from more orthodox theological categories. It also suggests that a summation of *religious education* in terms of the foundational questions might provide an analytic base for the classic expression *Christian education,* which developed largely in reaction to the theological and educational premises of *religious education.*

RELIGIOUS EDUCATION: A SUMMARY

The first generation of theorists of *religious education* devoted little explicit attention to the question of revelation. Yet one can ferret out implications from their stress on human experience and simultaneous deemphasis on divine revelation. Their commitments to reconstruction of the social order meant that they understood the fundamental locus of God's revelation to be in the world, particularly in social interaction. Though they did not reject the Scriptures or traditional forms of worship, neither played an important role. Coe disapproved of too much focus on the Bible, since he feared it would distract people from reality, and regarded true worship as seeing life objectively. His exclamation during a capital-labor struggle in the Kentucky coal mines witnessed to his understanding of revelation: "O, you metaphysicians! If there be a God, he is in Harlan County, Kentucky. Show us him, that we may worship! If you cannot find him in Harlan County, your talk about the universe in general will not bring us to our knees."[72]

Conversion, as understood in *evangelism,* was incompatible with these theorists' view of the divine-human relationship, since it rested on an authoritarian God and a passive creature. In *religious education,* growth replaced conversion as the key emphasis; in fact, the entire educational process obviated the need for conversion. The vocabulary of nurture, formation, development, and wholeness evoked an entirely different understanding of a person's relationship with God; words such as sin and guilt nearly fell into disuse. Furthermore, conversion became a subject of empirical study, and those who engaged in this research had often themselves undergone a sort of a conversion to the methods of science.

Their embrace of empiricism fostered a devaluation of the supernatural. Consequently, adherence to a creed was looked upon as dogmatism and the educational process was regarded as a necessary corrective to the indoctrinating ways of *evangelism.* Yet despite their critical perspective on assent to traditional creedal formulations, Coe and his colleagues considered cognition extremely important. They had serious reservations about the enthusiasm unleashed by revivals and sought to counter this emotionalism with rational, analytical discussion. The affective dimension was not without its importance, as they frequently affirmed the "whole child," but their commitment to scientific method entailed more respect for logic and critical thinking. Ironically, their appropriation of science was enthusiastic, their argument for rationality in religion passionate.

For theology, however, they had little enthusiasm. Clearly, the theorists of *religious education* were decidedly uninterested in metaphysical questions and directed virtually no energy into theological debates. Of course, they had a theology, as has been made plain above, but their preoccupation with education, including psychology and sociology, precluded much explicit theologizing.

The liberal theology upon which their assumptions rested exemplifies Niebuhr's category "Christ of culture," a "culture Christianity" allied with self-reliant humanism.[73] Conscious of their explicit commitment to reconstruction of the social order, leaders of the religious education movement equated education with salvation. Moreover, they directed their concerns toward "the salvation of world community rather than merely the salvation of a few select individuals."[74] Since they believed that there was no specifically "religious" subject matter, they designed curricula inclusive of a broad range of human concerns.

Proponents of *religious education* were clear and consistent in articulating their aim: the reconstruction of society, even if the precise meaning of that was less obvious. The faith in the democratic process gave this goal a distinctively American and generally white, middle-class cast and distinguished it from more orthodox aims. One educated another in faith because that was the most powerful means of changing the world and of creating a more just society.

Their epistemology provides some fascinating contrasts. On the one hand, the empirical enthusiasm reflected a tendency to quantify learning; after all, much of the psychology developed out of progressivist circles—particularly along the lines of Edward Thorndike—rested on the assumption that one could measure learning and intelligence. Coe's early work on cases of conversion contributed to the establishment of the scientific study of religion. It is necessary to acknowledge the ground-breaking character of his efforts, since his predecessors would not have presumed to apply scientific categories to God's work in a person's soul. Certainly hindsight reveals the naiveté of the liberal-progressivist movement: the knowledge discovered by the so-called scientific method is neither so objective nor so certain as its enthusiasts believed. Yet, coexisting with this predilection for "objective" knowledge was a profound sense that true knowledge overflowed into action. Dewey's aversion for dualism and his insistence upon the unity of theory and practice testified to this desire to understand knowledge as transformation. Coe's illumination of the ethical foundation of spirituality likewise manifests a recognition that knowledge is far more demanding that mere comprehension of information. Moreover, fundamental to *religious education* was a commitment to "learn by doing," thus a rejection of the dichotomy between knowledge and know-how.

In part, the orientation toward learning through activity grew out of and contributed to the significant role of the social sciences in *religious education*. The emergence of a psychology of learning and of developmental psychology proved crucial to this classic expression. Later, Freudian theory influenced progressive schools. Certainly the social sciences bore more weight than did theology in the development of religious education theory.

A 1912 curriculum for a Sunday school in New Haven, Connecticut—including an introductory essay by Coe—hints at the kind of curriculum characteristic of *religious education*. Instruction was initiated with very young children (the "cradle roll," ages one through three). For children six through eight years of age, the focus was on God's loving qualities and on the ways the man Jesus served others. The next age group studied the heroes of the Bible and the history of Christianity; teenagers began to utilize historical criticism in studying the Bible and were involved in social service. Older teens studied comparative religion and the principles of psychology.[75]

In *religious education* the teacher's role primarily involved design of activities and facilitation of growth. Teachers needed to know how to lead group processes (an emphasis particularly in the second generation of theorists) and were to avoid methods that smacked of indoctrination. They were looked upon as guides to their students rather than as authoritarian figures.

If the theorists made one thing clear, it was their realization that education was indeed a political activity. "Hidden," of course, in their curriculum was the uncritical regard for democracy and the arrogant belief that progress was being made steadily; what was not taught (the "null" curriculum) was traditional Christian doctrine.

As a classic expression, *religious education* reflects a radical departure both theologically and educationally from previous modes of educating in faith. The furor its radicality engendered leads to the next section: the classic expression *Christian education* resulted from its critique.

Figure 3

Religious Education

FOUNDATIONAL QUESTIONS	THE CLASSIC EXPRESSION *RELIGIOUS EDUCATION*
REVELATION	• Scripture and traditional forms of worship did not play as central a role. • Normative criteria for theology derived from dominant philosophical and scientific movements rather than from ancient texts. • God's immanence stressed. • Revelation found in social interaction.
CONVERSION	• Viewed primarily as growth. • Became subject of empirical study. • Family life and the educational process seen as making conversion unnecessary. • Danger of church falling into "uneducational evangelism."
FAITH & BELIEF	• Religious experience more important than dogma and creedal formulas. • Dogma "unscientific" and linked to authoritarian systems.
THEOLOGY	• Scientific models dominated theological ones. • Theological language "translated" into educational terms (e.g., Jesus the "supreme educator"). • Lack of interest in metaphysical questions. • Modern biblical criticism used. • Religious pluralism extolled. • Sin and guilt de-emphasized.
FAITH & CULTURE	• The sacred and secular seen as essentially harmonious. • Progress and democracy extolled. • Religion tended to be relegated to periphery as the domain of women and clergy. • Society seen as the prime educator.
GOAL OF EDUCATION	• The reconstruction of society. • Continuous growth. • Formation of the whole child.
KNOWLEDGE	• Attention to the link between theory and practice. • Emphasis on "objective" knowledge as discovered through empirical methods. • Respect for logic and cognition; distrust of emotionalism spawned by revivalism.

FOUNDATIONAL QUESTIONS	THE CLASSIC EXPRESSION *RELIGIOUS EDUCATION*
SOCIAL SCIENCES	· Very important. · Use exemplified reconciliation of scientific method with traditional Christianity. · Precedence given to psychology. · Interest in social science outweighed interest in theology.
CURRICULUM & TEACHING	· Child-centered curriculum replaced creed-centered curriculum. · Curriculum more inclusive and humanistic. · Curriculum less attentive to doctrine. · Emphasis placed on the *process* of teaching. · Teachers regarded as guides rather than as authorities.
EDUCATION AS POLITICAL	· Education seen as first and foremost among the ways of transforming society. · Social reform and educational form linked. · Uncritical regard for democracy.

NOTES

1. William Ellery Channing, *The Sunday School: A Discourse Pronounced Before the Sunday School Society* (Boston: James Munroe, 1838), 11.
2. Ibid., 9–10.
3. Cited in William Adamson, *Bushnell Rediscovered* (Philadelphia and Boston: United Church Press, 1966), 19.
4. Horace Bushnell, *Christian Nurture* (New Haven, CT: Yale University Press, 1967).
5. Ibid., 60.
6. Ibid., 61.
7. Ibid., 4.
8. Ibid., 15.
9. Ibid., 39.
10. Ibid., 41.
11. Ibid., 140.
12. Ibid., 158.
13. Ibid.
14. Ibid., 158–159.
15. Ibid., 328.
16. Ibid., 292.
17. Mary B. Cheney, *Life and Letters of Horace Bushnell* (New York: Harper and Brothers, 1880), 60.
18. Cited in Anne L. Kuhn, *The Mother's Role in Childhood Education: New England Concepts 1830–1860* (New Haven, CT: Yale University Press, 1947), 47–48.
19. Ibid., 30.
20. Ibid., 76.
21. Horace Bushnell, "The Age of Homespun," *Litchfield County Centennial Celebration* (Hartford, CT: Edwin Hunt, 1851), 112. Cited in Ann Douglas, *The Feminization of American Culture* (New York: Avon, 1977), 60.

22. Milton Powell, ed., *The Voluntary Church: American Religious Life (1740–1865) Seen Through the Eyes of European Visitors* (New York: Macmillan, 1967), 125. Cited in Douglas, *The Feminization of American Culture*, 48.

23. Kuhn, *The Mother's Role in Childhood Education*, 97.

24. Cited in Martin E. Marty, *Righteous Empire: The Protestant Experience in America* (New York: Dial, 1970), 195.

25. Langdon Gilkey, *Naming the Whirlwind: The Renewal of God Language* (Indianapolis, IN: Bobbs-Merrill, 1969), 77–78.

26. See William R. Hutchison, *The Modernist Impulse in American Protestantism* (Cambridge, MA: Harvard University Press, 1976), 158–59.

27. In Martin S. Dworkin, ed., *Dewey on Education*, Classics in Education No. 3 (New York: Teachers College Press, 1959), 34.

28. Ibid., 88.

29. Ibid., 52–53.

30. Ibid., 69.

31. Ibid., 30–31.

32. Ibid., 32.

33. John Dewey, *A Common Faith* (New Haven, CT: Yale University Press, 1934), 42, 51.

34. See Hutchison, *The Modernist Impulse*, 159.

35. See William James, *The Varieties of Religious Experience: A Study in Human Nature* (London: Collins, 1977). James derived his distinction between "onceborn" and "twiceborn" from F. W. Newman's 1852 *The Soul: Its Sorrows and Its Aspirations.* James's book is based on the Gifford Lectures delivered at Edinburgh in 1901–1902.

36. George Albert Coe, "My Own Little Theatre," in Vergilius Ferm, ed., *Religion in Transition* (New York: Macmillan, 1937), 93.

37. Ibid., 95.

38. George Albert Coe, "My Search for What Is Most Worthwhile," *Religious Education* 47 (1952):176.

39. George Albert Coe, *The Spiritual Life: Studies in the Science of Religion* (New York: Eater and Mains, 1900).

40. George Albert Coe, *The Religion of a Mature Mind* (Chicago: Revell, 1902).

41. Hutchison, *The Modernist Impulse*, 159.

42. George Albert Coe, *Education in Religion and Morals* (New York: Revell, 1904), 29–32.

43. "The Purpose of the Association," *Religious Education* 1 (1906):2.

44. Ibid., 406.

45. Ibid., 405.

46. George Albert Coe, *A Social Theory of Religious Education* (New York: Scribner, 1917). Available in a reprint in the American Education Series (New York: Arno Press and the New York Times, 1969).

47. Coe, *A Social Theory of Religious Education*, 1927, 181–83.

48. Ibid., 55.

49. Ibid., 102, 104.

50. Ibid., 116.

51. George Albert Coe, *What Is Christian Education?* (New York: Scribner, 1929).

52. Ibid., 28.

53. Ibid., 33.

54. Ibid., 73.

55. See Helen A. Archibald, *George Albert Coe: Theorist for Religious Education in the Twentieth Century* (Ann Arbor, MI: University Microfilms, 1975), 234.

56. Coe, *What Is Christian Education?* 296.

57. Ibid., 137.

58. See George S. Counts, *Dare the School Build a New Social Order?* American Education Series (New York: Arno Press and the New York Times, 1969).

59. George Albert Coe, *What Is Religion Doing to Our Consciences?* (New York: Scribner, 1943), 57.

60. See H. Shelton Smith, "George Albert Coe, Revaluer of Values," *Religion in Life* 22 (1952–53):46–57.
61. William Clayton Bower, *Character Through Creative Experience* (Chicago: University of Chicago Press, 1930), 13.
62. David Robinson, *The Unitarians and the Universalists* (Westport, CT: Greenwood, 1985), 278.
63. Sophia Lyon Fahs, *Beginnings of Earth and Sky* (Boston: Beacon, 1937), v.
64. Sophia Lyon Fahs, *Today's Children and Yesterday's Heritage* (Boston: Beacon, 1952).
65. Ibid., 177.
66. Ibid., 176–197.
67. Harrison S. Elliott, *Can Religious Education Be Christian?* (New York: Macmillan, 1940).
68. Ibid., 115.
69. Ibid., 80.
70. Ibid., 177.
71. Ibid., 278–79.
72. George Albert Coe, "The Social Value of Prayer and Worship," *The World Tomorrow* 15 (1932):176.
73. See H. Richard Niebuhr, *Christ and Culture* (New York: Harper & Row, 1951), 83–115.
74. Fahs, *Today's Children and Yesterday's Heritage*, 152.
75. See George Albert Coe, *The Core of Good Teaching* (New York: Scribner, 1912).

Bibliographic Essay

Religious Education

In addition to the general studies of American religious history cited in the previous bibliographic essay (especially Handy, Ahlstrom, and Marty), I have been especially assisted in this chapter by William R. Hutchison, *The Modernist Impulse in American Protestantism* (Cambridge, MA: Harvard University Press, 1976). Also instrumental in my interpretation of this period were Kenneth Cauthen, *The Impact of American Religious Liberalism* (New York: Harper & Row, 1962); Langdon Gilkey, *Naming the Whirlwind: The Renewal of God Language* (Indianapolis, IN: Bobbs-Merrill, 1969), esp. 85–91; David Tracy, *Blessed Rage for Order* (New York: Seabury, 1975); and Claude Welch, *Protestant Thought in the Nineteenth Century* (New Haven, CT: Yale University Press, 1972). A fine analysis is offered by Robert M. Crunden, *Ministers of Reform: The Progressives' Achievement in American Civilization, 1889–1920* (New York: Basic Books, 1982).

Lawrence Cremin, *The Transformation of the School: Progressivism in American Education, 1876–1957* (New York: Knopf, 1961) situates the educational history. Clarence J. Karier, Paul Violas, and Joel Spring, eds., offer a revisionist perspective on the era in their *Roots of Crisis: American Education in the Twentieth Century* (Chicago: Rand-McNally, 1973).

William E. Channing's convictions can be traced in *The Works of William E. Channing, D.D.*, 6 vols. (Boston: James Munroe, 1843). Horace Bushnell's *Christian Nurture* (New Haven, CT: Yale University Press, 1967) is essential reading; the first edition was published as *Views of Christian Nurture and of Subjects Adjacent Thereto* in 1847; Mary Bushnell Cheney's *Life and Letters of Horace Bushnell* (New York: Harper and Brothers, 1880) does much to fill out his person. William Adamson, *Bushnell Rediscovered* (Philadelphia and Boston: United Church Press, 1966) is useful. Two works that contribute to a fuller understanding of his time are Anne L. Kuhn, *The Mother's Role in Childhood Education: New England Concepts, 1830–1860* (New Haven, CT: Yale University Press, 1947) and Ann Douglas, *The Feminization of American Culture* (New York: Avon, 1977).

Martin S. Dworkin has compiled an excellent sampling from John Dewey in his *Dewey on Education*, Classics in Education No. 3 (New York: Teachers College Press, 1959). Other key Dewey works include: *Democracy and Education* (New York: Macmillan, 1916); *Art as Experience* (New York: Capricorn, 1934); *A Common Faith* (New Haven, CT: Yale University Press, 1934); and *Experience and Education* (New York: Collier, 1938).

Though less prolific than Dewey, George Albert Coe also contributed a substantial list of books during the course of his long career. Among the primary sources, I think the following indicate the extent of his thought: *The Spiritual Life: Studies in the Science of Religion* (New York: Eaton and Mains, 1900); *The Religion of a Mature Mind* (Chicago: Revell, 1902), *Education in Religion and Morals* (New York: Revell, 1904); *The Psychology of Religion* (Chicago: University of Chicago Press, 1916); *A Social Theory of Religious Education* (New York: Scribner,

1917; available also in reprint in the series "American Education: Its Men, Ideas and Institutions," [(New York: Arno Press and the New York Times, 1969]); *What Is Christian Education?* (New York: Scribner, 1929); "My Own Little Theatre," in Vergilius Ferm, ed., *Religion in Transition* (New York: Macmillan, 1937), 90–125; *What Is Religion Doing to Our Consciences?* (New York: Scribner, 1943). Of the periodical literature, these appear to be most representative: "Religious Education as a Part of General Education," *Proceedings of the First Convention of the Religious Education Association* (Chicago, 1903; reprinted in John H. Westerhoff, III, ed., *Who Are We? The Quest for a Religious Education* [(Birmingham, AL: Religious Education Press, 1978): 14–22]); "What I Have Seen and What I Hope to See," *Religious Education* 22 (1927):419–27; "What Is Religious Education?" *Religious Education* 18 (1933):92–95; "The Assault upon Liberalism," *Religious Education* 34 (1939):85–92; "The Definitive Dewey," *Religious Education* 35 (1940):45–50; and "My Search for What Is Most Worthwhile," *Religious Education* 47 (1952):170–76.

Regarding the secondary literature on Coe, Helen A. Archibald's *George Albert Coe: Theorist for Religious Education in the Twentieth Century* (Ann Arbor, MI: University Microfilms, 1975) ranks as definitive. Also of special note is H. Shelton Smith's appreciative retrospective, "George Albert Coe: Revaluer of Values," *Religion in Life* 22 (1952–1953):46–57. William James, *The Varieties of Religious Experience* (London: Collins, 1977 [original, 1902]) offers an important psychological perspective; George S. Counts, *Dare the School Build a New Social Order?* American Education Series (New York: Arno Press and the New York Times, 1969) argues a thesis in general education that Coe argued for *religious education.* Among other theorists identified with the classic expression *religious education,* Sophia Lyon Fahs has also contributed greatly. See her *Today's Children and Yesterday's Heritage* (Boston: Beacon, 1952); Edith Hunter, *Sophia Lyon Fahs: A Biography,* One Hundredth Birthday Edition (Boston: Beacon, 1976) not only provides an immensely readable account, but includes a complete bibliography of her writings. Also of great assistance is Elizabeth Baker's *Retrospect* (Boston: Unitarian Universalist Advance Study Paper No. 14A with Supplement, 1980), which the author kindly made available to me. William Clayton Bower's work also figures significantly, especially: *A Survey of Religious Education in the Local Church* (Chicago: University of Chicago Press, 1919); *The Curriculum of Religious Education* (New York: Scribner, 1925); and *Moral and Spiritual Values in Education* (Lexington, KY: University of Kentucky Press, 1952). Also Washington Gladden, "Bringing All the Moral and Religious Forces into Effective Educational Unity," *Proceedings of the Fifth Convention of the Religious Education Association,* in Westerhoff, *Who Are We?* 23–33; and Ernest J. Chave, *A Functional Approach to Religious Education* (Chicago: University of Chicago Press, 1947).

The work of Coe's successor at Union Theological Seminary, Harrison S. Elliott, is especially important: *Can Religious Education Be Christian?* (New York: Macmillan, 1940). It represents the most detailed presentation of *religious education* in response to the critics described in chapter 4.

Surveying the Territory: Christian Education

If the classic expression *religious education* served as both counterpoint and alternative to *evangelism,* then *Christian education* functioned as the critique and corrective to what were perceived as the excesses of liberalism. *Christian education* was, in a word, a theological thrust among Protestant educators that sought to emphasize the distinctiveness of a *Christian* education. Yet, despite its repudiation of many of the claims of the progressives, the *Christian education* movement did not return to the enthusiasms of *evangelism,* but contributed its unique emphases. Thus a third classic expression developed.

NEO-ORTHODOXY: A SOBER ASSESSMENT OF LIBERALISM

Much of the philosophical and theological thought of the nineteenth century that had so profoundly shaped Dewey and Coe appeared to take on a different cast to many who took up its study in the wake of World War I and the economic downturn of the late 1920s. Reinhold Niebuhr, one of the most significant theologians of the era, remarked that when the war had started (1914) he had been a "young man trying to be an optimist without falling into sentimentality. When it [the war] ended and the full tragedy of its fratricides had been revealed, I had become a realist without trying to save myself from cynicism."[1] Or as Halford Luccock later commented, it seemed as though an "elevator loaded with humanity, due to shoot upwards to some sixty-fifth story of a skyscraper" constructed by human technology had jammed and dropped: "In that drop it was not only General Motors and AT&T and other similar hopes of salvation that were deflated, but faiths as well."[2]

Much of the theological impetus for this reconsideration of Christian essentials originated in Germany, inaugurated by a commentary, Karl Barth's celebrated *The Epistle to the Romans,* first published in 1919 and revised in 1922. Thus began a Lutheran renaissance indebted to the existentialist thought of Danish philosopher Søren Aaby Kierkegaard (1813–1855) and manifested in the works of Karl Barth, Emil Brunner, Rudolf Bultmann, and Paul Tillich. Indeed, it appeared as if God were speaking German, so far-reaching was the effect of these theologians upon the Western world. Their viewpoint was termed "dialectical theology," since it emphasized the difference between divine and human categories, or, alternatively, "neo-orthodox theology," since its reinterpretation of Christianity both rejected the optimism of the liberals and the defensiveness of the evangelicals, particularly of the fundamentalists. Deeply sensitive to the divisions of the war-torn world, they judged the liberal enterprise to be tragically naive in its assessment of progress, particularly as imaged in evolutionary ascent, and sought to make reparation for this arrogance in their emphasis on the sinfulness and finitude of the human condition. Moreover, they judged the categories of orthodox thought to be inadequate insofar as they insufficiently reflected the personalist dimension of the encounter of the divine and human. Thus, they promulgated—albeit in new terms—some of the classic themes of the Reformation: biblical faith, transcendence, sinfulness, and the necessity of choice.

Neo-orthodoxy made its appearance in North America not only through the publications of Barth and his colleagues, but particularly through the teaching of Paul Tillich (who emigrated to the United States in 1933), Reinhold Niebuhr, his brother, H. Richard Niebuhr, and their sister, Hulda Niebuhr. Their positions at prominent theological schools exercised a profound influence upon generations of those working in Christian ministry. Tillich and Reinhold Niebuhr taught at Union Theological Seminary in New York City. Tillich taught there from 1933 to 1955, when he went to Harvard Divinity School, and then in 1962 he moved to the University of Chicago. Reinhold Niebuhr taught at Union from 1928 to 1962; H. Richard Niebuhr taught at Yale from 1938 to 1962. Many observers of theological education in the 1970s and 1980s decry its present state and hearken back to its heyday of the Niebuhrs and Tillich.

REINHOLD NIEBUHR'S INFLUENCE

Perhaps Reinhold Niebuhr's 1932 book *Moral Man and Immoral Society* most eloquently testifies to the neo-orthodox departure from liberal categories.[3] From the outset he took issue with the progressives, most especially with John Dewey, whom he accused of failing to understand the economic interests of the middle class; reason, claimed Niebuhr, was always to some degree the "servant of interest" in a social situation. Therefore, "social injustice cannot be resolved by moral and rational suasion alone, as the educator and social scientist usually believe."[4] What

Dewey and others of his worldview lacked was an understanding of the "brutal character of all human collectives, and the power of self-interest and collective egoism in all inter-group relations." They failed to see that the "limitations of the human imagination, the easy subservience of reason to prejudice and passion, and the consequent persistence of irrational egoism, particularly in group behavior, make social conflict an inevitability in human history, probably to its very end."[5] Individuals may be moral, but in groups a certain collective egoism exerts more power than does either reason or conscience.

Niebuhr's arguments with the liberals foreshadowed some of the criticism that would come later from Christian educators. His realism regarding the limits of reason clashed with Coe's great faith in scientific method. Furthermore, he judged the progressives' "evolutionary millennialism" to be the "hope of comfortable and privileged classes," and accused liberal Protestantism of sentimentality:

In spite of the disillusionment of the World War, the average liberal Protestant Christian is still convinced that the kingdom of God is gradually approaching, that the League of Nations is its partial fulfillment and the Kellogg Pact its covenant, that the wealthy will be persuaded by the church to dedicate their power and privilege to the common good and that they are doing so in increasing numbers, that the conversion of individuals is the only safe method of solving the social problem, and that such ethical weaknesses as religion still betrays are due to its theological obscurantism which will be sloughed off by the progress of enlightenment.[6]

Niebuhr did not share Coe's confidence that the power of religious education could reconstruct society. He considered even the wisest "social pedagogy" incapable of developing the sort of ethical attitudes made possible by personal, intimate, and organic contacts, though he did believe that a sense of justice was primarily a product of the mind rather than the heart. If ethical attitudes were to be formed at all, they would need to arise from intimate religious communities, that is, from situations that influenced a person's actions in a social rather than individual context. Hence, the power of the church as a countercultural community. But even then one ought not be unduly optimistic, since human moral resources were not the guarantors of God's reign: "A sentimental generation has destroyed this apocalyptic note in the vision of the Christ. It thinks the kingdom of God is around the corner, while he [Jesus] regarded it as impossible of realisation, except by God's grace."[7]

H. SHELTON SMITH: CRITIC OF THE RELIGIOUS EDUCATION MOVEMENT

Niebuhr's assessment of the world situation was in many respects paralleled by one of his contemporaries, H. Shelton Smith, the most judicious among those in the educational realm who confronted progressivism. Smith proposed in 1934 that "religious educators must reckon with Barthianism."[8] Despite his own reservations about a tendency among Barth and his followers to resort to "dogmatic supernaturalism," Smith saw in their work significant challenges to the customary thought of religious educators. First, in the Barthian stress on proclamation of the Word, the norm of Christian education became Jesus Christ as revealed in the Bible. Instead of "life situations" espoused by Dewey and Coe, the Bible constituted the subject matter of the curriculum. Second, Barthian pedagogy devolved on an anthropology of human sinfulness and thus entailed attentiveness to the need for conversion. Third, it rejected human autonomy as a principle of education and stressed God's authority instead. Fourth, it assigned education a more modest role; God's Word, not the teacher's strategies, revealed truth. Thus the Barthians rendered a "long-needed service" since they effectively battled with "easy-going liberalisms": that humans are the center and measure of all things; that evil is but an "anti-social appendix" from which people can be weaned by a "little more progressive teaching and preaching"; that it is not what people think but how they think; that Jesus was simply a good man who gave good advice; and that the Bible is a problem-solver for "life situations."[9]

In many respects, Smith's prime contribution to the field was his own commitment to "reckon" with the implications of neo-orthodoxy for education. While clearly sympathetic to the critique of liberalism, Smith nevertheless evidenced a genuine appreciation for the work of the progressives under whom he had begun his career in 1928 at Teachers College. Thus, on the occasion of Coe's death in 1951, he composed an article that discharged a "debt to a man who was one of my warmest friends, despite our disagreements at certain theological points."[10] Indeed, Smith's preeminence lay largely in his astute analysis of the theological assumptions underlying progressivist thought. His 1941 book, *Faith and Nurture*, is a foremost example of those critiques that would ground the classic expression of *Christian education;* when read in tandem with Harrison Elliott's 1940 apologia for the liberal perspective, *Can Religious Education Be Christian?*, it aptly summarizes an era.

Like Niebuhr, Smith took issue with the optimism of the liberals. "Paradoxically," he observed, "the generation that has been preoccupied with the study of man [woman] finds itself in the predicament of discovering that it does not really know man [woman]!"[11] Overawed with the newly developing social sciences of psychology, sociology, and anthropology, the progressives had ignored Christian theology and thus had concocted a superficial view of reality. In their dependence upon social science, they had insufficiently accounted for the sinful, broken character of the human condition; in their enthusiasm for empiricism they had obscured, and even in some cases denied, the ultimate ground of human existence; in their championing of immanence and denial of transcendence, they had replaced the cosmic source of human worth with the less forceful notion of the intrinsic worth of personhood in a democratic society.[12] Smith agreed with the progressives that persons were of infinite worth, but took issue with the way they understood the source of that worth. In Christian faith, he argued, human beings are not merely creatures of purely secular or natural forces but are, rather, divinely fashioned: "The ultimate root of the Christian worth of persons is therefore theocentric."[13]

SMITH ON THE THEOLOGY OF PROGRESSIVISM

In sum, Smith discerned two theological assumptions in the progressivist outlook (especially in Coe's thought): divine immanence and a "progress-making God."[14] The first theme was implicit in Coe's assertion in his 1904 *Education in Religion and Morals* that the religious growth of the child from birth took place "entirely within the kingdom of grace"—as if one's innate goodness were a logical deduction from God's immanence in human existence. Smith recognized that Coe was not an uncritical romantic, since he had acknowledged that the child had evil tendencies as well as good ones—even if he attributed those evil tendencies to the "warped mores of society." Still, Smith argued for the recognition that "a realistic understanding of human nature requires man [woman] to see himself [herself] as both child of God and sinner, and not merely as one or the other."[15] Smith, it should be noted, was not suggesting that Coe and his colleagues should return to the notion of total depravity ("Orthodoxy had committed itself to a doctrine of total depravity, and had thereby lost the consciousness of man's [woman's] godlikeness as implicated in the divine image"[16]), but that their view should reflect the balance that came from a recognition of divine transcendence. Similarly, Smith accused Coe of so fusing divine with human love that one could have no private relation with God, thereby effectively obscuring God's transcendence.

The second theme was implicit in Coe's embrace of evolution and its accompanying notion of human advancement. At stake here, Smith perceived, was whether or not Christianity contained within itself any element or principle of permanent validity. Coe claimed that there was: the principle of worth Jesus ascribed to persons. But Smith challenged the Christology that could lead Coe to say that "the loyalty of the Christian, accordingly, is loyalty not to one person, even Jesus, but to persons."[17] This, remarked Smith, represented the logical deduction of Coe's evolutionary theory of history and religion: "reasoning, as he does, from the premise of a continuously growing religion, he has to reject the classical Christian view of the finality of the Christian revelation."[18]

Furthermore, Coe's belief in moral progress led him to an overly optimistic interpretation of the human predicament.

In Smith's assessment, the theological assumptions of the progressives presented them with three options. One was to continue to reaffirm their present directions, a thematic present in Coe's later articles[19] and in the work of William Clayton Bower and Harrison Elliott. Another was simply to align forces with the naturalists and abandon any pretense of distinctively Christian approaches, as evident in the work of Ernest J. Chave.[20] The third option was a reconstruction of theological foundations in light of "more realistic" insights of current Christian faith—the option for which Smith held the most hope. Typically, Smith sought the middle road, as Susan Brooks Thistlethwaite observes:

Smith sought a position mid-way between the idea of conversion as a radical, unrepeatable experience as found in an older orthodoxy and a perfectionizing liberalism which had obscured the ambiguous character of this life of growth in the faith which was still subject to sin and perversity because the church, while the body of Christ, is also in and of the world.[21]

THEOLOGY AS THE "CLUE" TO CHRISTIAN EDUCATION

Smith had seen in the 1947 study of the International Council of Religious Education promise of this reconstruction, though he himself went in the direction of American religious thought and became less identified with the church's educational endeavors. But the study, published as *The Church and Christian Education*, provided the thrust for a new era of interest in theological foundations. This, in conjunction with the Biblical Theology Movement (a European-inspired emphasis on reading the Bible as the "history of salvation" *[Heilsgeschichte,]* established the groundwork for the curricula of *Christian education*.

Randolph Crump Miller's metaphor—theology as the "clue" to *Christian education*—served as motif of the era:

The clue to Christian education is the rediscovery of a relevant theology that will bridge the gap between content and method, providing the background and perspective of Christian truth by which the best methods and content will be used as tools to bring the learners into the right relationship with the living God who is revealed to us in Jesus Christ, using the guidance of parents and the fellowship of life in the church as the environment in which Christian nurture will take place.[22]

Miller's thesis had developed from an earlier assessment. "Someone," he proposed in 1943, "has to make a Christian out of John Dewey!"[23] Miller argued that educators had to come to some conclusions about the nature of God before developing curricula and offered his formula, "theology in the background: faith and grace in the foreground."[24]

JAMES SMART AND THE INFLUENCE OF BIBLICAL THEOLOGY

But for Old Testament scholar James Smart, who served as editor-in-chief for six years (1944–1950) of the Presbyterian church's influential *Faith and Life* curriculum, Miller's assertion was insufficiently attentive to the failure of Christian educators to be critical theologians. It was not enough, Smart claimed, merely to champion the rekindling of theology; what the field needed was serious rethinking of the foundations. It was to an examination of these fundamental principles that Smart's 1954 book, *The Teaching Ministry of the Church*, was devoted.[25]

Smart accused both conservatives and liberals of a rigidity of ideas and practice in the church school and cited the isolation of Christian education within the field of theology as the cause. He viewed theology as fourfold: biblical, systematic, historical, and practical. Religious education was included in the fourth part, along with homiletics, pastoral theology, and missions and evangelism. All were involved in the total structure of theology. Accordingly, Smart attempted to take up all phenomena touching upon the church's educational task in the light of what he considered the "essential Christian revelation" and, by so doing, model the teacher becoming a theologian.[26] His basic assumption was that the church's educational program should be a valid continuation of what was done by Jesus with his disciples and the early church. To insert the adjective "Christian" before education meant that whatever was done must be rooted and grounded in the gospel—a proposal that appeared to be simple, but that had revolutionary implications. If it were followed through relentlessly, Smart argued, radical changes would ensue in the church's educational program.[27] And from the progressivist standpoint his proposals were radical indeed; Smart's thesis that the church of Jesus Christ should be the focal point of the educational program represented a substantial departure from the Coe-Bower-Elliott tradition. Moreover, he maintained, the whole church educates, and its curriculum must encompass five aspects: Bible, worship, fellowship, history, and the exercise of discipleship.

Also foundational to Smart's curriculum design is a Christian anthropology, the starting point of which is the true humanity of Jesus Christ. It is to recognize that persons are in relationship to one another (the horizontal) and to God (the vertical). It is to acknowledge the place of conversion in *Christian education*. Smart opposed both the moralistic, evangelistic approach (in which the child was viewed as a sinner by nature from birth and had no hope except through conversion by means of a sudden, emotional crisis) and the liberal view that had no place for sin, repentance, and conversion (in which the child was to grow like a flower, stage by stage, until his or her character blossomed forth in its full Christian form, and thus needed only enlightenment, not redemption). Sounding distinctly Niebuhrian, Smart remarked about the liberal's reductionistic concept of conversion that it understandably led to a passionate concern with education (the prime means of delivering humankind from disorder) and transformation of the economic and social order, but "in a time such as the present, when the reality of evil as a force working from within men [women] compels the attention of the world, such romantic conceptions of human nature have a hollow ring."[28]

In fact, Smart continued, the awareness was beginning to dawn that good Christians, who had little they could call sin and no conscious need for repentance, had "actually substituted a very smug middle-class form of religion and morality for New Testament Christianity and may be considered, perhaps, the most stubborn obstacle to the rebirth of an evangelizing Church."[29] Conversion ought not to be reduced to moral and religious growth, though neither should it be set in opposition to it. For growth to take place, "there must first be a sowing of the seed of truth"—thus the centrality of Christian revelation in Smart's educational theory. And the conversion that takes place between the planting of the seed and the ripening of the grain does not lie within the sower's domain: it is God's mysterious work, God who educates. Thus educators cannot seek to control others' responses; they can, however, work as harvesters and midwives, ready to help persons as they pass from one stage of Christian development to the next. They are servants of God's word of revelation who need always be mindful that education is a process far vaster than anything they could organize.[30]

Smart's conclusion that the church's educational problem was at heart a theological problem had numerous ramifications:

If the arguments of these chapters are sound, they lead to some important practical conclusions. They call for reconsideration of the place of Christian education in the theological curriculum and of the place of basic theological disciplines in the curriculum of schools of education. They raise sharply the question of the unity of the ministry, and the right of those who are teachers rather than preachers to share in the full ministry when they are properly trained. They point to the importance of more thorough training in Bible, history, and doctrine for church school teachers. They call for a recognition by the congregation as a whole of its responsibility for teaching. Above all, they set a new aim for education, one that is significant for a Church that is interested in regaining its evangelizing power. The call we hear is simply the call to be the Church for which Jesus Christ lived and died, a royal priesthood, daring to put itself at his service to be used by him for his conquest of the world.[31]

H. Shelton Smith's analysis of the theological assumptions operative among progressivist religious educators and James Smart's proposed theological foundations established the principal contours of *Christian education*.

CHRISTIAN EDUCATION: A SUMMARY

Any summary of *Christian education* must begin with the relationship between religion and culture, since it was the neo-orthodox interpretation of the human situation that established the fundamental contours of *Christian education*. The awareness of finitude and sinfulness, together with a sense of the transcendent God's gracious judgment, seemed to exemplify what H. Richard Niebuhr termed the position of "Christ and culture in paradox"—a sense of the "whole edifice of culture" as "cracked and madly askew," yet a realization of being sustained by God in the midst of it.[32] This dualist position (a recognition of one's "caughtness" in a broken world and of one's graced existence) shaped a sharply theocentric outlook. The revelation of a transcendent God became a dominant theme, and this theme was played out in the distinctive emphasis of the Biblical Theology Movement: God's progressive revelation in history. This notion, indebted to the imagery of evolution, was anticipated in the Old Testament, became fulfilled in Jesus the Christ, and continued on in the life of the church. The Scriptures played a central role in education, though not in a fundamentalist manner, since the new biblical theology incorporated many of the insights of historical criticism. Thus much attention was devoted to the function of the Bible in the educational realm, a development analyzed by Sara Little in *The Role of the Bible in Contemporary Christian Education*.[33] Assent to creedal formulations, moreover, became more important than it had been during the reign of the progressives, because faith was seen as closely linked with classical statements of belief.[34] Conversion was likewise regarded theologically, as little interest was evidenced in its psychological dynamics, though Smart's mention of stages of Christian development may perhaps presage the interest of the 1970s and 1980s in faith development.

Quite clearly, theology was viewed as the key constituent, the identifying characteristic of *Christian* education. The attention given to world religions, to a psychology and sociology of religion among the proponents of *religious education* was seen as turning away from the essentials of Christianity. As a result, theology subsumed education, served as its "clue" and controlling partner. Relatively little attention was devoted to detailing educational processes, though among theorists whom one might associate with this classic expression in their early days, D. Campbell Wyckoff stands out as the most attentive to educational issues. Wyckoff's work on curriculum has been particularly significant. This work is based on a category system of six parts: (1) the objective of *Christian education*, its *why;* (2) the scope, *what* is to be taught and learned; (3) the context, *where* Christian education takes place; (4) the process, *how* it takes place; (5) the participants, *who* are involved; and (6) the timing, *when* Christian education happens.[35] Interestingly, Wyckoff reports that his experience at New College in the 1930s, which included study of Henry Nelson Wieman, Karl Barth, and Reinhold Niebuhr, changed him: "I had grown up in a liberal atmosphere, shot through with the imperatives of the social gospel. Now my theological thinking began to become more conservative and biblical without losing its educational focus or its concerns for social responsibility."[36] In many respects, Wyckoff's statement exemplifies the forces that shaped *Christian education* in its early days and suggests why he became one of its major theorists.

The theological critique of the progressives led to a suspicion of their entire educational stance as well, so in *Christian education* "learning by doing" tended to be replaced by transmissive modes. The emphasis on God's revelatory Word suggested a view of teaching as telling, as proclaiming "God's mighty acts"—a phrase popularized by George Ernest Wright's book *God Who Acts: Biblical Theology as Recital*.[37] Similarly, the dominance of theology resulted in less attention to the social sciences, though social psychology and developmental psychology enjoyed more importance than did psychoanalytic theories or sociological analysis. Education was quite clearly oriented toward the formation of faithful followers of Jesus Christ. While there was far less naiveté about the nature of democracy, neither was there much emphasis in the various curricula on developing a "critical consciousness." *Christian education* by and large was directed toward developing an ecclesial rather than a worldly holiness.

Christian education was reactionary insofar as it represented the confluence of neo-orthodox theologies with an antiprogressivist educational outlook. Its characteristic stresses on proclamation of the Word, divine transcendence and divine authority in revelation took up and promulgated the emphases of the so-called Biblical Theology Movement. Though its theological premises dominated its conversation with education, it quickly assumed a primary position among educators in the mainline churches. Not until the late 1960s, when so many developments in the world would lead to new directions within the churches as well, would *Christian education* be significantly modified.

Quite clearly, one attempting to map the North American religious scene would need to acknowledge the prominent place of *Christian education*. Yet its setting is only fully described in the context of the two classic expressions it mediates, namely *evangelism* and *religious education*. For the present, a turn to the fourth classic expression, *Catholic education–catechetics*, will complete this initial survey.

Figure 4

Christian Education

FOUNDATIONAL QUESTIONS	THE CLASSIC EXPRESSION *CHRISTIAN EDUCATION*
REVELATION	· God's transcendence emphasized. · God revealed progressively in history, as anticipated in the OT and fulfilled in Jesus Christ. · Scripture and the preached word dominant. · One's personal relationship with God emphasized.
CONVERSION	· Conversion inspired by God's graciousness. · Little interest in its psychological dynamics.
FAITH & BELIEF	· Creedal formulas and Christian doctrine assumed new importance. · Reformation themes reclaimed.
THEOLOGY	· "Theology in the background; faith and grace in the foreground." · Theology seen as the key constituent of the educational process of the church, the "clue" to education. · Theology subsumed education. · Emphases of the Biblical Theology Movement shaped curricula.
FAITH & CULTURE	· Awareness of finitude and sinfulness, of the culture as radically askew. · Dualistic: persons were caught in a broken world yet lived a graced existence. · Less stress on social reform and on the church's role in society. · Pessimism about human condition—liberals excoriated for naivete about progress.
GOAL OF EDUCATION	· Formation of faithful followers of Christ. · Development of an ecclesial commitment. · "Someone has to make a Christian out of John Dewey."
KNOWLEDGE	· Truth found in God's revealed word. · Importance placed on understanding Christian doctrine.
SOCIAL SCIENCES	· Dominance of theology relativized use of social sciences. · Some use of social and developmental psychology.
CURRICULUM & TEACHING	· Teaching essentially proclamatory and transmissive. · Scripture and doctrine dominated curriculum. · Stress given to the theological preparation of teachers.
EDUCATION AS POLITICAL	· Education for the sake of achieving salvation.

NOTES

1. Reinhold Niebuhr "What the War Did to My Mind," *Christian Century* 45 (1928):1161.
2. Halford Luccock, "With No Apologies to Barth," *Christian Century* 56 (1939):972.
3. Reinhold Niebuhr, *Moral Man and Immoral Society* (1932; reprint New York: Scribner, 1960).
4. Ibid., xv.
5. Ibid., xx.
6. Ibid., 79–80.
7. Ibid., 82. See also 28–29.
8. H. Shelton Smith, "Let Religious Educators Reckon with the Barthians," in John H. Westerhoff, III, ed., *Who Are We? The Quest for a Religious Education* (Birmingham, AL: Religious Education Press, 1978), 98. Originally published in *Religious Education* 24 (1934):45–51.
9. Ibid., 107.
10. H. Shelton Smith, "George Albert Coe: Revaluer of Values," *Religion in Life* 22 (1952–1953):46.
11. H. Shelton Smith, *Faith and Nurture* (New York: Scribner, 1941), 68.
12. Ibid., 69–79.
13. Ibid., 79.
14. See H. Shelton Smith, "Christian Education: Do Progressive Religious Educators Have a Theology?" in Arnold S. Nash, ed., *America at the End of the Protestant Era* (New York: Macmillan, 1951), 225–46.
15. Smith, *Faith and Nurture,* 95.
16. Ibid.
17. George Albert Coe, *What Is Christian Education?* (New York: Scribner, 1929), 94.
18. Smith, "Christian Education: Do Progressive Religious Educators Have a Theology?" 239.
19. See especially George Albert Coe, "The Assault upon Liberalism," *Religious Education* 34 (1939):85-92 and "Religious Education Is in Peril," *International Journal of Religious Education* 33 (1939):9–10.
20. See Ernest J. Chave, *A Functional Approach to Religious Education* (Chicago: University of Chicago Press, 1947).
21. Susan Brooks Thistlethwaite, "H. Shelton Smith: Critic of the Theological Perspective of Progressive Education, 1934–1950" (Ph. D. diss., Duke University, 1980), 137.
22. Randolph Crump Miller, *The Clue to Christian Education* (New York: Scribner, 1950), 15.
23. Randolph Crump Miller and Henry H. Shires, eds., *Christianity and the Contemporary Scene* (New York: Morehouse-Gorham, 1943), 197.
24. Miller, *The Clue to Christian Education,* 14.
25. James Smart, *The Teaching Ministry of the Church* (Philadelphia: Westminster, 1954).
26. Ibid., 70–71.
27. Ibid., 84.
28. Ibid., 164.
29. Ibid., 165.
30. Ibid., 165–69.
31. Ibid., 206–207.
32. H. Richard Niebuhr, *Christ and Culture* (New York: Harper & Row, 1951), 156.
33. Sara Little, *The Role of the Bible in Contemporary Christian Education* (Richmond, VA: John Knox, 1961).
34. See James D. Smart, *The Creed in Christian Teaching* (Philadelphia: Westminster, 1962).
35. See D. Campbell Wyckoff, *The Gospel and Christian Education* (Philadelphia: Westminster, 1959).
36. D. Campbell Wyckoff, "From Practice to Theory—And Back Again," in Marlene Mayr, ed., *Modern Masters of Religious Education* (Birmingham, AL: Religious Education Press, 1983), 96.
37. George Ernest Wright, *God Who Acts: Biblical Theology as Recital,* Studies in Biblical Theology 1/8 (London: SCM, 1952).

Bibliographic Essay

Christian Education

Since *Christian education* is necessarily understood as a critique of *religious education*, it shares general historical sources with that classic expression. Because *Christian education* is primarily a theological critique applied to educational situations, the works of the neo-orthodox theologians are fundamental. Karl Barth is, of course, a prime source: *The Epistle to the Romans*, 6th ed. (London: Oxford University Press, 1933) and *The Doctrine of the Word of God* (New York: Scribner, 1936). Also of importance is Emil Brunner, *The Mediator: A Study of the Central Doctrine of the Christian Faith* (New York: Macmillan, 1934) and *The Divine Imperative* (New York: Macmillan, 1937). In the United States, Reinhold Niebuhr achieved prominence as a most perceptive interpreter of the times: *Moral Man and Immoral Society* (New York: Scribner, 1932); *Reflections on the End of an Era* (New York: Scribner, 1934); *The Nature and Destiny of Man,* 2 vols. (New York: Scribner, 1941–1943); and "What the War Did to My Mind," *Christian Century* 45 (1928):1161–63. See also H[elmut] Richard Niebuhr, *The Kingdom of God in America* (Chicago: Willett, Clark, 1937); H. Richard Niebuhr, Wilhelm Pauck, and Francis P. Miller, *The Church Against the World* (Chicago: Willett, Clark, 1941); and Paul Tillich, *The Religious Situation* (New York: Henry Holt, 1932). Two very useful works are Charles Kegley and Robert W. Bretall, eds., *Reinhold Niebuhr: His Religious, Social, and Political Thought* (New York: Macmillan, 1956); and Arnold S. Nash, ed., *Protestant Thought in the Twentieth Century: Whence and Whither?* (New York: Macmillan, 1951).

Among those concerned with the implications of neo-orthodox thought for religious education, H. Shelton Smith certainly ranks as the foremost interpreter. See in particular his *Faith and Nurture* (New York: Scribner, 1941) and "Christian Education: Do Progressive Religious Educators Have a Theology," in Arnold S. Nash, ed., *America at the End of the Protestant Era* (New York: Macmillan, 1951), 225–46. Also his "Let Religious Educators Reckon with the Barthians," *Religious Education* 29 (1934):45–50, reprinted in John H. Westerhoff, III, ed., *Who Are We? The Quest for a Religious Education* (Birmingham, AL: Religious Education Press, 1978), 97–109. Susan Brooks Thistlethwaite, "H. Shelton Smith: Critic of the Theological Perspective of Progressive Religious Education" (Ph.D. diss., Duke University, 1980) provides an illuminating exposition of Smith's work.

Elmer G. Homrighausen likewise examined educational and pastoral implications: "Barthianism and the Kingdom," *Christian Century* 48 (1931):922–25. Especially important is Paul H. Vieth, ed., *The Church and Christian Education* (St. Louis, MO: Bethany, 1947), the report of the committee of the International Council of Religious Education (established 1944) on the place of theology in *Christian education.* Two other theorists contributed important works in the 1950s: James D. Smart, *The Teaching Ministry of the Church* (Philadelphia: Westminster, 1954) and Randolph Crump Miller, *The Clue to Christian Education* (New

York: Scribner, 1950). Since this was Miller's early work, it may be read against his own later interpretation, now available in two sources: "Theology in the Background," in Norma Thompson, ed., *Religious Education and Theology* (Birmingham, AL: Religious Education Press, 1982), 17–41; and "How I Became a Religious Educator—Or Did I?" in Marlene Mayr, ed., *Modern Masters of Religious Education* (Birmingham, AL: Religious Education Press, 1983), 65–86. The Mayr volume also provides a glimpse into the development of D. Campbell Wyckoff's career in his autobiographical essay, "From Practice to Theory—And Back Again," 87–114. That essay is helpful in reading Wyckoff's early works, *The Task of Christian Education* (Philadelphia: Westminster, 1955) and *The Gospel and Christian Education* (Philadelphia: Westminster, 1959). Another important work that skillfully delineates some of the theological perspectives of this era is Sara Little, *The Role of the Bible in Contemporary Christian Education* (Richmond, VA: John Knox, 1961). Miller, Wyckoff, and Little, along with colleagues such as C. Ellis Nelson, enjoy long careers in the field, and their later work will be taken up under the rubric of "contemporary modifications."

CHAPTER 5

Surveying the Territory: Catholic Education–Catechetics

Each of the previous classic expressions (with the exception of *evangelism,* which encompassed a Catholic revival movement in the parish missions of the latter part of the nineteenth century) has reflected American, Protestant concerns. This fourth classic expression, *Catholic education–catechetics,* however, reveals a distinctively Catholic approach to educating in faith. Moreover, its hyphenated title suggests a dual character. *Catholic education,* as Fayette Breaux Veverka has argued, might best be understood as a term expressive of a *paideia* (a normative set of educational values and ideals); it mirrored a particular way of construing the relationship between religion and education that developed in the context of the alienation (both religious and cultural) of U.S. Catholic immigrants and also reflected the siege mentality of a European-dominated, nineteenth-century Roman Catholicism. Though it came to expression in the Catholic school system, *Catholic education* itself embraced wider concerns about the relationship of faith to society and, therefore, should not merely be equated with Catholic schooling.[1]

TERMINOLOGY

Generally speaking, *Catholic education* prevailed as the most inclusive term until the years immediately following the Second Vatican Council (1962–1965), when the term "catechetics" (or "catechesis") emerged as the more dominant.[2] *Catechetics* might be regarded as a focusing of *Catholic education.* The twentieth-century origins of *catechetics* lie with the so-called kerygmatic movement—a European renewal movement of the 1930s grounded in a return to biblical and liturgical roots and immensely influential in establishing the milieu for Vatican II. More recently, *catechetics* has become a term advocated by some Roman Catholic and Protestant theorists as the most appropriate name for the broad range of activities involved in educating in faith. Others question, however, whether *catechetics,* with its Roman Catholic moorings, can appropriately be extended; I include myself among those who have reservations. Hence, the importance of examining the presuppositions upon which the terminology rests. Once again, the foundational questions provide the basis of analysis.

CATHOLIC EDUCATION

Though not among the documents generally regarded as the most significant, Vatican II's "Declaration on Christian Education" *(Gravissium educationis)* manifests the Catholic church's continuing interest in promulgating an explicit philosophy of education. Its conviction that "a true education aims at the formation of the human person with respect to his [her] ultimate goal, and simultaneously with respect to the good of those societies of which as a man [woman] he [she] is a member, and in whose responsibilities, as an adult, he [she] will share," reflects long-standing beliefs.[3] What the council participants voiced about education was in reality a philosophy well established in nineteenth- and twentieth-century papal teachings and made accessible in numerous books about "a Catholic philosophy of education." But, ironically, what the council participants did not entirely forsee was that the ecclesial revolution set in motion by the council changed the theological and philosophical assumptions upon which *Catholic education* rested. Vatican II represented a rethinking of "timeless truths" and the emergence of new categories. It therefore exercised a profound effect on ways of thinking about the relationship of faith and education.

CATHOLIC EDUCATIONAL PHILOSOPHY PRIOR TO VATICAN II

Earlier in the century such rethinking was hardly imaginable. The truth about education was eminently clear, precisely because the faith—the truths about God and humankind—were absolute and unchanging. The categories of scholastic thought, enshrined in Pope Leo XIII's decree of 1879, *Aeterni patris,* provided a clear "grammar of assent," thereby giving Catholics a sense of distinct identity and establishing principles upon which a philosophy of education could be developed. In brief such principles were as follows. The existence of a personal God could be proved by reason, as Thomas Aquinas had demonstrated. Moreover, this God had created humans as rational and free beings with both body and soul; the spiritual soul transcended the purely material and temporal order and was the higher dimension of human nature. Furthermore, God has endowed humanity with the gift of a "supernature," the source of a share in divine life. But Adam has fallen from this original state, and thus all his descendants needed to be redeemed by God's son, Jesus, and restored to the supernatural life by being incorporated into Christ and formed in his example and teaching. "The starting point in the Catholic philsophy of education, then, is the reality of the supernatural as revealed through and in Jesus Christ."[4]

Thus, wrote Pope Pius XI in his encyclical "The Christian Education of Youth" *(Divini illius Magistri,* 1929), education consists essentially in preparing persons for what they must be and for what they "must do here below in order to attain the sublime goal" for which they were created. There could be no true education not wholly directly to one's final end, no "ideally perfect education which is not Christian education."[5] Furthermore, Christian education was far more than merely imparting religious instruction; it was the *permeation* of all of life with God's grace. Only education that was Christian could embrace the whole sweep of human life—physical and spiritual, intellectual and moral, individual, domestic, and social—"in order to elevate, regulate and perfect it, in accordance with the example and teaching of Christ":

Hence the true Christian, product of Christian education, is the supernatural man [woman] who thinks, judges and acts constantly and consistently in accordance with right reason illumined by the supernatural light of the example and teaching of Christ. . . . For, it is not every kind of consistency and firmness of conduct based on subjective principles that makes true character, but only constancy in following the eternal principles of justice.[6]

Veverka has suggested that this selection from Pius XI's encyclical highlights three important features of the Catholic perspective on education that American educators developed extensively: first, that the primary purpose of education lies in the formation of Christians through developing the life of grace built upon an essentially good human nature; second, that Christian education is broad and all-encompassing and so necessarily includes a social dimension; and, third, that because there is a distinctive Catholic way of life, faith ought to suffuse and transform the culture. As they became translated into operative norms for Catholic schools, the three principles meant an understanding of the school as a means of regulating and perfecting human nature so that God's grace could build upon it, a recognition that the curriculum must be a source of learning about social responsibilities in American society, and an attempt to foster the development of a distinctively Catholic ethos.

The church teachings also provided a useful means of differentiating a true philosophy of education from a false one. For instance, John D. Redden and Francis A. Ryan in their 1942 work *A Catholic Philosophy of Education* set a Catholic philosophy of education—one derived not simply from natural sources, both empirical and rational, but from an "infallible and supernatural source, namely, divine revelation"—over against virtually all other modern philosophies: naturalist, socialist, communist, and experimental.[7] They maintained that a Catholic philosophy is universal, comprehending life as an integrated whole, and that it aims at the person's complete transformation, both as an individual and as a member of society. "Such transformation implies the enlightenment of the intellect, the discipline of the will, and very specifically, the acceptance of, and adherence to, *eternal values*" (emphasis added).[8] Other philosophies, in contrast, singled out one aspect or another of human nature, but denied, excluded, or ignored others. Naturalism reduced all elements of human experience to physiological and biological functions, socialism made society itself the ultimate end of education, nationalism promoted a country's material welfare as the fundamental objective of education, communism aimed merely to create a classless society, and experimentalism (progressivism) made an idol of reconstruction of experience as the basis of the social order.

A CRITIQUE OF PROGRESSIVISM

Perhaps the character and function of a Catholic educational philosophy became most transparent in the Redden and Ryan critique of the "experimentalists" (William James, C. S. Peirce, John Childs, and above all John Dewey). One of the most problematic topics from the Catholic standpoint was *experience*, since it seemed that metaphysics and tradition had thus ceased to function as guides to truth. By making the school an experimental laboratory, the Fordham University professors argued, much confusion about educational aims, methods, and products inevitably resulted. No longer was there a philosophy possessing the "essential truths and necessary wisdom required to interpret and evaluate educational ends and procedures."[9] Experimentalism, in its efforts to adapt to the changing conditions of life, had relativized truth:

Such a philosophy falsely interprets all reality. Its followers advocate adherence to no principles except those that serve immediately existing conditions and situations. They resolutely reject any authoritative interpretation that makes for stabilization, because they hold that a changing civilization produces the need for new, dynamic principles, or a reinterpretation of old principles. Experimentalism, therefore, denies the existence of absolute truth, and in its place, substitutes relative truth or what is called "progressive truth."[10]

Thus, at numerous points Redden and Ryan set up contrasting pairs. One set involved "fundamental principles": (1) progressive educational philosophy considered that children were ends in themselves; Catholic philosophy considered that they were ordained primarily to God and secondarily to society; (2) progressives believed that children developed outward from within by giving expression to inherent interests and capacities; Catholics believed that they developed not only from internal stimuli but also from the guidance and direction of constituted authority; (3) progressives championed children's making their own truth by choosing it for themselves through the continuous reconstruction of experience; Catholics maintained that there was but a single objective body of truth to which individuals must submit; (4) progressive philosophy led to the evaluation of human experience solely by its pragmatic or instrumental value; Catholic philosophy upheld the importance of deferred values (i.e., that done in light of eternity).

Another set of pairs that served as indicators of the clash between the philosophy of traditional *Catholic education* and progressive thought centered around topics such as the soul, origin of ideas, truth, knowledge, goodness, freedom of will, morality, democracy, and God. Redden and Ryan spelled out the experimentalist position, then used the Catholic, scholastic interpretation to identify the fallacies of experimentalism. For instance, the experimentalists argued that truth is relative and can only be accepted if it meets the test of experience; a supernatural base for truth is, therefore, untenable. But the scholastics taught that the terms of a truth (proposition) are unchangeable; in regard to the essence of things, the truth is necessarily unchangeable, since a thing must be that which it is. Because the intellect apprehends truth, an immediate judgment motivated by objective evidence cannot be false. The experimentalists had denied the absolute and unchanging norm of the eternal law. They had failed to comprehend the metaphysical and eternal truths derived from the essence of things.[11]

Not unsurprisingly, Redden and Ryan concluded that experimentalism presented a "false and exclusive view of the world, of man [woman], of morality, and of democracy," since it was postulated on an erroneous view of the "origin, purpose, and end of life and hence of the educative process." Moreover, only a Catholic philosophy of education could be viewed as truly progressive because it alone embraced "all desirable and reasonable features of 'progressive education' insofar as these contribute to the development and achievement of objectives, ideals, and values, consonant with the child's true nature, highest good and last end."[12]

A MORE POSITIVE JUDGMENT OF PROGRESSIVISM

Despite such assurance that experimentalism was incompatible with Catholic philosophy, not every Catholic educator assumed Redden and Ryan's negative stance. Most notable among the proponents of openness to the progressivist viewpoint was George Johnson, chairman of the Education Department at the Catholic University of America. Johnson argued:

It is true that there are eternal verities that never change, fundamental principles that remain valid no matter how circumstances may shift. But circumstances do shift and in their shifting require new interpretations and application of the eternal verities and the fundamental principles. Our faith in the absolute should not blind us to the existence of the relative.[13]

Thus, a number of Catholic educators embraced progressive practices, as many of their methods seemed capable of being synthesized into Catholic thought. Accordingly, the social sciences came into more extensive use, child-centered learning became more prevalent, and "learning by doing" entered into the vocabulary of numerous teachers. Even the teaching of religion was affected: as early as the 1920s, a clear dissatisfaction with rote memorization and abstract presentations of dogmatic formulations and catechism materials was evident.[14] By no means did progressivism dominate in Catholic schools; indeed, those that were characterized by an explicit openness to the spirit of John Dewey, such as Corpus Christi School on New York City's Upper West Side, attained a certain notoriety. Yet the fact that some Catholic leaders did indeed embrace progressivism indicated that the philosophy of *Catholic education* was not nearly so uniform as some of its proponents believed and that it in fact engendered differing interpretations.

CATHOLIC EDUCATION AND CATHOLIC SCHOOLS

The philosophy of *Catholic education* also contributed to the emergence of some mixed messages for students in the Catholic schools. On the one hand, the strong tradition of a distinctive Catholic ethos—including the prizing of rationality and logic—led to a certain sense of separatism. In many respects, of course, this was a natural outcome of a school system that had developed not only from an era of theological defensiveness (nineteenth-century Catholic theology was unabashedly condemnatory of the modern world), but also from the bigotry of the American scene. As immigration increased (e.g., 4.5 million Irish immigrants came to the United Sates between 1820 and 1920), so did the anti-Catholic virulence that had infected common schooling from its earliest days. As Bishop John Hughes of New York claimed, the public schools taught that "Catholics are necessarily, morally, intellectually, infallibly, a stupid race." He cited a textbook that stated that immigration could make America the common sewer of Ireland, "full of drunken and depraved Paddies."[15]

On the other hand, the social orientation of a Catholic philosophy gave an impetus to educating for democracy. Coupled with the immigrants' desire for acceptance, in the United States this too often meant an uncritical acceptance of American ways and the adoption of some of the cult of efficiency modes ("scientific management") spawned by the second generation of progressives.[16]

Eventually, at least in the United States, *Catholic education* came to be associated almost entirely with Catholic schools. Its distinctive philosophy, though worded in absolutist and ahistorical terms, had nevertheless sought to express the relationship of faith to society. Now, however, *Catholic education* was virtually equated with the development and maintenance of schools. Some of the philosophical concerns became submerged in the efforts to keep a financially marginal school system afloat and to sustain a humanist tradition in an increasingly technological society. And as the Catholic schools, in order to legitimize themselves in the nation's eyes, aspired to become more like the public schools, only the teaching of religion seemed to differentiate them. Lost (or perhaps obscured) was the sense in which a Catholic educational philosophy *permeated* everything—even if in practice this had too often been reduced to "Catholic arithmetic" problems ("If Harry says three decades of the rosary every day for a week, how many decades will he have recited?").

MORE SYSTEMATIC RELIGIOUS EDUCATION IN THE SCHOOLS

Thus began the efforts to become more systematic about religious education. Veverka has observed that the emergence of catechetics as a model of religious education coincided roughly with a new emphasis in Catholic schools on the teaching of religion as a distinct subject in the curriculum and with the founding of the Confraternity of Christian Doctrine (CCD) to educate public-school children in the faith. Prior to studying the development of catechetics, however, three preliminaries must be addressed: a look at *Catholic education* at work outside the school system in the Confraternity of Christian Doctrine; a summary of *Catholic education;* and a brief explanation of Vatican II, an event of profound consequence for dealing with questions about educating in faith.

THE CONFRATERNITY OF CHRISTIAN DOCTRINE ("CCD")

Even at the height of their development (5.6 million students in elementary and secondary schools in 1965), Catholic schools were never able to enroll every Catholic student. The Confraternity of Christian Doctrine offered an alternative. Originating early in the twentieth century (New York [1902], Pittsburgh [1907], and Los Angeles [1932]), the CCD offered a means of religious education for those not enrolled in Catholic schools. Although new to the United States, the roots of this organization were extensive, as it had been founded in 1536 in Milan by Castello de Castellano and given a great impetus by the cardinal archbishop of Milan, Charles Borromeo. Its purpose was straightforward: "to organize schools of Christian doctrine conducted by trained teachers, where youth and unlettered men and women may be instructed in the truths of the faith."[17] By 1584 the confraternity had some 40,000 children and adults involved in lessons taught by some 3,000 teachers. By 1710 more than 271 different confraternity units had spread throughout Europe.

The declining health of Catholic theology apparently also had its effects on the confraternity, since its influence waned in the later eighteenth century and into the nineteenth. But the efforts of Pope Pius X to revive it in the enyclical *Acerbo nimis* in 1905 not only restored the confraternity's importance, but led to its incorporation into the 1914 code of canon law, in which bishops were mandated to ensure the erection of the Confraternity of Christian Doctrine in every parish. In the

United States, of course, this took some time to accomplish. Under the leadership of Bishop Edwin O'Hara, who in the early 1920s had spurred the foundation of religious vacation schools for children in the rural areas, the CCD ultimately became organized on a large scale, with a national office opening in 1935.

One of the more important aspects of the confraternity is that through its inception in sixteenth-century Milan to the present day, it has been primarily the work of the nonordained. In fact, a 1978 study on women in ministry sponsored by the Center for Applied Research in the Apostolate (CARA) identified CCD work as the most common ministry of women in the United States.[18] Though directed almost exclusively to children and young people, it has also functioned, particularly in more recent years, as a stimulus for adult education, since teachers in search of better ways to instruct their classes have themselves participated in theological and educational workshops and courses. But that is to go ahead of the story, as such updating belongs primarily to the post–Vatican II era.

CATHOLIC EDUCATION: A SUMMARY

A review of the foundational questions offers a way of providing a summary of *Catholic education*. Revelation was of first importance: God was revealed in the church (as the classic formula put it, *"locutio Dei ad homines per modum magisterii"*—the word of God is spoken to men and women through the way of the magisterium). The inheritance of Thomism meant a special emphasis on assent to truth, since for Thomas Aquinas revelation was the saving act by which God furnished humankind with the truths necessary for salvation. Faith enabled believers to assent to the divine truths, which were given expression in the church's creeds. Thus, adherence to the church's teaching was seen as the primary mode of acceptance of God's revelation. To know meant to give assent to truth expressed in propositional form.

As H. Richard Niebuhr has shown, classical Thomistic thought offered a synthesist position on Christ and culture: God's rule was shown to be established in the nature of things, and salvation did not entail the destruction of the created order, since grace is built upon nature. Unlike both the "cultural Christian," for whom there were no distinctive Christian principles, and the radical who despised the non-Christian order, the synthesist was able to work with nonbelievers while maintaining the centrality of Christ. Yet, this effort "to bring Christ and culture, God's work and man's [woman's], the temporal and the eternal, law and grace, into one system of thought and practice tends, perhaps inevitably, to the absolutizing of what is relative, the reduction of the infinite to a finite form, and the materialization of the dynamic."[19]

The synthesist perspective, however, came to coexist with a more negative assessment of culture. As the church dealt with the political, social, and economic realities of the nineteenth century, it became increasingly defensive toward the wider culture and seemed to withdraw itself from the world. Thus, *Catholic education* had a Janus-like quality: on the one hand, it prized culture and learning and proclaimed that "nothing human was alien"; on the other, it looked severely on the Enlightenment's motto (from Kant), "dare to think for yourself" and condemned modernity. This paradox is at least partially explained in Langdon Gilkey's distinction that Catholicism had long honored speculative reason, but that its ecclesiology fostered a negative judgment of critical reason. Thus Catholicism became increasingly engaged in a war against modernity from the advent of the Enlightenment and the emergence of modern empiricism.[20] At least in its general contours, this acrimony characteristic of nineteenth- and early twentieth-century Catholicism bore a striking resemblance to the fundamentalist antipathy toward modernity.

Philosophy and theology were regarded as the epitome of human knowledge and undergirded the understanding of education; they also served as principles by which one could criticize the social sciences. The church regarded education as of supreme importance because it involved the formation of the whole person. Education was one of the prime means by which persons developed Christian character and, thereby, prepared themselves for heaven. Significantly, *Catholic education* transcended the schoolhouse. It was a view of education as an immersion in a culture, an all-embracing way of life.

At its best, Veverka has concluded, *Catholic education* "represented a public vision of religious education that understood that education was broader than schooling and that religion was broader than church or creed."[21] Certainly, *Catholic education* was prophetically "holistic" (to use the current jargon). Yet, as Veverka has also noted, its assumptions were based on a worldview that could no longer be sustained once Catholicism came to grips with (rather than condemned) modernity. Thus it was that Vatican II—the Catholic church's long-delayed confrontation with the modern era—led inevitably to a reconsideration of what it means to educate in faith.

THE SECOND VATICAN COUNCIL (1962–1965)

Rosemary Haughton's oft-quoted characterization of Vatican II as "that superbly destructive Council" suggests the turbulence it engendered. Volumes were written on the "changing church," and the precise character of change—how extensive it should be and how it ought to take place—did indeed seem to be the crux of the matter. Gilkey's assertion that in change one sees the "strange face of the hidden God, constituting, upsetting, destroying, challenging, judging, re-creating and calling us" provided a theological interpretation, but not all read such a positive message in change.[22]

Two dimensions of Vatican II seem especially pertinent for understanding the shift in emphasis that took place in *Catholic education–catechetics*. The first centers around its conciliatory tone and the second around the dissolution of the supernatural/natural schism that had so long predominated in Catholic philosophy and theology.

The tone of Vatican II differed dramatically from the twenty preceding councils, most of which had centered on the refutation of heresy or on the defense of the church against other errors and enemies. Pope John XXIII's opening address on 11 October 1962, "Mother Church Rejoices," *(Gaudet Mater Ecclesia)* invited the participants to deliberate in a spirit of charity and reconciliation. Gently chiding "prophets of gloom" who could see nothing but "prevarication and ruin" in the modern world, always contrasting it unfavorably with the past, the ailing Pontiff (who died just eight months later) spoke with a hopeful conviction that "in the present order of things, Divine Providence is leading us to a new order of human relations."[23] Rather than the church becoming obsessed with errors, it must be more open and welcoming, since "today the spouse of Christ prefers to make use of the medicine of mercy rather than severity. She considers that she meets the demands of the present age by demonstrating the validity of her teaching rather than by condemnation."[24]

This gracious tone is all the more striking when contrasted with the condemnation of the so-called modernists earlier in the century (the decree *Lamentabili* and the encyclical *Pascendi dominici gregis* in 1907). In effect, such a tone of openness refuted the "siege mentality" so characteristic of nineteenth-century Catholicism. By implication, a Catholic educational philosophy that defined itself as "true" and condemned all other systems as "false" stood now in need of rethinking. Triumphalism seemed now to be tragically empty.

Not unrelated was dualism's "fall from grace." Over the years, a two-storied world had come to dominate the Catholic worldview: nature and supernature. The former was constituted by the created order and thereby associated with nature, time, space, and matter and with what was relative and changing. In contrast, the supernatural order expressed God's eternal, absolute, and changeless nature; a chasm lay between it and the inferior realm of nature. The divinely founded church existed to mediate between this divine-human gap. Its God-given power and authority were bestowed to witness to God's intervention in the time and space of the ordinary world. And, even though the church was, to be sure, constituted by sinners, it nonetheless had a dual existence, since it shared God's absolute, changeless, and inerrant nature. Inevitably, this meant, particularly in the nineteenth century, the emergence of a clear "Christ against culture" position, in which the church understood itself as against modernity:

With truly lamentable results, our age, casting aside all restraint in its search for the ultimate causes of things, frequently pursues novelties so ardently that it rejects the legacy of the human race. Thus, it falls into very serious errors, which are even more serious when they concern sacred authority, the interpretation of Sacred Scripture, and the principal mysteries of the Faith. . . .

These errors are being daily spread among the faithful. Lest they captivate the faithfuls' minds and corrupt the purity of their faith, His Holiness, Pius X, by Divine Providence, Pope, has decided that the chief errors should be noted and condemned by the Office of this Holy Roman and Universal Inquisition.[25]

How different was one of the most important texts of Vatican II, "The Pastoral Constitution on the Church in the Modern World" *(Gaudium et spes)*, which begins:

The joys and the hopes, the griefs and the anxieties of the men [women] of this age, especially those who are poor or in any way afflicted, these too are the joys and hopes, the griefs and anxieties of the followers of Christ. Indeed, nothing genuinely human fails to raise an echo in their hearts. For theirs is a community composed of men [women]. United in Christ, they are led by the Holy Spirit in their journey to the kingdom of their Father and they have welcomed the news of salvation which is meant for every man [woman]. That is why this community realizes that it is truly and intimately linked with mankind [womankind] and its history.[26]

One may, of course, make too much of documents, especially if one quotes selectively. Moreover, there is little doubt that Vatican II's were uneven; like all political texts, they reflect compromise and consensus. Nonetheless, from the vantage point of over twenty years since the council, it appears all the more evident that this twenty-first ecumenical council stimulated a profound shift in the church's self-understanding. Though full justice can hardly be done here, a brief summary of the rethinking of key concepts is necessary because of their great significance for religious education. These are the concepts of truth, knowledge, salvation, humanity, conversion, and revelation.

As is evident in much of the previous matter of this chapter, preconciliar views of truth involved a notion of ahistorical propositions. But what emerged during Vatican II and after was a quite different perspective: truth, insofar as it is always and necessarily expressed in human language, is, therefore, always relative to culture, time, and place. By implication, all dogma is likewise embedded in human culture and thus is also relative: the teaching of the church may indeed be about an eternal God, but insofar as it is formulated in ever-changing language systems, it cannot be timeless. Even more, the Catholic experience does not exhaust the fullness of truth.

A renewed understanding of knowledge followed. Though the Catholic tradition had long valued rationality, modernity revealed that even reason had its limits. The "faith as assent" notion had been built on a supernaturalistic ecclesiology in which God's revelation to the church could not be questioned (e.g., Pope Pius X's remark in 1906: "The duty of the multitude is to allow itself to be led and to follow its leaders obediently"). But knowing clearly had existential dimensions. In one way, of course, the church had long acknowledged this by bestowing sainthood on those, such as the Curé of Ars, whose knowledge of God had little to do with native intelligence. But too often the honoring of the "little ones" had legitimized anti-intellectualism and played into an uncritical ecclesiology. But what the council stimulated was a renewed notion of knowing linked not simply with orthodoxy ("correct belief") but with orthopraxis ("correct action").

The reconsideration of truth and knowledge contributed to an understanding of faith as a liberating power and, thereby, to a renewed vision of salvation. The legacy of the nineteenth century had been a schism between life in this "vale of tears" and eternal life, between the sacred and the secular. But Vatican II provided an impetus to remove an "otherworldly" idea of salvation and replace it with a commitment to God's reign in history. The dichotomies between heaven and earth, between the material body and the incorruptible soul became blurred, as the church came increasingly to realize that salvation embraced the whole person.

It followed, therefore, that one's humanity was good, and that the hierarchical categories of supernatural and natural had done injustice to the essential integrity of the person. Most significantly, the ranking of the contemplative life over the active and the clerical state over the lay was called into question. With the council came the prevalence of expressions such as the "lay church" and the "age of the laity."

Related to this was increased emphasis on conversion, now understood not first and foremost as becoming a Catholic or returning to the church after having "fallen away," but as a deep change of one's life, a commitment to live anew in Christ. All persons were called to a continuous conversion of life, not simply those in the clerical or religious life.

And interwoven with expanded understandings of truth, knowledge, salvation, humanity, and conversion was a more dynamic view of revelation. To explicate that is to begin to trace the catechetical movement.

CATECHETICS

THE IMPORTANCE OF A NEW UNDERSTANDING OF REVELATION

Vatican II's "Constitution on Divine Revelation" *(Dei verbum)* reflected a significantly different orientation from earlier ecclesial statements on the topic. Particularly since the mid-nineteenth century, revelation had been regarded largely in neoscholastic categories as a body of propositional truth. In the neoscholastic view, as Avery Dulles has aptly summarized, revelation meant the whole process by which the "deposit of faith" was built up in biblical times and also the process by which the revealed deposit was communicated to believers in postapostolic times.[27] Thus, the church's role was to guard and expound authoritatively the truths God had revealed in Scripture and Tradition. The religious educator's role, accordingly, was to hand on the truths of the faith.

In contrast, Vatican II expressed a notion of revelation more indebted to personalist and biblical categories, a shift in understanding with profound consequences for educating in faith. This revised view was grounded in the conviction that the "invisible God (cf. Col. 1:15; 1 Tim. 1:17) out of the abundance of His love speaks to men [women] as friends (cf. Exod. 33:11; John 15:14–15) and lives among them (cf. Bar. 3:38), so that he may invite and take them into fellowship with Himself."[28] The council participants maintained that God's self-revelation, brought to completion in Christ, could be discerned as flowing from one divine wellspring, the source of the inextricably linked streams of sacred Scripture and sacred Tradition; no longer would the Council of Trent's notion of the two sources prevail. To change the metaphor, Tradition and Scripture were "like a mirror in which the pilgrim Church on earth looks at God."[29]

A NEW ATTENTION TO SCRIPTURE

Scripture, therefore, received a renewed emphasis; its role had been obscured in the abstractions of scholasticism and in the polemics of the Counter-Reformation (though the council did not explicitly acknowledge this). A new mandate was delivered: "easy access to sacred Scripture should be provided for all the Christian faithful."[30] In fact, four of the *Constitution's* six chapters focused on Scripture, thereby vividly reflecting the renewed linkage of the Bible with revelation. But an important distinction was made: the Scripture contains revelation but cannot itself be equated with revelation. One must recognize historical context, literary forms, and cultural influences because God's word is always necessarily expressed in human language. Moreover, one must take into account the living tradition of the church, upon whom the Spirit continues to breathe. Thus, Vatican II propounded that the Scriptures must be interpreted within the community of faith, not merely used to legitimize some private revelation.

The council's theology of revelation had, of course, not emerged from a vacuum. Indeed, it developed out of a lively ferment in European theology, including a renewal of Thomistic thought (termed transcendental Thomism, largely associated with Joseph Marechal, mentor of the renowned Karl Rahner) and the so-called kerygmatic theology. To that latter movement we now turn, since it was the matrix from which *catechetics* was born.

THE KERYGMATIC MOVEMENT

A renewed interest in the life of the early church inspired the formulations of kerygmatic theology, and a deep concern about what it meant to proclaim God's word in the contemporary world characterized its catechetical developments. For kerygmatic theology, one looks especially to the work of Josef Jungmann (1889–1975); for catechetical development, one recognizes the contribution of six International Catechetical Study Weeks (1959–1968) and the work of leading figures, such as Johannes Hofinger, Piere-André Liégé, D. S. Amalorpavadass, and F. H. Drinkwater. Both movements, however, emanated from a singular conviction that "liturgy is the summit toward which the activity of the Church is directed; at the same time it is the fountain from which all her power flows." This statement from Vatican II's "Constitution on the Sacred Liturgy" *(Sacrosanctum concilium)* was in large measure inspired by these key figures and movements.[31]

Jungmann was himself a liturgist par excellence. His work on the history of the Mass, originally published in 1948, remains the classic study and, indirectly, the source of his insights on what came to be called "kerygmatic theology." His study of the early church at worship led him to question what he perceived to be a lifelessness in the modern church. Jungmann's encounter with the vivid, proclamatory language of the Scripture fostered in him a reserve about the abstractions of scholastic theology. His recognition of the Christocentric character of the New Testament engendered hesitations about the multiplicity of devotions that had developed over the centuries. In short, Jungmann's immersion in liturgical studies set in motion an inquiry about the church's faithfulness to its roots. Perhaps in being preoccupied with a propositional notion of orthodoxy, it had lost the spirit of true glory-giving.

Jungmann proposed in 1936 a need to return to the sources.[32] First and foremost, this meant for him a renewed attention to the language and categories of Scripture. He believed that preaching and teaching must manifest much more sharply the "good news" of salvation in Christ and that the unity of God's plan needed to be made evident. Accordingly, he made "salvation history" *(Heilsgeschichte)* a central theme in his proposals: God's progressive revelation in history was anticipated in the Old Testament, brought to fulfillment in Christ in the New Testament, and continues in the church. By always emphasizing this motif, a proper hierarchy of truths would result. Christ would be the center from which all life in the church flowed. The history of salvation provided the "unchanging background and fixed framework for the multifarious searchings and struggles that pass across the stage of life."[33]

Similarly, Jungmann believed this theme would restore a dynamism to ecclesial life that had been lost in the more static thought of scholasticism. In their enthusiasm for syllogisms and abstractions, the neoscholastics had, in Jungmann's view, inadvertently obscured the clarity of God's plan. Theology, therefore, needed to be grounded in the *kerygma*, in the announcement of God's salvation at work in the world. Kerygmatic theology was not, he clarified in later years, a separate field of theology, but rather a recognition of theology's inherently proclamatory character.

Jungmann's work rankled traditionalists, who managed to remove his 1936 book from publication and thereby to block its translation. The English translation did not appear until 1962. Despite this harassment, Jungmann's ideas were widely circulated and accepted enthusiastically by many. This was due in large measure to the tireless travels of fellow Austrian Johannes Hofinger, who taught in such far-flung places as China, the Philippines, Australia, and the United States. Hofinger's articles and books, often done in conjunction with other religious educators, promulgated and extended Jungmann's fundamental theses.

The Jungmann-Hofinger tradition functioned as a key element in pre–Vatican II renewal, often simply referred to as the "kerygmatic movement." It developed from a keen sense of the need to return to the sources and resulted in a deepened appreciation for liturgical life and biblical scholarship. Two 1943 encyclicals, *Mystici corporis* and *Divino afflante spiritu,* respectively, encouraged this *ressourcement.* Significantly, this awakening came to expression also in an intensified interest in "proclaiming the Good News." It is this understanding of educating in faith that is called *catechetics,* and that must be understood as integral to the liturgical and biblical renewal—generally European in character—that preceded the council and then evolved dramatically in its wake.

CATECHETICS AND THE CATECHISM

A clarification about the relation of two terms "catechetics" and the "catechism" derived from the same root *(katechein,* to resound) is in order here. Ironically, the advent of the era of the first led to the demise, or at least a deemphasis, of the latter. The catechism—a manual of one's beliefs usually couched in questions and answers—reflected the transition from oral to written instruction and thus came into prominence with the advent of the printing press in 1438. The central figure in popularizing its usage was none other than Martin Luther, whose small and large catechisms of 1529 exercised great influence. In turn the Counter-Reformers, most notably Peter Canisius and Robert Bellarmine as well as the Council of Trent (1545–1563), authored catechisms to refute Luther and provide the Catholic corrective.

In the United States, one catechism enjoyed widespread usage: the *Baltimore Catechism,* so named because it resulted from the Third Plenary

Council of Baltimore. First published in 1885 and then revised in 1941, the *Baltimore Catechism* came to dominate instruction in the faith, though numerous alternative catechisms existed as well. Its question-and-answer format (the original edition contained 421 questions and answers and the revision, 515) trained generations of Catholics in ready answers to theological questions. Moreover, a product of the post–Vatican I (1869) era, it translated that council's truncated ecclesiology into simple categories and dissected much of the narrative of faith into stylized formulas for memorization.[34] Its effectiveness, of course, was evident, as pupils either "knew"—could recite, if not explain—the correct answers or not. But as theological understandings developed and as educators came to draw upon psychological insights—much of the material was inappropriately formulated for the various age levels—the catechism fell increasingly into disuse (though 250,000 copies were sold in 1970). *Catechetics,* on the other hand, represented a reclaiming of the oral character of educating in faith insofar as it derived from consideration of what it meant to be a "herald of the Good News." Kerygmatic renewal ultimately meant that the inadequacies of the catechism became more and more evident.

Though Jungmann had exercised great influence in establishing the fundamental contours of *catechetics,* its distinctive concerns and contents were shaped by various institutions and persons. Initially European, the involvement of missionaries in the International Catechetical Study Weeks opened a more global perspective. Originally closely tied to the language of salvation history, *catechetics* increasingly adopted a more political language regarding the "salvation of history." Once intimately linked with biblical scholarship, *catechetics* became less able to integrate its methods and insights as that discipline became more specialized, yet retained a characteristically central role for the Bible. From the beginning rooted in liturgical renewal, *catechetics* intensified its bond with liturgy through the restoration of the catechumenate. Thus, *catechetics* passed through a number of transitions in the postconciliar years. A look at these offers a chronological framework by which to examine the foundational questions.

PHASES OF THE CATECHETICAL MOVEMENT

A certain caution is in order, lest the transitions that follow be too readily regarded as distinct phases. Nonetheless, some differentiation can be made between the early kerygmatic stress on proclaiming "God's all-embracing salvific plan"—articulated most succinctly at the International Catechetical Study Week in Eichstätt (Austria) in 1960—and the somewhat later study weeks—Bangkok in 1962, Katigondo (Uganda) in 1964, and Manila in 1967—which devoted more emphasis to adaptation of the message of salvation to particular cultures and subcultures. The Eichstatt Study Week, it should be noted, explicitly spoke of adaptation to the "life and thought of peoples,"[35] but the later conferences debated and developed this more extensively. Moreover, the French "school" of catechetical theorists, including Joseph Colomb, Pierre Babin, Marc Oraison, and Marcel van Caster, integrated psychological insights into their work. The Belgian catechetical school, Lumen Vitae (founded in 1937 as the Catechetical Documentary Center), where many of these leaders taught and in whose journal they frequently published, likewise provided an impetus to draw upon psychological studies.

Similarly, an important transition appears to have been in progress between the pre-1968 International Catechetical Study Weeks and the 1968 session in Medellín (Colombia). The Medellín participants concluded that the unity of God's plan—the fundamental axiom of the kerygmatic movement—meant that there must be no dichotomy

between human values and relations with God; between man's [woman's] planning and God's salvific plan as manifested in Christ; between the human community and the Church; between human experience and God's revelation; between the progressive growth of Christianity in our time, and its eschatological consummation.[36]

Reflected here was a recognition that the proclamation of the Good News entailed specific consequences for the way people lived, particularly those who, as in Latin America, were economically deprived. This "Medellín shift" (including documents of the Second Conference of Latin American Bishops who met in Medellín in the week following the International Catechetical Study Week) represented a major development in thinking about the meaning of *catechetics*. Michael Warren argues, "If there has been any quantum leap in modern catechetics, it has not been one from content to person but rather one to a recognition of the relation of catechesis to political realities and to a realization that the beloved community has to attend to systemic evil found in social and political structures."[37]

A document, "Justice in the World," issued from the 1971 Synod of Bishops, affirmed the Medellín conclusions and has become one of the prime sources for rethinking modern catechetics. Its thrust is evident from its oft-quoted thesis:

Action on behalf of justice and participation in the transformation of the world appear to us as a constitutive dimension of the preaching of the Gospel, or, in other words, of the Church's mission for the redemption of the human race and its liberation from every oppressive situation.[38]

This statement of the inherently political character of the mission of the church—certainly remarkable when contrasted with a decree such as *Lamentabili*—had its theological roots in a more mature notion of evangelization. In fact, the renewed attention given in the 1950s and 1960s to the meaning of evangelization had enkindled new dimensions for *catechetics,* and in turn this rethinking contributed to a recognition of the broader role of the church in the world.

CATECHETICS AND EVANGELIZATION

Among those who sparked the reconsideration of evangelization was French theologian Piere-André Liégé, whose expanded notion of the "Ministry of the Word" as embracing both evangelization and *catechesis* exercised great influence. Liégé considered evangelization to be the "first impact with the Good News of God's coming in Christ to found his Kingdom in the power of the Holy Spirit to rouse personal conversion and lead to entrance into the Church by baptism."[39] In other words, for Liégé, evangelization entailed a "primordial word" that would lead to faith as conversion, the change of life engendered by the recognition and intention of God's call to a person. Here the kerygma ought to be presented in all its clarity, lest the person, in the process of coming to faith, be overwhelmed with doctrinal matters. But Liégé also recognized a second movement, as it were, in which faith would be enhanced by the wisdom of the community. This he termed "*catechesis*": that which "exposes the totality of contents in Revelation-Tradition in the unity of the Christian mystery."[40] He considered *catechesis* to be the continuation of evangelization, vitally linked with it since it was always to return the person to his or her initial act of conversion. *Catechesis* was synthetic, in that its function was to show Christianity as one organic whole, communal in that it was addressed to a people, and "indissociably dogmatic, moral, and liturgical."[41] It was incumbent, then, upon the catechist to bring out the aspects of the Christian mystery as much or more by their significance than by their explanation.

Liégé's distinction between evangelization and *catechesis* has continued in the postconciliar literature, though the sense of the former has continued to expand. In the apostolic exhortation on evangelization, *Evangelii nuntiandi,* published in 1975 after a worldwide Synod of Bishops on that same theme in 1974, four meanings of evangelization emerged: the announcement of the Good News to all; the process of transformation and renewal; the initial proclamation to non-Christians; and all the activities of word and deed by which the gospel is made known. It has two simultaneous and cyclic moments: the proclamation of the Good News and the living out of this message of salvation. Thus, significantly, evangelization transcends pronouncement and must be seen as linked to liberation from both material oppression and from personal selfishness. Many methods can be employed to evangelize: witness of life, liturgy of the Word, mass media, sacraments, "living preaching," *catechesis,* personal contact, and popular piety.

Generally speaking, then, the efforts that prepare and bring into life a person's first responsible adherence to the gospel can be encompassed under the term "evangelization." *Catechesis* denotes a more specific phase: the efforts intended to activate faith by means of instruction and, by so doing, to bring initial faith to maturity.

CATECHETICS DEFINED

The *General Catechetical Directory,* a 1971 document issued from Rome, defined "catechesis" as "that form of ecclesial action which leads both communities and individual members of the faithful to maturity of faith."[42] The *Directory* spells out the functions of *catechesis* (references are to the paragraph number):

To dispose persons to receive the action of the Spirit and to deepen their conversion (#22).

To help make communion with God a reality (#23).

To present the Christian message in such a way that the highest value of human life is safe-guarded by it (#23).

To foster and illumine the increase of theological charity (#23).

To contribute to the gradual grasping of the whole truth about the divine plan by preparing the faithful for the reading of Sacred Scripture and the learning of tradition (#24).

To promote active, conscious, and genuine participation in the liturgy (#25).

To teach the faithful to give a Christian interpretation to human events (#26).

To assist ecumenical dialogue (#27).

To help individual communities to spread the gospel and to establish dialogue with non-Christians (#28).

To direct peoples' hope to the future goods of the "heavenly Jerusalem" and to call them to "be willing to cooperate in the undertakings of their neighbors and of the human race for the improvement of human society" (#29).

To lend aid for the beginning and growth of faith throughout the course of a person's life (#30).

Quite clearly, the scope of *catechesis* was quite broadly defined. Some elaborations by D. S. Amalorpavadass of India at the 1971 International Catechetical Congress in Rome developed the *Directory's* outline. Amalorpavadass spoke of the education of the faith of the converted and of the baptized as being the end of *catechesis;* it "aims at awakening, nourishing, and developing the faith, while renewing, deepening and perfecting the initial conversion, making it ever more personal and actual."[43] Furthermore, he stated, this lifelong education of faith and its concomitant transformation of one's life had quite specific implications:

It should give a new world view, set up a different hierarchy of values, cause a change of attitudes, form the whole person, educate his or her liberty, guide him or her toward Christian maturity, integrate the person in the church-community, and lead that person to commit himself or herself to the tasks of society and integral development of humanity.[44]

The work of Liégé and Amalorpavadass, in particular, indicates the intimate relationship of *catechesis* with a conversion of life. The importance of conversion, in fact, suggests the appropriateness of utilizing the foundational questions to summarize *catechetics (catechesis)*.

CATECHETICS: A SUMMARY

The theology of revelation provides a fitting beginning to the summary, since it played such a crucial role in the development of catechetics. The ferment in European thought that ultimately came to expression in the documents of Vatican II, most particularly the "Constitution on the Sacred Liturgy," profoundly shaped the emphases of *catechetics*. The new vigor with which the Catholic church took up the study of Scripture, and its recognition of the unity of Scripture and Tradition meant that *catechetics* would necessarily be biblically grounded. Even to regard it as a form of the ministry of the Word situates *catechetics* in its biblical moorings. Moreover, to speak of it as a ministry of the Word is to testify to its inherent link with liturgical life, certainly one of the most singular characteristics of *catechetics*.

Indeed, from the outset of the kerygmatic renewal through the recent official documentation *Sharing the Light of Faith: National Catechetical Directory for Catholics of the United States* (1979), *catechetics* has been liturgically rooted. Certainly, this was one of Jungmann's most significant contributions, and succeeding theorists followed his orientation. From the earliest days of the renewal, there was a recognition that liturgy was, in the tradition of John Dewey, "learning by doing."[45] Liturgy involved a form of knowing that transcended the merely informative. As the framers of the 1960 Eichstätt principles put it:

The *liturgy* does more than communicate the Christian mystery to the mind of the participant. It uses sound pedagogical principles, namely the intuitive process, activity, teaching by experience, the imparting of values. It appeals to the entire person, the sensibilities, the intellect and the will. It is the means of impregnating the whole life with the Spirit of Christ.[46]

An even earlier article expressed it this way:

For the liturgy offers Christian doctrine, not in abstract definitions, but in intelligible and prayable form: it teaches how to pray and live religion. It obviously addresses itself to the whole man [woman]. While doing full justice to the rational element of Christian religion, namely to Christian dogma, it nevertheless is basically opposed to religious intellectualism. It also offers religious nourishment to the senses: in fact, it starts with the visual elements, and through visible sign and symbol it leads to the invisible content and mystery.[47]

As liturgist Aidan Kavanagh has concluded, liturgy teaches "nondiscursively, richly, ambiguously, elementally."[48] In fact, this way of teaching through liturgy is closely related to the understanding of conversion. Kavanagh himself proffered some distinctions that, while not universally accepted or utilized, nevertheless shed light on conversion and *catechetics/catechesis*. In differentiating three interrelated processes: "conversion therapy" (*catechesis*), didactic instruction (*catechetics*), and liturgical proclamation of the Word (homiletics), he argued that conversion must be the foundation of the two latter processes. His notion of *catechesis* as "conversion therapy" is particularly intriguing, since it is linked with the catechumenate (the period of preparation for Baptism). The catechumenate, Kavanagh writes,

has more in common with Alcoholics Anonymous and with other kinds of groups that deal with personality changes bound up with specific alteration in social role than it does with educational programs such as CCD. The catechumenate's purpose is not to instruct in a classroom manner, but to precipitate a series of personality crises through to a point of initial maturity robust enough to bear the rough-and-tumble sharing that faith as lived together requires. The catechumenate is where incipient faith is forced to become ecclesially explicit.[49]

Kavanagh's thesis not only indicates the centrality of conversion, but suggests as well the countercultural character of conversion. Conversion entails a realignment of one's values. Its Christocentric character means that the words and deeds of Jesus serve as the basis of one's reorientation. Furthermore, since *catechetics* ought to deepen conversion, it must extend one's commitment to discern God's ways in the social sphere and thereby involve people in the church's prophetic mission.

Implicit here is a sense of the church's ambiguous relation with culture. Unlike the turn-of-the-century documents that condemned the secular culture, the documents of Vatican II expressed an awareness of the goodness of all creation. Yet within those same documents, and indeed in a series of subsequent documents such as Pope Paul VI's encyclical of 1967, *Populorum progressio,* and the Synod's "Justice in the World," the church recognized the prevalence of sinful social structures. In H. Richard Niebuhr's categories, what seemed to be developing was a transformist position, in which the values engendered by faith served as the basis for making societal changes. The emergence of *catechetics* represented a more complex perspective on the role of the church in the world.

Another tension inherent in *catechetics* centers on the relationship between faith and belief. Whereas previously faith had been regarded primarily in intellectualist terms as an illumination of the soul that implied adherence to a body of propositional truths, now it took on a more existential character. Faith frequently was spoken of as summoning the adherence of the whole person and was linked with one's process of maturing. Catechetical ministry aimed to "make a person's 'faith become living, conscious, and active, through the light of instruction.'"[50] Yet there was also the "faith *which* one believes," that is, faith is expressed in both words and deeds; "as the community of believers grows in understanding, its faith is expressed in creeds, dogmas, and moral principles and teachings."[51] Thus, in catechetical ministry, one necessarily works in summoning people to mature in faith as they deepen in a sense of the community's professed faith—a task that has in practice meant at numerous junctures considerable tension between forces desiring more attention to the church's official teaching and those who have devoted less attention to doctrine in their attempt to foster a personal life of faith. The most vivid example of this difference may be seen in the work of a group known as Catholics United for the Faith, whose strident criticisms of mainstream catechetical theory have forced numerous confrontations. A newspaper, *The Wanderer,* emanating from St. Paul, Minnesota, also testifies vociferously to sharp differences of judgment about the relationship of faith to belief.

Despite these serious rifts, all groups would grant the importance of theology in catechetical theory, even while differing on theological premises. In fact, critics such as Catholics United for the Faith seem to reflect the theological and philosophical convictions that antedate Vatican II and that had provided the foundation for a theory of *Catholic education* as explicated earlier in this chapter. But what is especially significant in terms of this study is the great importance given by all catechetical theorists to theology, particularly since a number of prominent theorists placed themselves outside the catechetical "school" predominantly because of what they perceived as an overemphasis on theology and an inattentiveness to education. Their critique will be taken up in chapters 6 and 7; for the present, one must at least take note of the overwhelming importance of theological understandings and categories in *catechetics* and the consequent devaluation of educational studies.

One might say that there appears even a certain discomfort with educational language, such as curriculum, instruction, and so forth, lest *catechetics* appear too linked with schooling models and, therefore, betray an excessively cognitive end. Theorists such as Robert Hater and Michael Warren have argued that the language of "religious education," precisely because it is so closely associated with a school model of learning, does not do justice to the process of deepening in faith and is not as appropriate to the experience of conversion as is the language of *catechetics/catechesis.*[52] These arguments provide at least a partial explanation for the fact that catechetical theory in general has given little sustained attention to matters of curriculum and teaching.

The question of the role and significance of the social sciences has become an increasingly important matter in *catechetics.* The use of a phrase such as "maturity of faith" signals a receptivity to developmental psychology, a field that first came to prominence in *catechetics* among the French school and has continued to play an important role since the advent of the stage theories of Erik Erikson, Lawrence Kohlberg, and James Fowler. *Sharing the Light of Faith* explicitly addresses this topic in its eighth chapter:

Because the life of faith is related to human development, it passes through stages or levels; furthermore, different people possess aspects of faith to different degrees. This is true, for example, of the comprehensiveness and intensity with which they accept God's word, of their ability to explain it, and of their ability to apply it to life. Catechesis is meant to help at each stage of human development and lead ultimately to full identification with Jesus.

The Church encourages the use of the biological, social, and psychological sciences in pastoral care. . . . Manuals for catechists should take into account psychological and pedagogical insights, as well as suggestions about methods. . . .

These sciences do, however, help us understand how people grow in their capacity for responding in faith to God's grace. They can, therefore, make a significant contribution to catechesis. At the same time, catechists should not be uncritical in their approach to these sciences, in which new discoveries are constantly being made while old theories are frequently modified or even discarded.[53]

Sociology is also pertinent to catechetical theory, at least as evidenced in the opening chapter of *Sharing the Light of Faith,* which describes some specific cultural and religious characteristics that affect educating in faith in the United States. Empirical studies of Catholic schools and of the religion of youth and children were important sources for this study.[54]

But what seems to be missing in catechetical theory—and here is a clue to education as a political activity—is any sense of critical ecclesiology. Contemporary *catechetics* seems to account only for the process of being socialized into the believing community. Critics—among whom I count myself—claim that catechetical theory is an inadequate base for one's entire understanding of what it means to educate in faith. *Catechetics* highlights the affective, experiential activity of coming to faith in a specific tradition, but it is not inclusive enough to embrace the totality of religious education.

A review of the foundational questions suggests a number of lively developments spawned by the classic expression *Catholic education–catechetics.* That is likewise the case with the three classic expressions surveyed in earlier chapters, *evangelism, religious education,* and *Christian education.* We turn now to examine how all four classic expressions have been modified in the contemporary setting.

Figure 5

Catholic Education-Catechetics

FOUNDATIONAL QUESTIONS	THE CLASSIC EXPRESSION *CATHOLIC EDUCATION-CATECHETICS*
REVELATION	· God revealed in the Church's life. · Revelation interpreted by the magisterium. · Linked with Church's liturgical life. · Appreciation of the mystery of God. · *Revelation expressed in more personalist and biblical categories.*
CONVERSION	· Becoming a Catholic or returning to the Church after having "fallen away." · *A deep change of one's life, a commitment to live anew in Christ.* · *To evangelize people is to call them to a realignment of their values; to catechize them is to deepen this conversion.* · *Catechesis is "conversion therapy."*
FAITH & BELIEF	· Faith enabled believers to assent to divine truths, which were expressed in the Church's creeds. · *Faith understood in more existential terms.* · *Faith linked with one's process of maturing.*
THEOLOGY	· Life of the mind important, so importance assigned to philosophy and theology. · Taught to majority of Catholics primarily through the catechism. · Emphasized doctrine. · Tended to be apologetic. · *Seen as grounded in the kerygma, the announcement of God's salvation at work in the world.* · *Scripture, interpreted historically within community of faith, became more significant.*
FAITH & CULTURE	· Distinction made between supernatural and natural. · Modernity suspect. · Recognition of the goodness of created order. · *Affirmation of the link between the Church and world.* · *Recognition of the way cultural forms have shaped doctrine and liturgy.* · *Realization of systemic evil.*
GOAL OF EDUCATION	· To form the whole person. · To permeate all of life with God's grace. · To achieve a person's complete transformation, both as an individual and as a member of society. · *To activate faith by means of instruction so as to bring initial faith to maturity.* · *To renew and deepen one's conversion.*

FOUNDATIONAL QUESTIONS	THE CLASSIC EXPRESSION *CATHOLIC EDUCATION-CATECHETICS*
KNOWLEDGE	· To give assent to truth expressed in propositional form. · *To complement orthodoxy with orthopraxy.*
SOCIAL SCIENCES	· Reserve about appropriateness of incorporating social sciences; distrust of emphasis on experience. · *Use encouraged, though not uncritically.* · *Receptivity to developmental psychology.*
CURRICULUM & TEACHING	· Teaching essentially transmissive—handing on of the truths of the faith. · Curriculum largely shaped by the catechism. · Curriculum rich in sacramental life—liturgy a prime teacher. · Separate school system gave a distinct identity. · *Teaching seen as proclaiming "Good News."* · *Teaching seen as involving dialogue.* · *Curriculum expanded to include human experience.*
EDUCATION AS POLITICAL	· Social orientation of Catholic philosophy gave an impetus to educating for democracy. · *Evangelization seen as including liberation from both material oppression and personal selfishness.* · *"Action on behalf of justice and participation in the transformation of the world" seen as constitutive of the preaching of the Gospel.*

The developments associated with the Second Vatican Council (1962–1965) are italicized.

NOTES

1. Fayette Breaux Veverka, "Defining a Catholic Approach to Education in the United States, 1920–1950," (paper presented to the Association of Professors and Researchers in Religious Education, Anaheim, CA., 19 November 1983).
2. For clarification on these interrelated terms, see this chapter's bibliographic essay.
3. Walter M. Abbott, ed., *The Documents of Vatican II* (New York: Guild, America and Association Presses, 1966), 639.
4. Neil G. McCluskey, *Catholic Viewpoint on Education* (Garden City, NY: Doubleday, 1959), 79.
5. In *Papal Teachings on Education* (Boston: Daughters of St. Paul, 1960), 203.
6. Ibid., 244.
7. John D. Redden and Francis A. Ryan, *A Catholic Philosophy of Education* (Milwaukee, WI: Bruce, 1942), 518.
8. Ibid., 519.
9. Ibid., 493.
10. Ibid., 492.
11. Ibid., 524.
12. Ibid., 533.
13. George Johnson, "The Need for a Catholic Philosophy of Education," in Charles A. Hart, ed., *Aspects of the New Scholastic Philosophy* (New York: Benziger Brothers, 1932), 297. Cited in Veverka, "Defining a Catholic Approach," 23.

14. See Veverka, "Defining a Catholic Approach," 27.
15. Cited in David B. Tyack, *The One Best System: A History of American Urban Education* (Cambridge, MA: Harvard University Press, 1974), 85.
16. See Fayette Breaux Veverka, "The Ambiguity of Catholic Educational Separatism," *Religious Education* 80 (1985):64–100.
17. Cited in Joseph B. Collins, "The Beginnings of the CCD in Europe and Its Modern Revival," *American Ecclesiastical Review* 168 (1974):695–706, reprinted in Michael Warren, ed., *Sourcebook for Modern Catechetics* (Winona, MN: Saint Mary's Press, 1983), 149.
18. Doris Gottemoeller and Rita Hofbauer, eds., *Women and Ministry: Present Experience and Future Hopes* (Washington, DC: Leadership Council of Women Religious, 1981).
19. H. Richard Niebuhr, *Christ and Culture* (New York: Harper & Row, 1951), 145.
20. Langdon Gilkey, *Catholicism Confronts Modernity: A Prostestant View* (New York: Seabury, 1975), 23.
21. Veverka, "Defining a Catholic Approach," 32.
22. Langdon Gilkey, *Reaping the Whirlwind: A Christian Interpretation of History* (New York: Seabury, 1976), 34.
23. In Abbott, ed., *Documents of Vatican II*, 712.
24. Ibid., 716.
25. *Lamentabili sane*, 3 July 1907, in Anne Fremantle, ed., *The Papal Encyclicals* (New York: Putnam, 1956), 202.
26. In Abbott, ed., *Documents of Vatican II*, 199–200.
27. Avery Dulles, *Models of Revelation* (Garden City, NY: Doubleday, 1983), 44.
28. In Abbott, ed., *Documents of Vatican II*, 112.
29. Ibid., 115.
30. Ibid., 124.
31. Ibid., 142.
32. Josef Jungmann, *Die Frohbotschaft und unsere Glaubensverkündigung* (English translation, William A. Huesman and Johannes A. Hofinger, eds., *The Good News Yesterday and Today* [New York: Sadlier, 1962]).
33. Josef Jungmann, *Announcing the Word of God* (London: Burns and Oates, 1967), 17.
34. Walter Ong suggests that print encourages a sense of closure and that, among its other effects, the catechism virtually eliminated paradox in its embrace of clarity. See his *Orality and Literacy: The Technologizing of the Word* (London: Methuen, 1982), 132.
35. General Conclusion #11, from the International Catechetical Study Week in Eichstätt, Austria, 1968, in Johannes Hofinger, ed., *The Art of Teaching Christian Doctrine* (Notre Dame, IN: University of Notre Dame Press, 1957), 270.
36. General Conclusion #12, from the International Catechetical Study Week in Medellín, 11–17 August 1968, reprinted in *Lumen Vitae* 24 (1969):346.
37. Michael Warren, "Introductory Overview," in Warren, ed., *Sourcebook*, 27.
38. In Joseph B. Gremillion, ed., *The Gospel of Peace and Justice: Catholic Social Teaching Since Pope John* (Maryknoll, N.Y.: Orbis, 1976), p. 514.
39. Piere-André Liégé, "The Ministry of the Word: From Kerygma to Catechesis," *Lumen Vitae* 17 (1962):21–36, reprinted in Warren, ed., *Sourcebook*, 324.
40. Warren, ed., *Sourcebook*, 325.
41. Ibid., 327.
42. *Directorium Catechisticum Generale*, in English translation (Washington, DC: United States Catholic Conference, 1971), #21.
43. D.S. Amalorpavadass "Catechesis as a Pastoral Task of the Church," *Lumen Vitae* 27 (1972):259–80, in Warren, ed., *Sourcebook*, 342.
44. In Warren, ed., *Sourcebook*, 342. Warren has in some instances made the language more inclusive; this paragraph is one example, as the pronouns are exclusively male in the original.
45. See Leo Dworshak, "Learning by Doing," in *Education and Liturgy: Proceedings of the 1957 North American Liturgical Week* (Elsberry, MO: The Liturgical Conference, 1958), 28–33.

46. General Conclusion #10, in Hofinger, ed., *The Art of Teaching*, 269.
47. Johannes Hofinger, "Catechetics and Liturgy," *Worship* 24 (1954–1955):92.
48. Aidan Kavanagh, "Teaching Through the Liturgy," *Notre Dame Journal of Education* 5 (1974):41.
49. Ibid., 43.
50. *Sharing the Light of Faith: National Catechetical Directory for Catholics of the United States* (Washington, DC: United States Catholic Conference, 1979), #32. The citation within is taken from the "Decree on the Bishops' Pastoral Office in the Church" (*Christus dominus*), #14, in Abbott, ed., *Documents of Vatican II*, 406.
51. *Sharing the Light of Faith*, #59.
52. See Robert J. Hater, *Religious Education and Catechesis: A Shift in Focus* (Washington, DC: National Conference of Diocesan Directors of Religious Education, 1981); Michael Warren, "Catechesis: An Enriching Category for Religious Education," *Religious Education* 76 (1981):115–27, reprinted in Warren, ed., *Sourcebook*, 379–94.
53. *Sharing the Light of Faith*, 174–75.
54. See Andrew M. Greeley, William C. McCready, and Kathleen McCourt, *Catholic Schools in a Declining Church* (Kansas City, MO: Sheed and Ward, 1976); R. H. Potvin, D. R. Hoge, and H. M. Nelsen, *Religion and American Youth* (Washington, DC: United States Catholic Conference, 1976); H. M. Nelsen, R. H. Potvin, and J. Shields, *The Religion of Children* (Washington, DC: United States Catholic Conference, 1976).

Bibliographic Essay

Catholic Education–Catechetics

My thinking on the relationship of Catholic education to catechetics has been greatly shaped by conversations with Fayette Breaux Veverka and in particular by her paper "Defining a Catholic Approach to Education in the United States, 1920–1950" (presented to the Association of Professors and Researchers in Religious Education, Anaheim, CA, 19 November 1983) and "The Ambiguity of Catholic Educational Separatism," *Religious Education* 80 (1985):64–100. Thus I went to sources of a classic Catholic philosophy, including the collection *Papal Teachings on Education* (Boston: Daughters of St. Paul, 1960); William F. Cunningham, *The Pivotal Problems of Education* (New York: Macmillan, 1940); Neil G. McCluskey, *Catholic Viewpoint on Education*, Catholic Viewpoint Series (Garden City, NY; Doubleday, 1959); William J. McGucken, *The Catholic Way in Education* (Milwaukee, WI: Bruce, 1934); and John D. Redden and Francis A. Ryan, *A Catholic Philosophy of Education* (Milwaukee, WI: Bruce, 1942). Also extremely illuminating was Mary Perkins Ryan's *Are Parochial Schools the Answer? Catholic Education in the Light of the Council* (New York: Holt, Rinehart and Winston, 1964), a book that anticipated by a number of years the tensions between schooling and the religious education of adults.

Three historical works of value include James Hennesey, *American Catholics* (New York: Oxford University Press, 1981); Jay P. Dolan, *The American Catholic Experience: A History from Colonial Times to the Present* (Garden City, NY: Doubleday, Image Books, 1985); and Mary Jo Weaver, *New Catholic Women: A Contemporary Challenge To Traditional Religious Authority* (San Francisco: Harper & Row, 1985). Primary references are collected in John Tracy Ellis, ed., *Documents of American Catholic History*, 3 vols. (vols. 1 and 2 reprints of a 1967 publication; Wilmington, DL: Glazier, 1987).

Also of great usefulness throughout the chapter were Richard P. McBrien, *Catholicism*, 2 vols. (Minneapolis, MN: Winston, 1980); Langdon Gilkey, *Catholicism Confronts Modernity: A Protestant View* (New York: Seabury, 1975); Avery Dulles, *Models of Revelation* (Garden City, NY: Doubleday, 1983) and "The Meaning of Faith Considered in Relationship to Justice," in John Haughey, ed., *The Faith That Does Justice*, Woodstock Studies 2 (New York: Paulist, 1977), 10–46; Gerald A. McCool, *Catholic Theology in the Nineteenth Century: A Search for a Unitary Method* (New York: Seabury, 1975); T. Mark Schoof, *A Survey of Catholic Theology 1800–1970* (New York: Paulist, 1970); and Leonard Doohan, *The Lay-Centered Church: Theology and Spirituality* (Minneapolis, MN: Winston, 1984).

Another collection of valuable historical essays is contained in John H. Westerhoff and O. C. Edwards, eds., *A Faithful Church: Issues in the History of Catechesis* (Wilton, CT: Morehouse-Barlow, 1981), particularly the essay by Mary Charles Bryce, "Evolution of Catechesis from the Catholic Reformation to the Present," 204–35.

Among the key documents on catechetics, the following publications from the United States Catholic Conference (Washington, DC) must be recognized as foundational: *The General Catechetical Directory (1971); To Teach as Jesus Did* (1972); *Basic Teachings for Catholic Religious Education* (1973); *The Rite of Christian Initiation* (1977); and *Sharing the Light of Faith: National Catechetical Directory for Catholics of the United States* (1979). Berard Marthaler has written commentaries on both the *General Catechetical Directory* and *Sharing the Light of Faith;* see his *Catechetics in Context* (Huntington, IN: Our Sunday Visitor, 1973) and *A Commentary on the National Catechetical Directory* (Washington, DC: United States Catholic Conference, 1981). Also of use is Anne Marie Mongoven, *Signs of Catechesis: An Overview of the National Catechetical Directory* (New York: Paulist, 1979).

The important synodal statement "Justice in the World" (1971) is available in Joseph Gremillion's fine collection, *The Gospel of Peace and Justice: Catholic Social Teaching Since Pope John* (Maryknoll, NY: Orbis, 1976). Other documents of importance are the two apostolic exhortations: Pope Paul VI's *"Evangelii Nuntiandi,"* in Austin Flannery, ed., *Evangelization Today* (Northport, NY: Costello, 1977); and Pope John Paul II's *"Catechesi Tradendae,"* in *Origins* 9 (1979):330–48. And, of course, one's whole understanding of this era must be predicated upon the work of the Second Vatican Council, so firsthand acquaintance with its sixteen documents is a prerequisite; see Austin Flannery, ed. *Vatican Council II: The Conciliar and Post Conciliar Documents,* 2 vols. (Collegeville, MN: Liturgical Press, 1975, 1984).

Among the important secondary literature, Gabriel Moran's two volumes on revelation contributed mightily to the integration of new understandings into catechetics; no account of the post–Vatican II catechetical scene is adequate without his *A Theology of Revelation* and *A Catechesis of Revelation* (both New York: Herder and Herder, 1966). Mary Charles Bryce's detailed history of the *Baltimore Catechism* is required reading: *The Influence of the Catechism of the Third Plenary Council of Baltimore on Widely Used Elementary Religion Text Books from Its Composition in 1885 to Its 1941 Revision* (Ann Arbor, MI: University Microfilms, 1971). Michael Dujarier has contributed two historical works essential to understanding the restoration of the catechumenate: *A History of the Catechumenate: The First Six Centuries* (New York: Sadlier, 1979) and *The Rites of Christian Initiation* (New York: Sadlier, 1979). Jacques Audinet's "Catechesis" in Karl Rahner, ed., *Encyclopedia of Theology: The Concise Sacramentum Mundi* (New York: Seabury, 1975), 176, also provides an important historical perspective.

I have written at length on the origins of the kerygmatic movement in my *Biblical Interpretation in Religious Education* (Birmingham, AL: Religious Education Press, 1980). The notes therein can guide readers to the extensive literature on the kerygmatic era. I recommend every reader's direct encounter with Josef Jungmann's *The Good News Yesterday and Today,* ed. Johannes Hofinger and William Huesman (New York: Sadlier, 1963). Hofinger's autobiographical essay, "Catechetical Sputnik," in Marlene Mayr, ed., *Modern Masters of Religious Education* (Birmingham, AL: Religious Education Press, 1983) offers a warm, personal perspective on this important era. Michael Warren's compendium, *Sourcebook for Modern Catechetics* (Winona, MN: Saint Mary's Press, 1983) contains key articles documenting the development of catechetics. It also reflects Warren's personal predilection for catechetical models, a conclusion with which I had earlier taken issue in my article, "The Standpoint of Religious Education," *Religious Education* 76 (1981):128–41. Other significant interpretations of *catechetics* can be found in Kenneth Barker, *Religious Education, Catechesis and Freedom* (Birmingham, AL: Religious Education Press, 1981); and R. M. Rummery, *Catechesis and Religious Education in a Pluralist Society* (Huntington, IN: Our Sunday Visitor, 1979). Rummery's work is especially helpful in laying out the different curricular implications of *religious education* in contrast to *catechesis*.

A fascinating perspective on the era of the so-called experiential catechetics is found in Didier-Jacques Piveteau and J. T. Dillon, *Resurgence of Religious Instruction* (Birmingham, AL: Religious Education Press, 1977). Among the authors who set the stage for that era were Pierre Babin, *Options* (New York: Herder and Herder, 1967); Marcel van Caster and Jean LeDuc, *Experiential Catechetics* (New York: Paulist, 1969); Marcel van Caster, *The Structure of Catechetics* (New York: Herder and Herder, 1965) and *Values Catechetics* (New York: Paulist, 1970).

The relation of evangelization to *catechetics* is laid out in Alfonso Nebreda's *Kerygma in Crisis* (Chicago: Loyola University Press, 1965), in which he suggests the necessity of "prevangelization" so as to prepare people for the conversion the Good News demands. Also of interest is Johannes Hofinger, *Evangelization and Catechesis* (New York: Paulist, 1976), in which he suggests that though distinguishable in theory, the two are closely related in reality.

The importance of the relationship between liturgy and catechetics is addressed by Mary Charles Bryce, "The InterRelationship of Liturgy and Catechesis," *The American Benedictine Review* 28 (1977):1–29. See also, Virginia Sloyan, "Liturgical Dimension of Catechetics," *The American Ecclesiastical Review* 160 (1969):255-61; Paul Marx, *Virgil Michel and the Liturgical Movement* (Collegeville, MN: Liturgical Press, 1957); and Jeremy Hall, "The American Liturgical Movement: The Early Years," *Worship* 50 (1976):474–89. Notable also is Aidan Kavanagh, "Teaching through the Liturgy," *Notre Dame Journal of Education* 5 (1974):35–47.

One of the more difficult distinctions to pin down with precision is the relation of the "cousin" terms *catechesis* and *catechetics*. I cannot find a consistent usage. Berard Marthaler, in the "Introduction" in Warren's *Sourcebook for Modern Catechetics,* offers the opinion that *catechetics* is to *catechesis* as ethics is to ethos, and as statistics is to data: *"catechetics* studies practice in order to formulate and test theory . . . no definition of *catechesis* has won universal acceptance. *Sharing the Light of Faith* associates it with endeavors which range from community building to prayer, from initiation into the Christian community to fostering attitudes, behaviors, and knowledge contributing to spiritual and moral maturity. Almost every pastoral ministry has its catechetical dimension" (pp. 15–16). In a different vein, John Westerhoff has argued that one should differentiate the two this way: *catechetics* has typically emphasized content to the exclusion of persons and their experiences, e.g., catechisms; whereas *catechesis* is a pastoral ministry uniting present experiences and the faith tradition ("Risking a Conclusion," in John H. Westerhoff, III, ed., *Who Are We? The Quest for a Religious Education* [Birmingham, AL: Religious Education Press, 1978], 268). He elaborates on his definition of *catechesis* in his two essays "The Challenge: Understanding the Problem of Faithfulness" and "Framing an Alternative Future for Catechesis," in Westerhoff and Edwards, eds., *A Faithful Church*, 1–9 and 293–14, respectively. Here his usage is so broad one wonders if there is anything religious that *catechesis* does not somehow embrace. In the Warren collection, Westerhoff appears to have left behind his previous sharp distinction, seemingly using the two terms interchangeably, though with what appears to be a decided preference for *catechesis* ("Catechetics: An Anglican Perspective," 428–35). Such confusions made my own decision about usage seem somewhat arbitrary; in the end I chose to speak more generally about *catechetics*, in part because it has been the more familiar term (at least until the restoration of the catechumenate) and also because I decided to follow Warren's lead in entitling his volume—the best collection for an understanding of this classic expression—*A Sourcebook for Modern Catechetics*.

In large measure concern about terminology reflects substantive issues that will be taken up later in this work, including issues centering around socialization and liturgy. Thus, I shall append further bibliographic references in later chapters.

CHAPTER 6

Extending the Survey: Contemporary Modifications of the Classic Expressions

In chapters 2 through 5, I have narrated the development of four "classic expressions" or ways of educating in faith arising from a particular history in which specific theological perspectives intersect with certain educational understandings. If the analysis was properly carried out, then readers should at various junctures have experienced an "aha": a recognition of the "staying power" of many of the concerns and characteristics of the four major ways Protestants and Catholics have educated in faith in twentieth-century North America.

It is my task now to trace the pathways of each of the classic expressions through the late 1960s into the 1980s. By so doing, I will follow up each classic expression by showing the core of continuity that still exists—albeit often modified—amidst ever-increasing diversity. The procedure, therefore, in this sixth chapter will be to take up in turn each of the four classic expressions (*evangelism, religious education, Christian education, Catholic education–catechetics*) as they exist today.

EVANGELISM

The rather broad definition given to *evangelism*—preaching or teaching the Scriptures in such a way as to arouse conversion—and its twofold manifestation in revivalism and evangelicalism suggest that this classic expression might well encompass a range of understandings of educating in faith. Particularly since the advent of the phrase "born-again Christian" into the vocabulary of the United States, the evangelical presence has become increasingly prominent. Moreover, it has become a political power to be reckoned with, attested to by the rapid growth of the evangelical-fundamentalist Right in organizations such as the Moral Majority, Christian Voice, Religious Roundtable, and National Conservative Political Action. Other groups, such as the Sojourners Fellowship, however, claim to be truly evangelical, even as they espouse political views and create modes of life that differ sharply from more prominent evangelical groups. The Sojourners Fellowship represents an alternative interpretation of evangelical traditions that is at once a critique of mainstream American society and of the evangelical Right. In addition, many evangelicals align themselves in positions less identifiable with perspectives they perceive as extreme, i.e., neither fundamentalist nor radically countercultural, and so identify with more centrist views.

The spectrum of contemporary evangelical life thus has hues of many colors, and its fascinating mosaic serves as a warning against simplistic generalizations. Because the differences tend to cluster to a significant degree around varying judgments on the nature of scriptural revelation (especially on its inerrancy) and on social ethics (especially on the question of Christ and culture), theology provides a useful analytic framework for understanding evangelicalism.

As the previous chapters have made clear, theology alone does not account for varying standpoints on educating in faith. One must also inquire into what constitutes educational philosophies consonant with contemporary evangelicalism. To a certain extent, this educational inquiry must proceed by way of inference, since the debate has generally been framed in theological terms. Nonetheless, questions about evangelical education must be pressed. Despite the frequent lack of an explicit educational philosophy, evangelicals educate in faith powerfully and pervasively.

Once education, and not merely theology, becomes a significant factor in analysis, three patterns may be seen: religious education as transmission of the truth; religious education as faith shared in a countercultural, apostolic community; and religious education as mission. These three patterns, though not mutually exclusive, may nonetheless be associated with the Right, Left and center, respectively, of evangelicalism.

Prior to sketching these patterns, however, a word on revivalism is appropriate, since it figures prominently in each, though in varying fashion. Revivals are not only a religious phenomenon but also an important means of educating. They must, therefore, be considered part of the total configuration of the educational institutions of modern-day evangelism. Without recognition of their formative role, the pattern is incomplete.

RELIGIOUS EDUCATION AS TRANSMISSION OF THE TRUTH

If, in an earlier era, revivalist preachers roused their hearers by means of pulpit artistry, those contemporary preachers associated with transmission of the truth—most notably Jerry Falwell, Pat Robertson, Robert Schuller, Rex Humbard, and Jim Bakker—engage their listeners by means of electronic empires. Their television programs ("Old Time Gospel Hour," "P.T.L. [Praise the Lord] Club," "700 Club," "Hour of Power") reach an estimated fourteen million people weekly; another forty-seven million hear them weekly on the radio.[1] In many instances, callers may phone telephone prayer-counseling centers; journals and newsletters champion various conservative causes, and computers keep track of all callers and subscribers for solicitation of funds. Theologian Harvey Cox remarks, "The love affair between conservative religion and the mass electronic media is the most significant recent religious event in the United States."[2]

For Jerry Falwell's followers the term "fundamentalist" is an honorable epithet. This implies not simply a judgment about the Bible, which Falwell says is "absolutely infallible, without errors in all matters pertaining to faith and practice, as well as in areas such as geography, science, history, etc."[3] The title "fundamentalist" also connotes opposition to what they regard as the bane of modernity, "godless, secular humanists." Indeed, what seems to be the most significant dynamic in fundamentalism is its militant standpoint against modernity. Because fundamentalists believe that God's truth as revealed in the Bible is perspicacious and immutable, they judge the relativism of a pluralistic society to be heretical. They scathingly denounce liberals and humanists who, they believe, have erred by departing from a literal interpretation of Scripture and by tolerating or approving of evils such as abortion, homosexuality, equal rights for women, and evolution. The fundamentalist commitment is to "saturation evangelism," using every medium—church services, television, video cassettes, radio, newsletters and journals, rallies, private schools, and computerized Bible programs—to transmit God's truth. By so doing, the perversions of what they regard as this "evil time" are countered.

The private school has become one of the prime means for fundamentalists to renew society. Critical of the moral neutrality of the public school system (including its ban on school prayer, its teaching of humanistic values and sex education, and its alleged preference for global interdependence rather than for national patriotism), fundamentalists intensified efforts to develop an alternative. Between 1971 and 1981, the number of students enrolled in fundamentalist Christian schools increased from 140,000 to 450,000. The schools provide a means for inculcating moral absolutes and reflect a clear "Christ against culture" stance. As one woman, a Nebraskan who conducts a school for her three daughters, remarks: "The girls like to be with other children, but they don't want to be with children who are taught contrary to our thinking." Among her curriculum materials are "truth packs," which take issue with liberal values—equality for women, socialism, abortion, and premarital sex.[4]

There is a certain irony in the fundamentalists' enthusiastic embrace of the technology of television, mass computer mailing, and sophisticated marketing techniques. Cox's assessment is worth quoting:

Jerry Falwell and other religious traditionalists who have embraced network color television, the ultimate form of modern mechanical reproduction, may have struck a mortal blow to exactly what they are trying to defend, the "old time Gospel" and traditional religion. The move from the revivalist's tent to the vacuum tube has vastly amplified the voices of defenders of tradition. At the same time it has made them more dependent on the styles and assumptions inherent in the medium itself. . . .

The contradiction between traditional religion and the mass media seems unavoidable. The deepest contradiction lies in the question of the nature of a genuine religious community. . . . Despite their efforts to include viewers through letters, telephone calls, and a folksy style on camera, something essential is missing in a television congregation. By buying into the mass-media world so heavily fundamentalism may have unintentionally sold out to one of the most characteristic features of the very modern world it wants so much to challenge.[5]

The revivalists of the Great Awakenings (1730–1760 and 1800–1830) sought a change of heart, not a mere change of opinion. Likewise do the fundamentalist leaders challenge their audiences and congregations to be "born again," to proclaim Jesus as their Lord and Savior, and to join the "Lord's army" in battle against the "principalities and powers." Their weapon is God's truth as found in a literal interpretation of the Bible; it sets them apart from the rest of society (a "Moral Minority"?) and provides the basis for a renewed order. As Falwell comments in *The Fundamentalist Journal,* which he edits:

America needs the impact of a genuine spiritual revival led by Bible-believing pastors. . . .

In reality, the Bible-believing church members of America are very close to one another theologically. They stand on the fundamentals of the faith. They believe the Bible is the Word of God; they believe in heaven, in hell, and in life after death. They believe that Jesus died for our sins, rose from the dead, and is coming again. They are the "bread and butter" Middle Americans who are holding this country together.

As pastors, we have an obligation to God and to His people to lead them according to the truths of Scripture. America is ripe for revival for the first time in this century.[6]

RELIGIOUS EDUCATION AS FAITH SHARED IN A COUNTERCULTURAL, APOSTOLIC COMMUNITY

Like Falwell, Jim Wallis, one of the founders of the Sojourners Fellowship and editor of its journal *Sojourners,* believes this country is in need of a revival, though his reasons differ:

Today America is bound by sin. As a people we have become captivated by greed, power, selfishness, and pride. We have been poisoned by years of unrepented racism, materialism, violence, and oppression. We have ignored the cries of the victims of our many sins—the poor, people of color, and women. We no longer trust in God but in our wealth and military might, and the fruit of our idolatry is a nuclear arms race that threatens the world with extinction.

Mere political solutions will not be enough. Calls for social change without the call to faith will only lead to discouragement and despair. And evangelism that does not address the crisis we face is unfaithful to the gospel.

A revival of genuine biblical faith in this country is the one thing that could most undermine the injustice and violence that have become endemic in the American system. Social justice and peace will only come as the fruits of spiritual transformation. Our hope is for a mighty outpouring of the Holy Spirit which brings repentance and conversion.[7]

The radical character of Wallis's call for a revival becomes apparent when placed in the context of the history of the Sojourners Fellowship. Their life together began in Chicago in 1970, where, against the backdrop of the war in Vietnam, seven or eight seminary students at Trinity Evangelical Divinity School gathered together to explore what it meant to be biblical Christians at that painful period in U.S. history. Though from diverse backgrounds, they shared an evangelical faith that fostered a growing sense that commitment to Christ meant in some way involvement in the social-political order. Disillusioned with the church, since it seemed merely to be one more institution conforming to the establishment, a "chaplain to all the injustice and profit-making violence of American society,"[8] they directed their energies to the publication of the *Post American,* a journal critical of the violence and greed they believed had overtaken the nation. The cover of the first issue pictured a statue of Christ removed from the cross and draped in an American flag with the caption, "And they crucified him." The responsiveness they encountered led to the realization that that radical meaning of the gospel could reach thousands of people.

Their recognition entailed a commitment to the development of a community wherein their social-political orientation could be deepened by supportive relationships and common worship. After years of struggle, a clarity about priorities and directions emerged, and in 1975 a core group of about twenty moved to Washington, DC, the place where both the prophetic and pastoral dimensions of their life could mature. They also chose to rename their magazine *Sojourners,* since that title evoked one of the central biblical metaphors for God's people, who are to live in the world as strangers and pilgrims because of their commitment to God's reign.

The Sojourners Fellowship, a community that publishes a monthly journal and works actively for the poor by means of food cooperatives, lobbying, neighborhood recreational programs, and dayschool tutoring programs, clearly identifies itself as countercultural. Yet its "Christ against culture" stance differs from that of the evangelical Right, which, though rejecting what it terms "godless, secular humanism" nevertheless accepts the "gospel of success." The evangelical Right's enthusiastic support of capitalism, military build-up, and patriotism suggests that its "Christ against culture" position coexists with a "Christ in culture" position that is quite comfortable with mainstream life. The Sojourners Fellowship, on the other hand, quite consistently maintains its sense of being set against all secular orders. Seeking to imitate Christ in all things and to live only by his values and priorities, the Sojourners Fellowship believes that justice can be achieved neither by a blind conformity to the American way of life nor by political reforms, but only by a biblically based response to the oppressed. As sojourners they see themselves as aliens, demythologizing and debunking all ideological idolatry, whether Marxist or capitalist, liberal or conservative.[9] To transform society—to seek conversion on the corporate as well as individual level—to them means the creation of an alternative "political" structure: "Change comes, we [Sojourners Fellowship] suspect, more through the witness of creative and prophetic minorities who refuse to meet the system on its own terms but rather act out of an alternative social vision upon which they have based their lives."[10]

As a monthly journal, *Sojourners* is the fruit of community life rather than the product of an editorial board and staff. Its articles represent their vision of "costly discipleship" and encompass topics such as spirituality, peacemaking, economics of oppression, liberation (of the poor, of people of color, and of women), and parenting for peace and justice. They make much less use of "televangelism" than do other evangelical groups, although they do make available documentary films for rental or purchase. But what is especially interesting is the community's recent decision to make the revival a major educational tool. To quote again from the same editorial by Jim Wallis with which this section began:

In the last few years the changing nature of speaking invitations and my own sense of direction has led me away from university and seminary lectures, conference speaking, and issue-oriented seminars, and toward city wide, ecumenical preaching events. These have been sponsored by coalitions of churches—evangelical, Catholic, mainline Protestant, black churches, historical peace churches, and various peace and justice groups, and have usually lasted one or two days.

Our intention now is to make the direction more explicit and expand the idea into preaching campaigns in various cities for up to a week in length. The revivals would include successive nights of preaching—at least three and perhaps as many as seven. We hope these events would be highly visible, attract large numbers of people, and make gospel preaching publicly controversial again. They would be designed to call people away from the ruling American myths, illusions, and lifestyle; from the sins of the people and the sins of the nation; from injustice and war; and from individual selfishness. They would call people to Christ, to personal transformation and to the biblical vision of justice and peace [emphasis added].

Today some call for spiritual renewal in a vacuum while others speak of social issues without recognizing the need for conversion. We will preach spiritual revival in the face of military madness, oppressive affluence, and abandonment of the poor. Our hope is for revivals that would have a powerful impact on a city or region spiritually, socially, economically, and politically. We hope that out of revival many will turn to Christ and, as a result, a whole new level of public activity for the sake of the poor, for peace, for racial justice and reconciliation would emerge.

I was raised in the evangelical tradition and, after a long pilgrimage, have come to understand that I am still an evangelist at heart. Therefore, the idea of these preaching campaigns reflects both the vision of our community and a clear sense of my own personal calling.[11]

The Sojourners Fellowship has no explicit program in religious education that I am aware of, but quite obviously it understands its very existence as an alternative community of faith to be a way of educating people to the meaning of the gospel. By its witness to a simple life-style and sharing of goods, its advocacy on behalf of and involvement with the poor, its work in journalism and now its leadership in revivals throughout the nation, Sojourners Fellowship educates in faith as surely as any other Christian group with a fully developed educational program.

RELIGIOUS EDUCATION AS MISSION

In a sense, all evangelical groups think of religious education as mission. The urgency of seeking conversion of sinful people to Christ is one of the major elements of evangelicalism. Yet, as the earlier sections of this chapter evidence, mission has quite a different meaning for Falwell's disciples, for instance, than it does for the Sojourners Fellowship. In part, this is attributable to varying understandings of conversion. For Falwell, conversion implies a personal submission to Christ's lordship in an experience of being "born again"; for the Sojourners, it implies not only the individual's discipleship, but also the transformation of society, a turning away from violence, racism, and injustice.

But not all evangelicals identify with these two positions. Some seem uncomfortable with the interpretation of the issues made by the televangelists and embarrassed by their preoccupation with fund-raising. Yet they also appear ill at ease with the countercultural position of the Sojourners Fellowship. This centrist group is committed to evangelical doctrine; most explicitly accept the doctrinal statement of the National Association of Evangelicals, formulated in 1943:

1. We believe the Bible to be the inspired, the only infallible, authoritative Word of God.
2. We believe that there is one God, eternally existent in three Persons: Father, Son, and Holy Spirit.
3. We believe in the deity of our Lord Jesus Christ, in His virgin birth, in His sinless life, in His miracles, in His vicarious and atoning death through His shed blood, in His bodily resurrection, in His ascension to the right hand of the Father and in His personal return in power and glory.

4. We believe that for the salvation of lost and sinful man [woman] regeneration by the Holy Spirit is absolutely essential.
5. We believe in the present ministry of the Holy Spirit, by whose indwelling the Christian is enabled to live a godly life.
6. We believe in the resurrection of both the saved and the lost; they that are saved unto the resurrection of life and they that are lost unto the resurrection of damnation.
7. We believe in the spiritual unity of believers in our Lord Jesus Christ.[12]

The acceptance of this statement, however, has not settled all matters theological; among many of these evangelicals, for whom schools such as Fuller Theological Seminary in California and Gordon-Conwell Seminary in Massachusetts serve as intellectual centers, there is considerable rethinking about the function of biblical authority and of the role of social concerns. But what is especially apparent when one tries to examine their most prominent understanding of religious education is the importance placed on witness, a desire to share the Good News in credible ways. Moreover, mission implies "fellowship" and congregational life—community.

This means great attention to the development of fellowship groups for Bible study and support (e.g., Young Life, InterVarsity Fellowship); it means that a graduate student specializing in Christian education (their preferred terminology) may take courses in media, group dynamics, and Christian camping.

The theorist who has best articulated this is Lawrence O. Richards, who argues that evangelicals can no longer limit their educational thinking to how they will deal with Scripture in the classroom or to how the teacher communicates, but to the "total life of believers as they function within the Body." Christian educators must consider "every interaction—the boards and committees, the growth and action groups, the congregational services, the phone calls and the fishing trips—settings in which to facilitate the development of ministering relationships that affirm the unity and love of the Body.[13] Consequently, says Richards, the Christian educator should be considered as a "designer of the life of the Church," and curricula should be designed more for structuring roles and relationships than for communication of content. Process is important, since the way in which the curriculum structures teaching/learning situations may well have more impact on learners than specific content.[14]

Ultimately, this implies an understanding of Christian education as socialization, the induction and formation of persons in a believing community. Accordingly, the Christian educator is not merely a writer of lessons and a teacher-trainer, but a "facilitator of community" who "requires a mastery not of formal education but of nonformal education—a discipline closer to sociology and anthropology than to education"[15] That is not to deny the fundamental importance of the theological disciplines that grow out of a recognition of Scripture as God's "reality revelation." These guide the Christian educator and the congregational leaders in their care for the community of faith.[16]

To educate in faith with an emphasis on mission means assigning a priority to "outreach" programs and to processes for building community. It does not preclude revivalism—Billy Graham still inspires massive gatherings—but places its emphasis on "fellowship" as a key element in education.

The differences among these three patterns ought not to be exaggerated, but they do indicate the complexity and liveliness of *evangelism* today. As a classic expression, *evangelism* testifies to the centrality of the experience of conversion in educating in faith and to the urgency of witnessing to the gospel.

RELIGIOUS EDUCATION

Each of the classic expressions is a mosaic, bringing various elements into the harmony of a single design. *Religious education,* for instance, encompasses Channing's Unitarianism, Bushnell's preference for nurture within the family over adolescent conversion, and the Dewey-Coe-Elliott commitment to education as reconstruction. These elements have continued through the present day in the educational commitments of the Unitarian Universalist church and its "cousin" traditions, such as the Ethical Culture Society; in the work of the Religious Experience Research Unit at Manchester College, Oxford; and in the work of theorists Paulo Freire and Gabriel Moran. A look at each in turn provides a glimpse of the current "state of the art" of *religious education.*

RELIGIOUS EDUCATION IN THE UNITARIAN TRADITION

Under the leadership of editor-consultant Sophia Lyon Fahs and the American Unitarian Association's Director of Religious Education, Ernest Kuebler, the New Beacon Series flourished. Its breadth—a curriculum inclusive of humankind's religiosity—and emphasis on developmentalism continued under Dorothy Spoerl, successor to Fahs. A psychologist and minister, Spoerl collaborated with Fahs and extended her work along humanistic lines.[17]

A new emphasis became discernible in 1965 with the advent of Hugo J. Hollerorth as Curriculum Director of the Unitarian Universalist Association (the two traditions had merged in 1961). Influenced especially by the existentialism of Paul Tillich, Hollerorth evidenced much interest in creating curricula that explored the "search for meaning" amid life's difficulties, complexities, and ambiguities. Thus, he led the way in publishing a multimedia curriculum with kits such as "Decision Making" (so that children can discover the power of reason and the insight gained from creative interaction); "Man [Woman] the Culture Builder" (so that children can discover some intellectual understandings of the world, including different customs and mores); "Human Heritage" (so that children can appreciate biological and cultural evolution); "Freedom and Responsibility" (so that the young can realize the potentiality of human beings to be with one another in relationships of love, sensitivity, and freedom); "Man [Woman] the Meaning Maker" (so that the young can become better able to communicate); "About Your Sexuality" (so that the young can develop a "life-enhancing orientation" to their sexuality); and "The Haunting House" (so that children can affirm their need for places of solitude, dreaming, and intimacy).[18]

Particularly useful is Hollerorth's statement of the philosophy that undergirds this multimedia curriculum, *Relating to Our World.* Herein Hollerorth lists three objectives of religious education in the Unitarian Universalist tradition:

1. To help children and young people become aware of and comprehend the multitude of powers within the self as well as those which impinge upon them from the environing world. These include powers with which they are endowed as human beings, such as biological needs and psychological desires, as well as those powers in the form of cultural expectations, traditions and evolutionary inheritances which impinge upon them as they move about the world and interact with it.
2. To help children and young people discover and become skilled in using the *process* which is the Unitarian Universalist religion [emphasis added]. This includes helping them discover and become skilled in the use of the human mind; creative interaction with themselves, with other human beings, and with nature; being with people in a relationship of freedom, love, sensitivity, honesty, independence, and adventurousness; the employment of the full range of human knowledge; and the use of diversity of thought.
3. To help children and young people use the *process* which is the Unitarian Universalist religion for relating to and dealing with the ways they are affected by the world as intellectual, moral, sentient, aesthetic and moral beings [emphasis added]. This includes helping them use the process for: fathoming the meaning of their experience; making responsible choices; sorting out feelings, understanding them, and evolving a disposition toward the world; gathering up the fragments of human existence and seeing life in its wholeness; confronting the precariousness of existence and the certainty of death and understanding their place in the drama of life.[19]

Elizabeth Baker sees in such objectives a shift in educational direction. Hollerorth's existentialist understanding of the person as torn and buffeted by myriad powers marks a change from the Dewey-influenced New Beacon Series in which each action was seen as an experience of a unified self seeking to resolve its conflicts through intelligent action. Moreover, Hollerorth's description of Unitarian Universalism as a process rather than as a system of meanings with which certain processes are compatible resulted in materials oriented to the present and the personal, with very little historical material available. His orientation seems also to be less grounded in a coherent educational philosophy; consequently, he gave little attention to developmentalism or pedagogy.[20]

Perhaps such differences have roots in the nature of Unitarian Universalism, which, according to Judith Hoehler, has three distinct "faith stances": the Judeo-Christian, the theistic, and the humanist. All three are authentic insofar as they incorporate the themes characteristic of Unitarian Universalism—free will, anti-Trinitarianism, reason, transcendentalism, universal salvation, and humanism. They are, nevertheless, mutually exclusive insofar as they emphasize certain of the themes to a greater or less extent and thereby differ substantially in regard to worship and religious education.[21] For instance, in the Judeo-Christian tradition, members see in Jesus Christ the revelation of what the God-human relationship should be and thus give the Bible a central role in curriculum. Because the theistic stance, on the other hand, is more tentative in its language about God and more directly linked to transcendentalism, it is (as was the New Beacon Series) more inclusive in its materials and draws upon a wider range of stories and symbols. The humanist stance emphasizes the power of human reasoning and scientific knowing. In its use of the Bible, it tends either to criticize the naiveté of a literalist rendering of Genesis or to approach it along the lines of Bible-as-literature. Hoehler concludes that the denomination cannot have one core curriculum.

Her typology provides a guide to *Stone House Conversations*, a work illustrative of the pluralism among Unitarian Universalist educators. The book consists of conversations by UUA's Religious Education Advisory Group and Staff. Thirteen of the participants have contributed a brief paper. Each addresses the following: "What is Unitarian Universalism?" "What are the objectives of UU religious education?" "What content and experiences should be included in the curriculum so as to fulfill these objectives?"[22] The theistic stance seems most prevalent, but readers also find consideration of what it might mean to stand in the Judeo-Christian tradition.[23] The work articulates as well a humanistic philosophy that suggests four organizing principles of the curriculum: the theory of evolution, scientific method, democratic process, and radical pluralism.[24] *Stone House Conversations* bears witness to the pluralism within Unitarian Universalism and reflects one of the directions in which the religious education movement developed.

RELIGIOUS EDUCATION AND THE
RELIGIOUS EXPERIENCE RESEARCH UNIT

George Albert Coe was a pioneer in empirical research on religion, certainly a mode of study that has developed rapidly in the past quarter century. It has led, for example, to the foundation of the Society for

Scientific Research in Religion and to the appropriation of the behavioral sciences, especially developmental psychology, for education in faith. Thus, names such as Jean Piaget and Lawrence Kohlberg have become familiar to many religious educators, and the work of James Fowler and his colleagues on stages of faith development has become one of the most important new developments in the field. This empirical research will be discussed more fully in the following chapter, but here it is important simply to note Coe's link with this particular direction.

Another, though less well-known, type of religious research emanates from Manchester College, Oxford, where British scientist Sir Alister Hardy founded the Religious Experience Research Unit in 1969 as a means of challenging his fellow scientists to give recognition to the role of religious experience in human life. Now under the direction of Edward Robinson, some of the research resonates with Horace Bushnell's respect for the religious character of childhood.

One of Robinson's research projects involved the formulation and compilation of a questionnaire designed to elicit people's views on their early experiences of the religious dimension of life. Originally, Hardy had invited all who felt that their lives had in any way been affected by "some power beyond themselves" to give an account of the experience and its effect on their lives. Of the more than 4000 respondents, about 15 percent related events and experiences going back to their earliest years. This piqued Robinson's interest. He decided to follow up that particular set of respondents to learn more about how children experience the world. Thus, he sent out approximately 500 questionnaires, asking questions such as, "How do you think that you owe your early religious ideas or feelings to the influence of your family, or to any other individuals who were helpful, whether as models to be imitated or just as sympathetic people to talk to?" Another question asked, "How far do you feel that your early idea of God was derived from what you saw in your parents?" Others asked about the influence of schooling and of organized religion in the development of religious awareness; about the emergence of a "socially induced conscience" in relation to one's religious feelings; about times when one felt a growing sense of self-identity; about awareness of death; and about the way childhood looks from the vantage point of adulthood.

Responses to these questions and Robinson's own reflections constitute his 1977 work, *The Original Vision: A Study of the Religious Experience of Childhood.*[25] It is a work that shows Robinson as a kindred spirit of Bushnell, as Robinson's thesis reveals: "I believe that what I have called the 'original vision' of childhood is no mere imaginative fantasy but a form of *knowledge* and one that is essential to the development of any mature understanding.[26]

Robinson sets his work over Piaget's, who Robinson suggests had an impoverished view of childhood, since his starting point was the incapacity of children to see the world as adults see it, thereby regarding children as "inefficient adults." Rather, Robinson argues on the basis of his research that the child's experience has its own validity. Many childhood experiences, he claims, are self-authenticating, having in themselves an absolute authority needing neither confirmation nor sanctions from other sources. Moreover, these experiences contribute to the person's sense of self and must be considered to be essentially religious. Perhaps Robinson's most significant comment is that no understanding or definition of the term "religious" is possible "without a sympathetic insight into all that is here included in the concept of childhood."[27]

A focus on one aspect of Robinson's research may best illuminate his project. In response to his query about the influence of church worship and organized religion, 31 percent of the respondents answered that they had been influenced "quite positively"; 25 percent, "if anything, positively"; 30 percent, "not at all, or a little each way"; 9 percent, "if anything, negatively"; and 5 percent, "quite negatively." The statistics take on more meaning when amplified by the responses themselves, which indicate, says Robinson, that children respond to religion as they do to poetry. For example, one respondent wrote, "The great festivals of the church quickened a sense of nostalgia in me, almost as if I had once known something which I had now lost." Another wrote: "I remember some sense of something I could not identify. . . . I can clearly remember even now it was nothing to do with liturgy, or atmosphere, or religiosity, but it was awesome." Robinson comments: "Looking back on childhood people often find it hard to put their finger on any particular incidents or special moments when a corner was consciously turned; they can still be aware that a great deal was going on.[28] Robinson continues:

I have so far quoted little from those who reacted negatively to organized religion in all its forms. They were a minority, though a substantial one (over a quarter of the younger correspondents). But many are quite outspoken, and their rejection is often total. Religion may be accepted when it offers a language, a means of interpretation, for an awareness of something already sensed, however dimly, to be real; but when it is seen merely to be presenting ready-made solutions—no. "There seemed nothing in the church that bore any correspondence with my own experience." That alone, it is implied, is real; that alone is authentic.

I have more than once let fall a reference to the idea of authenticity. . . . Here the reality of which we are assured is not that of the experience itself, nor does it belong wholly to some transcendent order which somehow ratifies the validity of the experience. What is authenticated is the selfhood of the person to whom the experience comes: a rather different matter, it might seem. Yet when we ask what exactly it is that confers this secret and unquestionable sanction, its source is often no less mysterious and elusive than before. Religion may support this emergent self-awareness: it cannot dictate to it. No Church God can ultimately be acknowledged unless He is acceptable to this inner authority.[29]

One of Robinson's more interesting comments concerns the nature of religious experience. He does not assign it an *a priori* definition, but rather tries to see what it has meant in a person's life. Whatever else it may mean, Robinson suggests, one element constitutes religious experience: that it lead to growth. "It is not enough for the experience to occur; one must say 'yes' to it." He expands:

"Religious experience," writes one correspondent, "is any experience that causes me to feel that there is a 'something-more-than' situation." Stripped of its mystique, the transcendent is no more than the sense of this "something more." Meaning, after all, is to be found not in the meaningful object or situation itself but always beyond it. . . . Many people to-day find themselves more deeply moved, in a way they will describe as in some sense religious, by Van Gogh's old boots than by the sublime vision of Michelangelo. And this significance of the insignificant is a theme central to the biblical, the Christian tradition. The still small voice, the grain of mustard seed, the one coin lost, the single sparrow dead—these are the stuff of which religious experience is made.[30]

Robinson's research has been taken up in particular by Maria Harris, whose work on education and art reflects a profound sense of the power of the image, story, and symbol in shaping one's religious experience— a theme that will be detailed in the next chapter.

Otherwise, Robinson's findings appear as yet to have made little impact in the United States. Nonetheless, Bushnell's convictions about the significance of childhood religious experience appear to have found an important new articulation.

RELIGIOUS EDUCATION AND PAULO FREIRE

Though the Brazilian-born Paulo Freire (b. 1921) does not work explicitly within the field of religious education, his theories have proved enormously influential for a number of contemporary religious educators—most notably, William Bean Kennedy, Malcolm Warford, Letty Russell, and Thomas Groome—and thus are pertinent. Moreover, Freire represents a point of view essentially harmonious with George Albert Coe insofar as both understand education as a means for the transformation of society.

This is not to imply that Freire has been influenced by the Dewey-Coe tradition. Freire has formulated his theory on quite different sources and circumstances. Nor is it to claim that Freire would feel comfortable with Coe's naive assertions about the "democracy of God" taking root in U.S. life or with the latter's liberal optimism. To the contrary, Freire, particularly as a citizen of the Third World, would be very critical of this dimension of Coe's thought. But what the two share is quite striking: a deep conviction that education is inherently political and never neutral. Education either domesticates or it frees people. Freire and Coe hold in common the conviction that a liberating education has a reconstructive character: it involves a commitment to overcome the forces of oppression and thereby to reconstruct society. Furthermore, both regard education as a religious activity without locating "religious" education exclusively within the church.

Freire's point of departure is the person's vocation to be fully human and the concomitant realization that numerous forces exist to deny one's humanity—thus his commitment to overcome these oppressive forces by helping people to come to a critical awareness of their causes and, in turn, to struggle to transform the situation. He sees as the central problem how one helps the oppressed to participate in developing the pedagogy of their liberation so that they can live in the fullness of humanity.

His method for doing this is often simply referred to as a "pedagogy for the oppressed." Freire's pedagogy begins with a critique of "banking education." His metaphor has by now become quite well known and bears a resemblance to Coe's notion of "transmissive" (as opposed to creative) education. "Banking education" means projecting absolute ignorance onto others so that the teacher is the expert and the student a passive receptacle. Thus the teacher dominates the educational process, controlling all the talk, making all the decisions, and confusing the authority of knowledge with his or her professional authority. As a consequence, Freire maintains, the more the students strive to store the "deposits" given to them, "the less they develop the critical consciousness which would result from their intervention in the world as transformers of that world." In other words, "the more completely they accept the passive role imposed on them, the more they tend simply to adapt to the world as it is and to the fragmented view of reality deposited in them."[31]

In contrast, Freire proposes "problem-posing" education, so that a "critical consciousness" can emerge and oppressive situations can be transformed. "Problematizing" entails questioning what has been taken for granted or presented as "the way things are" rather than as one perspective on the world. It rests on the recognition that reality is indeed socially constructed—as Peter Berger and Thomas Luckmann have argued[32]—and that the way things have traditionally been named is not the only possibility. Problematizing, furthermore, rests on the acknowledgment that the teacher does not possess all the answers. Because of this, genuine educational situations must be characterized by dialogue, an attitude that is incompatible with self-sufficiency: "At the point of encounter there are neither utter ignoramuses nor perfect sages; there are only men [women] who are attempting, together, to learn more than they now know."[33]

Freire's early work with problem-posing education was directed primarily to literacy programs. His method of helping peasants to read by means of investigating their situations, generating key themes (often using slides, photographs, and tape discussions) and codifying those themes into significant vocabulary words ("generative words," e.g., "shanty," "plow," "slum," "work") contrasts sharply with literacy programs built upon simplistic, meaningless sentences and vocabulary. For the rural poor of Brazil, Freire's literacy programs were enormously effective; in a ten-month period in the mid-1960s, for instance, his teams taught thousands of peasants to read, often in as little as a month and a half. But not only did they learn to read words. They learned to read their own life situations with a more critical eye. This led to Freire's arrest and imprisonment in 1964 and to exile in Chile; after five years working with Eduardo Frei's Christian Democratic government in Chile, he taught at Harvard and became a special adviser in education to the World Council of Churches in Geneva—a position that facilitated his influence on religious educators.

Freire's influence on the field can perhaps be summarized by two words integral to his work: "conscientization" *(conscientização)* and "praxis." The first denotes the process of coming to critical awareness of the social, political, and economic contradictions of "reality." The second refers to his commitment—not unlike John Dewey's—to keep theory and practice in a dialectic so that one acts reflectively and thinks for action. To be critical is to live in the "plenitude of the praxis," that is, to let one's action encompass a critical reflection that increasingly organizes one's thinking, thereby leading one to a move from purely naive knowledge of reality to a level enabling one to see the "causes of reality."[34] Both the process of conscientization and the concept of praxis have become vital terms in contemporary religious education, as I will show in chapter 7.

Now, however, it is important to recognize the pathway of thought that moves from Coe to Freire. The two come from dramatically different worlds, but their common commitment to fashion an educational process for transformation of society rather than merely for the conversion of the individual has given rise to significant developments in religious education. Surely Coe would have applauded Freire's conviction that "salvation can be achieved only *with* others,"[35] and Freire's work is at one with Coe's belief that religious education ought to be directed toward creating a new world.[36]

RELIGIOUS EDUCATION AND GABRIEL MORAN

Gabriel Moran's prolific writings defy easy categorization. By including his work among the pathways of *religious education* on the contemporary scene, I do not claim to do justice to the full scope of Moran's writings. The sheer range of his thought offers a wide spectrum of creative ideas. But here one significant aspect of Moran's work emerges for analysis, namely, his challenge to conceptualize religious education in a way that is larger than what church people do to hand on their faith to a younger generation. In Moran's conviction that theological language ought not to dominate religious education and in his conviction that religious education itself is communal and directed toward the world, one sees once again a manifestation of Coe's thought. Again, this is not to imply a line of direct influence, but rather to demonstrate a kinship flowing from some shared assumptions.

Moran, as did Coe, has little use for what the latter called "transmissive education" and what he speaks of as "officials of a church indoctrinating children to obey an official church." Moran prefers to underscore the communal character, defining religious education as the "whole religious community educat[ing] the whole religious community to make free and intelligent religious decisions vis-à-vis the whole world."[37] Like Coe's successor, Harrison S. Elliott, Moran has little confidence in "Christian education," which he considers to have been "largely an escape out of the educational mainstream":

Neo-orthodox theology insisted that Christianity is based upon a "revealed word": a pure message which can be distinguished from human experience and religion. The educational application of that theology is "Christian education," whose main task is "proclaiming a message of salvation." All the educational techniques and educational psychology that are put in the service of that message do not make the undertaking an educational one.[38]

Similarly, Moran accuses the catechetical movement in Catholicism of sharing in that same movement away from the risks of education. Thus Moran has long championed the term "religious education" as the most appropriate term for the field. In fact, Moran would keep the term "education" (which, Dewey-like, he conceives of as the "systematic planning of experience for growth in human understanding") in tension with "religion."[39] One must not only speak an ecclesiastical language—one characterized by theololgical terminology and spoken largely among those of one's particular denomination—but also an educational language, so as to extend religious education beyond the parochial and ecclesiastical.

Thus, like Coe but not precisely for the same reasons, Moran believes that theology makes but a "modest contribution" to the process of thinking more systematically and insightfully about religion and the religious. Religious education entails thinking through the meaning of one's own life as religious, and it must be done in relation both to those who share that life and to those who do not.

Consequently, the language of religious education must necessarily be sensitive to two factors: the inherent tension between the inner language of one's own religious group and the inner language of other religious groups; and the tension between the inner language of religious groups and language that lies beyond devotion to any religious group, that is, the public character of the field. For instance, it is insufficient to approach terms such as "faith" and "revelation" only in a theological manner. Moran maintains that though theology may indeed contribute to the context of religious education (but not to its method, structure, and institutional forms), it has some serious limitations with regard to contributing to a systematic and comprehensive study of the religious. First, it is too closely associated with the inner language of the Christian churches. Second, despite the wide variations within Christian theological methods, theology is still only one model for speaking about the religious dimension of life.[40]

Other aspects of Moran's thought will be taken up in the later chapters. But at least let it be recognized here that Moran's predilection for the term *religious education*—a manifestation of his high regard for the role of education and the limitations of theology—places him squarely in the Coe-Elliott trajectory.

CHRISTIAN EDUCATION

Perhaps the chief characteristic of *Christian education* as a classic expression was the significant role assigned to theology, particularly biblical theology. As the Biblical Theology Movement declined in the wake of developments in historical criticism and "postcritical" biblical study, the neo-orthodox categories that had dominated became less influential. Thus, for instance, Randolph Crump Miller sought to bring the categories of process theology to bear on religious education[41] and has modified his earlier claim about theology being the "clue" to religious education. Theology and educational theory must have equal voice, says Miller now—a significant shift from a position he had espoused consistently since 1952.[42] C. Ellis Nelson, drawing upon different perspectives from the various New Testament communities in *Where Faith Begins*, showed that the congregation's life itself constitutes a curriculum and so integrated cultural anthropology and sociology to develop his thesis that the meaning of faith is developed by the congregation's members out of their history and mutual interactions in relation to events taking place in their lives.[43] In short, the dialectical theology that had characterized the classic form of *Christian education* has been replaced by other theological perspectives, with greater appropriation of the social sciences. Yet that appropriation is done with careful attentiveness to biblical studies, as Nelson's *Where Faith Begins* and Letty Russell's *Growth in Partnership* exemplify.[44] The trend toward use of the social sciences is critically assessed from the theological point of view in works such as Craig Dykstra's critique of Lawrence Kohlberg's theory of moral development[45] and in Sara Little's work on teaching.[46] Thus, even in its contemporary pathways, *Christian education* retains the prominence given to biblical and theological categories.

In general, *Christian education* has become the term most frequently utilized to describe the process of educating in faith. This broadened usage reflects a variety of theological and educational views not necessarily indebted to the Barthians. Its widened theological base and openness to the social sciences suggest its adaptability, but they also help to account for a certain lack of clarity and unity about its nature and purpose.

In one sense, therefore, the term "Christian education" no longer means what it once did—assigning priority to theology in the church's curriculum. Its wide embrace of variant perspectives complicates mapping its contemporary modifications. Many theorists today, Catholics as well as Protestants, situate their work under the rubric of *Christian education* but do not assume the same neo-orthodox critique. Hence, the relative brevity of this section, which will trace only the key elements of continuity and discontinuity of the classic expression *Christian education*.

CONTEMPORARY CHRISTIAN EDUCATION:
ELEMENTS OF CONTINUITY WITH ITS CLASSIC FORM

One of the constants of *Christian education* is its attentiveness to revelation, and especially to Scripture. This is immediately apparent, for instance, in C. Ellis Nelson's *Where Faith Begins,* a study of the formative power of the congregation's life of faith. Nelson stresses that revelation, by disclosing the real meaning of tradition, enables a person to transcend the self and to stand outside the culture. Revelation, he reminds his readers, is not a discovery, but comes from outside oneself—a critique of the schema of progressive revelation so characteristic of the liberals.[47] Scripture plays a central role, since Nelson illustrates his theses about the function of faith in a congregation's life by demonstrating how faith functioned in the various communities among whom the biblical writings originated. Though Nelson draws far more extensively upon historical-critical biblical study than did his predecessors in *Christian education,* Nelson is no less indebted to the Bible than they were. Similarly, Letty Russell's key metaphor for educating in faith, partnership, is grounded in modern biblical studies. So is Thomas H. Groome's proposal that the ultimate purpose of Christian education is the Kingdom of God in Jesus Christ.[48]

Another central factor continuous with the classic expression *Christian education* is the importance assigned to the church. Not only does Nelson make understanding the process by which faith develops in the community of believers a prerequisite to the educational process, but John H. Westerhoff sets the church's way of passing on faith over the "schooling-instructional paradigm." Westerhoff questions reliance upon philosophy, social science, and general education rather than upon theology.[49] Though he contends that he is proposing a new paradigm in championing an emphasis on the community of faith rather than on schooling, Westerhoff's thesis stands squarely in the neo-orthodox tradition insofar as it questions the undue influence of disciplines other than the theological.[50]

More recently, Craig Dykstra has taken up the emphasis on the church, developing five theses especially harmonious with Nelson's earlier work.[51] The question at the center of Dykstra's inquiry—in what way is Christian education given a distinctive shape by being in and of the church?—is addressed in his definition of the field:

Christian education is that particular work which the church does to teach the historical, communal, difficult, counter-cultural practices of the church so that the church may learn to participate in them ever more fully and deeply. It is the dialogical process of teaching and learning (involving inquiry, interpretation, reflection, and care) through which the community comes to see, grasp, and participate ever more deeply in the redemptive transformation of personal and social life that God is carrying out.[52]

Dykstra notes that the practice of Christian education does not alone make the church, but he argues that it does facilitate people's recognition of what the church is, so that they might grasp something of its dynamics and nature and thereby participate more intensely in its life. Moreover, Christian education is not merely for the sake of increasing ecclesial membership but is a means by which the church participates in God's redemptive activity.

The emphasis devoted to revelation, Scripture, and church indicates elements of continuity with *Christian education* in its classic manifestation. Certainly, the work of the theorists cited above cannot only be categorized under this rubric alone, since there are other dimensions to their proposals not so readily linked to the neo-orthodox elements. Nonetheless, contemporary theorists in the field of Christian education have drawn deeply upon their predecessors.

CONTEMPORARY CHRISTIAN EDUCATION IN
DISCONTINUITY WITH THE CLASSIC FORM

Perhaps the element least harmonious with earlier theorists is the significance assigned to *process* rather than to *proclamation*. Many who write on Christian education today are far less inclined to stress the authoritative character of the revealed Word; rather, their interest lies in the revelatory process, in the dynamic by which faith takes root and develops.

This is evident especially among those who place importance upon curriculum and teaching, most notably D. Campbell Wyckoff, Sara Little, Mary Elizabeth Moore, and Charles R. Foster. Wyckoff and Little span, in a very real sense, the transition from *Christian education* in its classic form to the contemporary form presently under discussion. One might say that they are among the major catalysts in this reshaping: throughout their careers they have manifested a keen interest in process.

As Little writes in her most recent book, teaching is an intentional activity the church can use to help persons find meaning in a chaotic world; teaching is a response to "faith asking the intellect for help."[53] Unlike those who criticize reliance upon educational studies, Little appropriates them in her argument that intentional teaching is essential to the formation of beliefs:

Beliefs which engage the thinking powers of the person as they emerge out of and inform faith, sustained, reformed, and embodied by the faith community, can be an important factor in bringing integration and integrity to life. Teaching that contributes to the formation of this kind of belief necessitates the selective use of a variety of models with clear purposes, and presupposes the existence of a context that supports and interacts with intentional teaching.[54]

Accordingly, Little draws upon educational literature to design teaching strategies to enhance believing. She chooses models that stimulate thinking, encourage interaction, facilitate indirect communication, foster personal awareness, and hold together action and reflection.

Though less specific than Little, both Moore and Foster develop harmonious theses, assigning the educational process a place of honor. Since their work will be drawn upon in later chapters, I simply make note here of the appropriateness of including them among Christian educators who highlight the pedagogical process.

Christian education encompasses a spectrum of interests, emphases, and themes. It, therefore, resists easy analysis.

CATHOLIC EDUCATION–CATECHETICS

In many respects *Catholic education* has become virtually synonymous, particularly in common parlance, with Catholic schools. As a consequence, discussion of its philosophical-theological grounding tends to be interwoven with justification of the schools. Nevertheless, it is possible to sort out some significant strands of thought characteristic of a contemporary understanding of Catholic education inclusive of the schools but not restricted to them. Flowing from this is an articulation of *catechetics (catechesis)* as a way of socializing neophytes into the life of the community of faith. Accordingly, one must turn first to the self-understanding of Catholic educators and then to those theorists whose catechetical theory rests (at least implicitly) on that viewpoint.

A POST–VATICAN II PHILOSOPHY OF CATHOLIC EDUCATION: A NEW ERA

In the years since the Second Vatican Council, Catholics—at least in the United States—have witnessed a number of significant changes on the educational scene. Their schools, constituting the largest private system in the world, have undergone and successfully withstood, many would argue, a crisis of identity, including a reduction in both the number of schools and enrollments and development of a new sense of mission.[55] The traditional emphasis on the religious education of children through the agency of the parochial school and the Confraternity of Christian Doctrine has been expanded to include adults, thus creating a fresh configuration of educative agencies and giving renewed significance to the life of the parish. Furthermore, the 1972 restoration of the catechumenate, a result of conciliar discussion,[56] in the *Rite of Christian Initiation of Adults* (RCIA) has not simply fostered intense discussion about the pros and cons of infant baptism but also engendered much exploration about the communal character of Catholicism. It is this latter scrutiny that has led to enthusiastic claims about the RCIA as the "most important advance in postconciliar liturgical reform in Roman Catholicism . . . [that] will have the greatest impact upon how we Catholics understand ourselves as Church."[57] More recently, Catholics in North America have begun to investigate the potential of the so-called base communities of many Third World nations for educational revitalization. This investigation harmonizes to a considerable extent with intense interest in smaller, more personal communal groupings as the primary experience of ecclesial life and, accordingly, as the matrix for the education of its members.

A POST–VATICAN II PHILOSOPHY OF CATHOLIC EDUCATION: A HYPOTHESIS

Is there an all-embracing Catholic educational philosophy undergirding these postconciliar developments? What expresses the convictions at the root of the identity of the Catholic school, the attention to the education and formation (especially in the catechumenate) of adults and the interest in base communities?

In the absence of a single, definitive statement embracing these interrelated dimensions of Catholic education, a hypothesis might appropriately be offered. The educational philosophy of post–Vatican II Roman Catholicism derives, first, from the characteristics of Catholicism itself; second, from the statements and publications of various official and quasi-official bodies (e.g., national episcopal conferences, groups such as the National Catholic Educational Association); and, third, from the corporate life of various forms of Catholic communal life (e.g., schools as "faith communities," diocesan agencies, justice centers, and other alternative educational institutions), especially as these communities struggle to formulate and embody ideals in "mission statements." Together they form a certain consistent pattern that deserves more detailed analysis.

CHARACTERISTICS OF CATHOLICISM:
THE CENTRIPETAL FORCE OF ITS EDUCATIONAL PHILOSOPHY

The basic weave is established by the nature of Catholicism, sketched by Protestant theologian Langdon Gilkey and expanded in turn by Richard P. McBrien. Gilkey identifies five uniquely Catholic characteristics. First, a sense of *peoplehood* pervades Catholicism; it encompasses many races and cultures and fosters community rather than individualism. Second, it honors *tradition:* there is a continuity in the formation of its people and an importance given to past experience. Third, what Gilkey terms *caritas* is in the marrow of Catholicism. This may well be its most intangible characteristic; by it Gilkey means a sense of humanity and grace in its corporate life that overflows into a love of life, a celebration of the body, and a certain tolerance for human sinfulness. Fourth, Gilkey recognizes *sacramentality* as special to Catholicism, that is, a conviction about the presence of God and of grace mediated through symbols in the ordinary, workaday world. Finally, he observes the importance of *rationality:* "the insistence that the divine mystery manifest in tradition and sacramental presence be insofar as is possible penetrated, defended, and explicated by the most acute rational reflection."[58] McBrien, building upon Gilkey's five characteristics, identifies both a philosophical focus, *Christian realism* (the world is mediated by meaning), and three theological foci: the principles of *sacramentality* (God is present and operative in and through the visible, concrete, created order); *mediation* (God uses signs and instruments to communicate grace); and *communion* (our way to God and God's to us is mediated through community).[59]

Rosemary Haughton enfleshes the Gilkey-McBrien analysis in her study *The Catholic Thing,* in which she argues that the Catholic enterprise has been the attempt to "integrate the whole of human life in the search for the kingdom of God."[60] Her thesis might be regarded as a statement at the core of Catholic educational philosophy not unlike the following articulation by a more than a hundred participants in an NCEA-sponsored symposium in 1967:

Education is, in one sense, the central mission of the Church. Through education, broadly conceived, man [woman] becomes more truly human. This is also the work of the Church: to put man [woman] in touch with reality in its deepest dimensions. Even when education is understood in a narrower, more formal sense and apart from specifically religious formation, it concerns the Church because it affects man's [woman's] understanding of himself [herself] and of the meaning of life.[61]

DOCUMENTS FOR A CATHOLIC EDUCATIONAL PHILOSOPHY

Perhaps the most comprehensive declaration on Catholic education in the United States comes from an episcopal pastoral letter *To Teach as Jesus Did: A Pastoral Message on Catholic Education.*[62] In a spirit similar to the citations above, the bishops maintain that "education is one of the most important ways by which the Church fulfills its commitment to the dignity of the person and the building of community."[63] They further assert that the church's educational mission "is an integrated ministry embracing three interlocking dimensions: the message revealed by God *(didache)* which the Church proclaims; fellowship in the life of the Holy Spirit *(koinonia)*; [and] service to the Christian community and the entire human community *(diakonia)*."[64] This triad—message, community, service—remains central to continuing reflection about the meaning of Catholic education.[65]

To Teach as Jesus Did seems to have been an especially formative document. Its influence lies particularly in its vision of "total Catholic education," in its advocacy of adult education, and in its proposal that Catholic schools embody a "faith community." First, the letter addresses the range of educational agencies and instruments under church sponsorship: adult education, family-centered education, campus ministry, Catholic colleges and universities, Confraternity of Christian Doctrine (CCD) and other parish programs, and Catholic schools and youth ministry. This broad compass provides a sense of the scope of Catholic education within the context of the threefold rubric of message, community, and service. Thus, it effectively counters the equation of Catholic education with formal schooling and implicitly challenges each agency to define itself in relation to the whole configuration. Second, the pastoral voices a major shift in priorities in its argument that the "continuing education of adults is situated not at the periphery of the Church's educational mission but at its center."[66] Furthermore, the bishops reveal a new sense of the dialogical character of adult education: "Those who teach in the name of the Church do not simply instruct adults, but also learn from them; they will only be heard by adults if they listen to them."[67] Such a statement reveals a significant shift from the days when the laity operated out of the old formula of "pay, pray, and obey."

Third, the inclusion of the Catholic school within the document appears to have been an impetus to its proponents to think more comprehensively about its possibilities and place it within the whole context of Catholic education. This meant viewing the school as community in which religious truth and values might be integrated with life; it also provided a foundation for the development of "service projects," that is, the insertion into the curriculum of projects by which the students could serve others in direct, tangible ways, since "the first goal of Catholic education [is] to link love of God with love of neighbor."[68]

THE COMMUNITY'S SEARCH FOR MEANING:
EXEMPLARS OF CATHOLIC EDUCATIONAL PHILOSOPHY

Much of the discussion of the issues raised by the 1972 letter has continued in the pages of *Momentum*, the NCEA's quarterly journal founded in 1970. Here, for instance, one finds an attempt to articulate a contemporary notion of "permeation":

When the people of a school share a certain intentionality, a certain pattern or complex of values, understandings, sentiments, hopes and dreams, that deeply conditions everything else that goes on, including the math class, the athletic activities, the dances, coffee breaks in the teachers' lounge, everything.[69]

"Permeation," as Michael O'Neill suggests, reflects the reality at the heart of Catholic education as a classic expression: one's "religious" education is not merely gained in religion class, but in the intentionality shaping the whole educational experience. Religion can and ought to be studied in a classroom setting, but, more than that, the "religious life"—ultimate questions about life, love, death, suffering, sex, intimacy, God[70]—*suffuses* the curriculum (and not merely the explicit curriculum). When this happens, the process should form "truly liberating communities in which to educate our young."[71]

THE CATHOLIC SCHOOL AS A COUNTERCULTURAL INSTITUTION

Such language reveals the present focus on shaping the Catholic school as a countercultural institution. Primarily, this has meant an intensified effort to give priority in the schools to justice and peace education, an emphasis that enlarges the concept of the school as a "faith community" insofar as it extends the community's awareness of the systemic implications of linking love of God with love of neighbor. As a consequence, Catholic schools seem to be undergoing a change in identity from the period earlier in the century when only their religion classes (and budgets) differentiated them from the public schools. Now, for instance, many school leaders, cognizant of the significance of the statement from the Synod of Bishops in 1971 that "action on behalf of justice and participation in the transformation of the world fully appear to us as a constitutive dimension of the preaching of the Gospel. . .,"[72] have turned their attention to ways of explicitly incorporating the knowledge and values prerequisite for the formation of a more just social order. For example, the NCEA sponsors workshops and offers materials for faculty on the "infusion method," a way of integrating fundamental concepts about justice and peace into the whole curriculum rather than separating them into a particular unit or course.[73] Moreover, it publishes and distributes curricular resources such as the two-volume *Seeking a Just Society,* an educational design with materials for school boards, faculty, parents, and religion coordinators, as well as for homilists.[74]

This emerging sense of the Catholic school as a countercultural community of faith has necessitated both increased professionalism in the teaching of religion and also sustained attention to the "formation" of faculty and staff members. While the former has meant more adequate theological preparation, the latter emphasizes the religious and spiritual dimensions of the teacher's life so that he or she can contribute to the development of the community of faith in the school:

While it [teacher formation] includes professional education as necessary to the total preparation process, it is a broader concept which endeavors to foster knowledge and understanding of such areas as basic teachings of Catholic education, revelation, scripture, traditions and documents of the Church. It further considers a knowledge of principles of spiritual growth and development and how these relate to Christian value education. *But more important, the Christian formation of teachers is a process enabling educators to be persons with Christian attitudes and qualities so that they can become witnesses of the Gospel, witnesses of the Church, proclaimers of the message and sharers in the fellowship of the Spirit in order to "give witness to Christ, the unique Teacher, by their lives as well as by their teaching"* [emphasis added].[75]

Similarly, a monograph commissioned by the Chief Administrators of Catholic Schools (CACE) concludes that teachers should themselves be evangelized, i.e., converted to discipleship as a follower of Christ; catechized, i.e., willing to probe the meaning and relevance of the Christian life; bonded to the church, i.e., have a strong sense of Catholic identity; involved in sacraments and prayer; touched by social awareness; and in search of ways to integrate the behavioral sciences with the religious dimension of life so that they move toward full human development.[76] Interestingly, "teacher formation" has become one of the prime means of educating adults in the church and thus a way of joining the school's function with the concerns about adult education first articulated in *To Teach as Jesus Did*.

THE LANGUAGE OF MINISTRY AND CATECHETICS

The emphasis on teacher formation has tended to utilize the language of ministry; the teacher, for instance, becomes the "Catholic educational minister." Several consequences, both positive and negative, seem to flow from this shift from educational to ministerial language. First, the priority assigned to the teacher's religious and spiritual formation suggests a correlative priority on the school as an agency of moral formation. In the past, this has meant a devaluation of the intellectual life, but whether this need necessarily be the case today remains an open question. Certainly, it is possible to see tensions between the professional competency of teachers and their growth in faith and between their witnessing to the faith and teaching in a way that facilitates a *critical* (i.e., discerning) appropriation of faith. This raises the need to look anew at the ever-present temptation of indoctrination, an issue that will be taken up in later chapters. It further suggests the importance of a theology of revelation, particularly regarding how one understands the role of the church as an authoritative interpreter of revelation. Second, ministerial language signals a concern about "total education," in which the school holds a place in the total configuration of educational institutions in the church. To view teaching in a school as a ministry is to provide a way of incorporating it into the broad spectrum of ministerial activities; thereby, the school is less isolated. Put more positively, such language contributes to an inclusive view of Catholic education in which the school is one agency among others—albeit a vital one. It would seem also to foster a more cohesive sense of identity and express an awareness of the distinctive mission of a Catholic school. Less happily, ministerial language may encourage an ecclesiastical exclusivity and ultimately reflect a separation of the Catholic school from the public forum.

It is premature to make conclusions about the newfound emphasis on formation and ministry; at this juncture, one might simply point out the emergence of an increasingly evident pattern in Catholic educational philosophy. The classic synthesis of faith and culture is now seen as happening within a community oriented toward discipleship. Conversion, understood as a response to God's call and a lifelong deepening of one's commitment to the following of Christ, figures as the central element and means that persons will live in tension with many of society's values. The Catholic school, with its attention to permeation, infusion, and formation, exemplifies the changed meaning of conversion.

Linked with the language of ministry is the language of *catechetics (catechesis)*, which has taken on new importance in the post–Vatican II philosophy of Catholic education. Here the communal character of the philosophy is again evident, especially in the thesis of Berard L. Marthaler, that *catechesis* is fundamentally the experience of socialization (i.e., the interaction of an individual with a collective) into the faith of the community.[77] As Marthaler sees it, *catechesis* awakens, nourishes, and develops faith; raises one's consciousness by uncovering the mysteries dwelling beneath the surface of everyday life and by enabling one to read and interpret signs (biblical, liturgical, doctrinal, existential); and transmits the wisdom of tradition, especially the sacramental view of the universe. Accordingly, this way of educating in faith has three corresponding objectives: facilitating maturity of faith; giving one a sense of belonging; and impressing the community's meanings and values upon its members so that the symbol system resonates within each individual. In short, Marthaler argues that *catechetics* is at heart "community education," consisting of a "fragile network of interlocking and mutually supportive institutions and agencies, professional leaders and private citizens, formal and informal influences, through which a person comes to identify with the Church."[78] Its task is not simply to enable persons to internalize the symbol system, but also to provide them with a way of interpreting the meaning of human life and of patterning their actions.

Marthaler's argument takes on a particular cogency in light of the communal orientation of Catholic educational philosophy. What his theory lacks, however, is a more encompassing understanding of religious education in which members are not only socialized into the traditions of the community, but also become able to discern ways that traditions can become distorted or absolutized. To draw once again upon H. Richard Niebuhr's typology, *catechetics* as a theory of socialization tends to incorporate a less transformist notion of Christ and culture. *Catechetics* does not examine critically the accretions that have grown up around the faith community's existence. Modern catechetical theory, for example, certainly is rooted in ecclesial teaching on justice as "constitutive"of the preaching of the gospel, but it is less apt to direct one's attention to the unjust structures within the ecclesial community as well as outside of it.

Catechetical language, however, does highlight the affective dimension of knowing and the centrality of the community in forming people in faith. Like the more recent language of ministry, it is integral to the *Rite of Christian Initiation of Adults.*

THE RITE OF CHRISTIAN INITIATION OF ADULTS

In particular, three aspects of the RCIA stand out as especially harmonious with a Catholic educational philosophy: "sponsorship" as formative in coming to faith; knowledge as including the affections; and pedagogy as process-oriented.

The *Rite's* emphasis is clearly on the role of the community in leading people to faith; this suggests education as "sponsorship." Just as the schools have initiated processes by which they might develop as communities of faith, so, too, have parishes committed to the RCIA. In fact, much of the literature on this rite indicates that its proper implementation largely depends upon the quality of communal life in the parish.

Moreover, the RCIA is explicitly regarded as a formation process in which persons are led toward a conversion of life. Recall the comments cited earlier from Aidan Kavanagh on the catechumenate as "conversion therapy."[79] It places a primacy on the affectional character of knowledge not unlike Jonathan Edwards's view in which one has a change of heart, not of opinion. In a similar vein, proponents of the rite place an emphasis on the experiential quality of the teaching. They tend, in fact, to consider any educational language about instruction and curriculum as inappropriately didactic, a judgment resulting from a tendency to understand education reductionistically as well as an indication of the dichotomy that has developed between the specializations of liturgy and religious education. Yet, clearly, the RCIA is a way of educating the person in faith, not only neophytes but their sponsors as well, and it mirrors the major emphases emerging in Catholic schooling. While it is indeed a liturgical rite, it ought also to be regarded as an expression of Catholic educational philosophy; it is further testimony to the inextricable link in the Catholic tradition between liturgy and education.

THE "BASE COMMUNITY"

The primacy accorded the notion of "faith community" in postconciliar Catholic education takes on new meaning in the so-called basic or grass-roots communities. Often referred to as "CEBs" (an acronym formed from their Spanish title, *Communidades Ecclesiales de Base*), these are small groups of Christians, usually poor and almost always marginal to the power structure of society. These Christians form communities whose members together engage in reflection—often based on biblical stories—in order to act for justice. Originating in Brazil (where recent estimates suggest there may now be as many as 100,000 of these vibrant, small groups) in the late 1950s, faith communities exist throughout Latin America and Africa, and to a lesser extent in Holland, Italy, and North America.[80] The creation of a communal context for reflection is oriented toward the reordering of society; the base communities offer a way for those whose voice is seldom heard to join in solidarity so as to cry out against injustice. The knowledge these communities seek is one that gives rise to action. Hence, their focus is on *praxis*, that is, on the dialectical movement of action and reflection. As they retell the biblical stories, the stories of their own struggles are illuminated; for example, illiterate peasants hear resonances in Mary's Song (Luke 1:46–55) to which more prosperous Christians are deaf. The Magnificat becomes a way of the poor hearing that God fills the hungry with good things— thus engendering a hope that energizes them to participate in God's activity.[81]

Since the CEBs exist primarily as communities of the poor struggling for justice, they are, as Maurice Monette has pointed out, "educative" but not "educational," because their purpose is a changed society rather than the education of its members.[82] They represent a more radical community of faith; their members work directly to challenge and reform the social order to its roots. Hence, their pedagogy is "radical," often rooted in Freire's "pedagogy of the oppressed" in which illiterate people literally learn to "read" their lives with acuity:

This methodology avoids the fragmentation common in liberal education. It does not divorce one's reality from the study and preaching of the gospel, instruction concerning the social encyclicals, social analysis, and action on behalf of social justice. The point of departure is one's situation in the world, which in turn is subjected to social analysis and theological analysis.[83]

The basic Christian communities offer an alternative model of "faith community." They illustrate the way powerless people (often encouraged by those who have had more formal preparation in religious and theological education) have appropriated for themselves the reality at the heart of a Catholic education: through education, men and women become more human and the world more humane. Theirs is a brave manifestation of the "Catholic thing," as Haughton uses the phrase.

Though more radical in their political orientation, the CEBs also bring to consciousness the educative function of communal movements such as Marriage Encounter, cursillos (a three-day period of spiritual renewal), charismatic renewal groups, "consciousness raising" groups, and support groups for those who are divorced or bereaved. None of these is primarily educational, yet each in fact does lead its members to new levels of awareness through the experience of community. Though little analysis has been done to date, groups such as these offer to adults education that emphasizes the affective character of knowing. They often become an impetus toward deepened study and new ways of participating in the mission of the church.

PEACE AND JUSTICE CENTERS

One further agency deserves mention as an expression of contemporary Catholic educational philosophy: justice and peace offices that have sprung up throughout the country. Some are diocesan sponsored; others, such as the Center for Concern in Washington, DC, the Catholic Connection in Boston, and the Justice and Peace Center of Southern California, are supported by religious communities and contributions (time and money) from church members. These offices prepare curricular materials, engage in symbolic action, and offer workshops for those seeking to deepen their understanding of Christian responsibility in a broken world. One organization expresses its charter this way:

The Catholic Connection is a reflection/action center which exists to educate the Catholic community of Greater Boston particularly, and an increasing number of Catholics beyond this area, to the social teachings of the Church and to motivate its members to work for just public policies in the areas of Peace, Central America and Urban Housing and Homelessness. It emphasizes social justice (dealing with the causes of injustice), as distinguished from social action (dealing with the results of injustice).[84]

The Catholic Connection, for instance, sees its mission as involving the formation of communities of faith "from which people will act to educate others and to influence public policy for a more just and peaceful world."[85] Similarly, a national organization such as Network engages in lobbying, both in direct work with legislators and with their constituents, by informing them of the justice-related issues coming up in the House and Senate. All of these groups educate, though outside the boundaries of schools, with a clear emphasis on the justice dimension of Catholic education.

Though hardly in the mainstream, the existence of these groups is especially significant to postconciliar Catholic education. They represent, in Niebuhrian terms, a vision of faith transforming culture; their praxis orientation, like that of the CEBs, suggests that true knowledge is transformative. They place emphasis not only on theological understanding but also on the skills of social analysis. Staff members of peace and justice centers are often leaders in the production of curricular materials and generally are committed to dialogical and process-oriented pedagogies. Their marginality in terms of budget and diocesan *realpolitik* often indicates a certain tension with the institutional church, but it is clear that such centers operate within the boundaries of Catholic notions of education.

To the outsider, postconciliar Catholic educational philosophy may seem amazingly consistent in its emphasis on faith communities oriented toward the creation of more just societies. But the Catholic penchant for documentation may be misleading, insofar as it suggests more coherence than exists in reality. To the insider, aware of all the finitude, obstacles, and contradictions, the pattern of such a philosophy may be painfully incoherent in the struggles of daily work. But there is little question that institutions, widely varied in their educational tasks, take seriously the rhetoric, however sinfully short they may fall.

In this chapter, I have traced the pathways of the classic expressions in the last twenty years. I recognize that these pathways form their own patterns, sometimes overlapping each other for a time, sometimes intersecting another, but more often simply forging their own ways.

Within *evangelism* I have identified three points—roughly labeled "Right," "Left" and "center"—on a theological-educational spectrum:

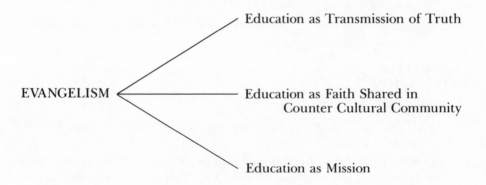

EVANGELISM

Education as Transmission of Truth

Education as Faith Shared in Counter Cultural Community

Education as Mission

In defining the contours of *religious education,* I have shown four distinct developments, each reflecting a component of the classic expression. Unitarian Universalism moves along the path of low Christology, stress on social ethics, and embrace of evolutionary theory. Edward Robinson's research on religious experience stands in the trajectory of Horace Bushnell's attention to the religious life of the child. The work of Paulo Freire provides a Third World perspective on George Albert Coe's conviction that education must transform the social order. Gabriel Moran is also "kin" to Coe in assigning theology a less prominent role in religious education theory.

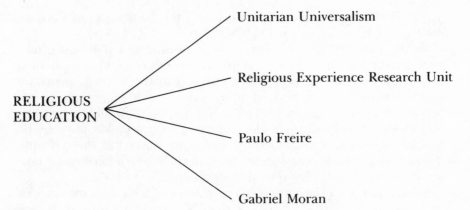

RELIGIOUS
EDUCATION

Unitarian Universalism

Religious Experience Research Unit

Paulo Freire

Gabriel Moran

The classic expression *Christian education* has developed so diversely that I could categorize its contemporary modifications only in terms of their continuity, especially in the prominence given to biblical studies, and discontinuity, the new emphasis assigned to educational process.

CHRISTIAN
EDUCATION

Contemporary Modifications in Continuity

Contemporary Modifications in Discontinuity

Finally, I identified four manifestations of Catholic educational philosophy in the post–Vatican II era. The Catholic school, the *Rite of Christian Initiation of Adults,* the base communities, and peace and justice centers constitute a contemporary network of interrelated institutions.

CATHOLIC
EDUCATION–
CATECHETICS

Catholic Schools as Counter Cultural

*Rite of Christian Initiation of
Adults* (RCIA)

Base Communities

Peace and Justice Centers

NOTES

1. As this is being written, the controversy over leadership of the P.T.L. Club is unresolved. To what extent Jim and Tammy Bakker's "fall from grace" will result in a diminished leadership role in evangelical circles is not clear.
2. Harvey Cox, *Religion in the Secular City: Toward a Postmodern Theology* (New York: Simon and Schuster, 1984), 43.
3. Jerry Falwell, *Listen, America!* (New York: Bantam, 1980), 54.
4. Cited in *Time* (8 June 1981):55.
5. Cox, *Religion in the Secular City*, 69–70.
6. Jerry Falwell, "Time for Revival," *Fundamentalist Journal* 2 (February 1983):8.
7. Jim Wallis, "A Hope for Revival," *Sojourners* 13 (March 1984):4–5.
8. Jim Wallis, "Crucible of Community," *Sojourners* 6 (January 1977):16.
9. Jim Wallis, *Agenda for a Biblical People* (New York: Harper & Row, 1976), 134.
10. Jim Wallis, cited in Robert K. Johnston, *Evangelicals at an Impasse: Biblical Authority in Practice* (Atlanta, GA: John Knox, 1979), 93.
11. Wallis, "A Hope for Revival," 5.
12. Statement of Faith of the National Association of Evangelicals, printed in the pamphlet *Leadership through Cooperation* (Wheaton, IL: National Association of Evangelicals, n.d.).
13. Lawrence O. Richards, *A Theology of Christian Education* (Grand Rapids, MI: Zondervan, 1975), 15.
14. Ibid., 317–20.
15. Lawrence O. Richards, "Experiencing Reality Together: Toward the Impossible Dream," in Norma Thompson, ed., *Religious Education and Theology* (Birmingham, AL: Religious Education Press, 1982), 215.
16. Ibid.
17. Elizabeth Baker judges Spoerl's work to be less theistic than Fahs's (*Retrospect*, Unitarian Universalist Advance Study Paper #14 [Boston, 1980], 21).
18. Summarized in full in Hugo J. Hollerorth, *Relating to Our World* (Boston: Unitarian Universalist Association, 1974), 14–35.
19. Ibid., 13.
20. Baker, *Retrospect*, 27–28.
21. I have culled this from two of Judith Hoehler's 1981 sermons, "The Unitarian Universalist Dilemma" and "To Be Specific," both of which are included in *Religious Education Futures Papers* (Boston: Unitarian Universalist Association, n.d.).
22. Hugo Hollerorth, ed., *Stone House Conversations* (Boston: Unitarian Universalist Association, 1979).
23. Ibid., 29; cf. 76 and the discussion on 78–83.
24. Ibid., 121–22; cf. the discussion on 124–30.
25. Edward Robinson, *The Original Vision: A Study of the Religious Experience of Childhood*, U.S. ed. (New York: Seabury, 1983). The questionnaire and statistical charts of the responses are found on pp. 159–71.
26. Ibid., 16.
27. Ibid.
28. Ibid., 94.
29. Ibid., 96.
30. Ibid., 147.
31. Paulo Freire, *Pedagogy of the Oppressed* (New York: Seabury, 1974), 60. Original Portuguese edition, 1968.
32. See Peter Berger and Thomas Luckmann, *The Social Construction of Reality: A Treatise in the Sociology of Knowledge* (Garden City, NY: Doubleday, 1966).
33. Freire, *Pedagogy of the Oppressed*, 79.
34. Ibid., 125–26.
35. Ibid., 142.
36. See George Albert Coe, *What Is Christian Education?* (New York: Scribner, 1929), 28.
37. Gabriel Moran, *Religious Body* (New York: Seabury, 1974), 150.

38. Ibid., 152–53.
39. Gabriel Moran, "Two Languages of Religious Education," *The Living Light* 14 (1977):10.
40. Gabriel Moran, "From Obstacle to Modest Contributor," in Thompson, ed., *Religious Education and Theology*, 42–70. Cf. his *Interplay: A Theory of Religion and Education* (Winona, MN: Saint Mary's Press, 1981), 9–78.
41. See Randolph Crump Miller, *The Theory of Christian Education Practice* (Birmingham, AL: Religious Education Press, 1980), 22–46.
42. Randolph Crump Miller, "Theology in the Background," in Thompson, ed., *Religious Education and Theology*, 31. Cf. his *Theory of Christian Education Practice*, 153–64.
43. C. Ellis Nelson, *Where Faith Begins* (Atlanta, GA: John Knox, 1967).
44. Letty Russell, *Growth in Partnership* (Philadelphia: Westminster, 1982).
45. Craig Dykstra, *Vision and Character: A Christian Educator's Alternative to Kohlberg* (New York: Paulist, 1981). Cf. Donald M. Joy, ed., *Moral Development Foundations: Judeo-Christian Alternatives to Piaget/Kohlberg* (Nashville, TN: Abingdon, 1983).
46. Sara Little, *To Set One's Heart: Belief and Teaching in the Church* (Atlanta, GA: John Knox, 1983).
47. Nelson, *Where Faith Begins*, 84–85.
48. See Russell, *Growth in Partnership;* Thomas H. Groome, *Christian Religious Education: Sharing Our Story and Vision* (San Francisco: Harper & Row, 1980), 49.
49. John H. Westerhoff, *Will Our Children Have Faith?* (New York: Seabury, 1976), 24.
50. Ibid., 30. Westerhoff sees liberation theology, on which he models his work, as a synthesis of liberal and neo-orthodox theology.
51. Dykstra notes the influence of his mentor D. Campbell Wyckoff in the latter's essay, "Understanding Your Church Curriculum," *The Princeton Theological Seminary Bulletin* 68(1970): 82–83.
52. Craig Dykstra, "Ecclesial Education" (paper presented to the Association of Professors and Researchers of Religious Education on the Eastern Seaboard, Princeton, NJ, 26 April 1985), 23.
53. Little, *To Set One's Heart*, 5–7.
54. Ibid., 9–10.
55. Catholic schools reached their all-time peak enrollment in 1965–1966 with some 5.6 million pupils enrolled in elementary and secondary schools. At that time they constituted 87 percent of the nonpublic school enrollment. Less than twenty years later, in 1981–1982, the Catholic school population was slightly over 3 million, 64 percent of nonpublic school enrollment. See Thomas C. Hunt and Norlene M. Kunkel, "Catholic Schools: The Nation's Largest Alternative School System," in James C. Carper and Thomas C. Hunt, eds., *Religious Schooling in America* (Birmingham, AL: Religious Education Press, 1984), 1–34.
56. See the following texts of Vatican II: *The Constitution on the Sacred Liturgy*, #64; *Decree on the Church's Missionary Activity*, #14; *Decree on the Bishops' Pastoral Office in the Church*, #14.
57. Edward K. Braxton, "Adult Initiation and Infant Baptism," in William J. Reedy, ed., *Becoming a Catholic Christian: A Symposium on Christian Initiation* (New York: Sadlier, 1979), 188.
58. Langdon Gilkey, *Catholicism Confronts Modernity: A Protestant View* (New York: Seabury, 1975), p. 22.
59. Richard P. McBrien, *Catholicism*, 2 vols. (Minneapolis, MN: Winston, 1980), 2:1183-84.
60. Rosemary Haughton, *The Catholic Thing* (Springfield, IL: Templegate, 1979).
61. "Statement of the Washington Symposium on Catholic Education," in Russell Shaw and Richard J. Hurley, eds., *Trends and Issues in Catholic Education* (New York: Citation Press, 1969), 308.
62. *To Teach as Jesus Did: A Pastoral Message on Catholic Education* (Washington, DC: United States Catholic Conference, 1973).
63. Ibid., #13.

64. Ibid., #14.
65. See, for instance, Hunt and Kunkel, "Catholic Schools," in Carper and Hunt, eds., *Religious Schooling in America*, 14–16.
66. *To Teach as Jesus Did*, #43.
67. Ibid., #44.
68. "Statement of the Washington Symposium," in Shaw and Hurley, eds., *Trends and Issues in Catholic Education*, 30.
69. Michael O'Neill, "Toward a Modern Concept of Permeation," *Momentum* 10 (May 1979): 49.
70. See Michael O'Neill, "A Second Spring for American Catholic Education," *Momentum* 12 (October 1980): 34.
71. Mary Peter Traviss, "The Catholic School as a Liberating Community," *Momentum* 11 (February 1980): 44.
72. "Justice in the World," in Joseph P. Gremillion, ed., *The Gospel of Peace and Justice: Catholic Social Teaching Since Pope John* (Maryknoll, NY: Orbis, 1976), 514.
73. See Loretta Carey, "Adapting the Infusion Method," *Momentum* 13 (October 1982): 40–42; Michael S. Griffin, "Tested Approaches for Implementing the Infusion Method in Justice and Peace," *Momentum* 15 (December 1984): 53–54.
74. Edward van Merrienboer with Veronica Grover and William Cunningham, *Seeking a Just Society: An Educational Design* (Washington, DC: National Catholic Educational Association, 1978). One volume deals with materials by levels, the other by topics. See especially pp. 31–36 in both volumes, where the authors detail their assumptions.
75. Russell Bleich et al., *The Pre-Service Formation of Teachers for Catholic Schools: In Search of Patterns for the Future* (Washington, DC: National Catholic Educational Association, 1982), vii.
76. Alfred A. McBride, *The Christian Formation of Catholic Educators* (Washington, DC: National Catholic Educational Association, 1981).
77. Berard L. Marthaler, "Socialization as a Model for Catechetics," in Padraic O'Hare, ed., *Foundations for Religious Education* (New York: Paulist, 1978), 64–92.
78. Ibid., 80.
79. See chapter 5, subsection "Catechetics: A Summary."
80. Caution is needed about the precision of the numbers. Peruvian theologian Gustavo Gutiérrez remarked that "when my people say 100,000, they mean *many, many* communities" (public lecture, Boston College, 17 October 1986).
81. See Ernesto Cardenal, *The Gospel in Solentiname*, 4 vols. (Maryknoll, NY: Orbis, 1976–1982).
82. Maurice Monette, "Justice, Peace and the Pedagogy of Grass Roots Christian Communities," in Padraic O'Hare, ed., *Education for Peace and Justice* (San Francisco: Harper & Row, 1983), 87.
83. Ibid., 90.
84. Taken from a 1983 Grant Proposal, appearing in a document for the Catholic Connection Reflection/Planning Days (30 June–1 July 1984).
85. Taken from the *Original Document of the Catholic Connection* (1980). Both this reference and the preceding have been provided by Margherita Cappelli, formerly of the Catholic Connection staff.

Bibliographic Essay

Contemporary Modifications of the Classic Expressions

Some of the literature essential for explicating *evangelism* as a classic expression was also useful here, especially George M. Marsden, *Fundamentalism and American Culture: The Shaping of Twentieth Century Evangelicalism: 1870–1925* (New York: Oxford University Press, 1980) and William McLoughlin, *Revivals, Awakenings and Reform* (Chicago: University of Chicago Press, 1978). Two massive works on evangelical theology have provided useful background: Carl F. H. Henry, *God, Revelation and Authority: God Who Speaks and Shows*, 4 vols. (Waco, TX.: Word, 1976–1979) and Donald G. Bloesch, *Essentials of Evangelical Theology*, 2 vols. (San Francisco: Harper & Row, 1978–1979). Also providing helpful information were Donald Dayton, *Discovering an Evangelical Heritage* (New York: Harper & Row, 1976); Robert K. Johnston, *Evangelicals at an Impasse* (Atlanta, GA: John Knox, 1979); Richard Quebedeaux, *The Young Evangelicals* (New York: Harper & Row, 1974) and *The Worldly Evangelicals* (New York: Harper & Row, 1978); Jack B. Rogers, *Confessions of a Conservative Evangelical* (Philadelphia: Westminster, 1974); and Jim Wallis, *Agenda for a Biblical People* (New York: Harper & Row, 1976). Two insightful biographies are Marshall Frady, *Billy Graham: A Parable of American Righteousness* (Boston: Little, Brown, 1979) and David E. Harrell, *Oral Roberts: An American Life* (Bloomington, IN: Indiana University Press, 1985).

Sociologist James Davison Hunter provides an astute analysis of the evangelical world, particularly of its institutions of higher education, in *Evangelicalism: The Coming Generation* (Chicago: University of Chicago Press, 1987). Frances Fitzgerald, *Cities on a Hill: A Journey Through Contemporary American Culture* (New York: Simon and Schuster, 1986) offers a fascinating analysis of Jerry Falwell's Liberty Baptist Church. Harvey Cox's *Religion in the Secular City: Toward a Postmodern Theology* (New York: Simon and Schuster, 1974) also gives astute commentary on evangelical fundamentalism. Daniel C. Maguire's *The New Subversives: Anti-Americanism of the Religious Right* (New York: Continuum, 1982) excoriates the evangelical Right as "a distinct threat to the American way" (p. 1). Their use of media is studied in two works: Ben Armstrong, *The Electric Church* (New York: Nelson, 1979) and Jeffrey K. Hadden and Charles E. Swann, *Prime Time Preachers: The Rising Power of Televangelism* (Reading, MA: Addison-Wesley, 1981). Journalist Dick Dabney has written on Pat Robertson in "God's Own Network," *Harper's* 261 (August 1980):33–52. Their work is placed in perspective by Robert Wood Lynn's historical study, "The Unnoticed Revolution: Mainline Protestantism and the Media Society" (unpublished manuscript, 1975), which shows the long-standing involvement of evangelicals in journalistic enterprises.

The story of the Sojourners community is available primarily through the issues of their journal, *Sojourners* (formerly the Post-American). Jim Wallis has contributed his autobiography to the Abingdon series (*Revive Us Again: A Sojourner's Story* [Nashville, TN: Abingdon, 1983]).

Key recent works on religious education from evangelical circles include Lawrence O. Richards, *A Theology of Christian Education* (Grand Rapids, MI: Zondervan, 1975) and G. Temp Sparkman, *The Salvation and Nurture of the Child of God: The Story of Emma* (Valley Forge, PA: Judson, 1983); Jim Wilhoit, *Christian Education and the Search for Meaning* (Grand Rapids, MI: Baker, 1986); and Timothy Arthur Lines, *Systemic Religious Education* (Birmingham, AL: Religious Education Press, 1987); and Robert W. Pazmiño, *Foundational Issues in Christian Education: An Evangelical Perspective* (Grand Rapids, MI: Baker, 1988).

In addition to the works cited in the notes on Unitarian Universalist religious education, see Harold Rosen, *Religious Education and Our Ultimate Commitment: An Application of Henry Nelson Wieman's Philosophy of Creative Interchange* (Lanham, MD: University Press of America, and Boston: Unitarian Universalist Association, 1985). See also the work of Catholic educator Padraic O'Hare, "Religious Education as Inquiry: The Thought of Henry Nelson Wieman," *Religious Education* 70 (1975):317–22.

A considerable body of literature about Paulo Freire's work has developed over the past decade. One must begin, of course, with his own writing. In addition to *Pedagogy of the Oppressed* (New York: Seabury, 1974), see *Education for Critical Consciousness* (New York: Continuum, 1973 [original 1969]); *Cultural Action for Freedom* (Cambridge, MA: Harvard Educational Review and The Center for the Study of Development and Social Change, 1970); "Conscientization," *Cross Currents* 23 (1974):23–31; and *Pedagogy in Process* (New York: Seabury, 1978). For secondary literature, see Denis E. Collins, *Paulo Freire: His Life, Works and Thought* (New York: Paulist, 1977); Regina A. Coll, *Paulo Freire and the Transformation of Consciousness of Women in Religious Congregations* (Ann Arbor, MI: University Microfilms, 1982); John L. Elias, *Conscientization and Deschooling: Freire's and Illich's Proposals for Reshaping Society* (Philadelphia: Westminster, 1976); Henry A. Giroux, *Theory and Resistance in Education* (South Hadley, MA: Bergin and Garvey, 1983); and Daniel S. Schipani, *Conscientization and Creativity: Paulo Freire and Christian Education* (Lanham, MD: University Press of America, 1984). See also Suzanne C. Toton, *World Hunger* (Maryknoll, NY: Orbis, 1982).

The work of Gabriel Moran will emerge with frequency in the second part of the book; for now I simply mention my earlier attempt to lay out the pattern of his thought in my *Biblical Interpretation in Religious Education* (Birmingham, AL: Religious Education Press, 1980), esp. 149–60.

The pastoral letter by the U. S. National Conference of Bishops, *To Teach as Jesus Did* (1972), is examined extensively in a series of articles in two issues of the *Notre Dame Journal of Education* 6 (Fall and Winter 1975), the first centering on educational developments since the pastoral's publication and the second examining alternative modes of schooling. The fall issue also contains articles on service programs. Furthermore, the pastoral has served as a catalyst for two workbooks designed to help put the pastoral in practice: Charles Brady and Mary Sarah Fasenmyer, eds., *Giving Form to the Vision* (Washington, DC: National Catholic Educational Association, 1974) and Ted Wojicki and Kevin Convey,

Teachers, Catholic Schools, and Faith Community: A Program of Spirituality (New York: Le Jacq, 1982). The latter illustrates the effort to engage in teacher "formation."

Pertinent in this regard are two NCEA monographs, Alfred McBride, *The Christian Formation of Catholic Educators* (1981); and Russell Bleich et al., *The Pre-Service Formation of Teachers for Catholic Schools: In Search of Patterns for the Future* (1982). Relevant as well is James Hawker's essay on "Schools as an Evangelizing Community: Guidelines Regarding Teachers, Pupils, Parents," which, together with an essay by Thea Bowman, "Religious and Cultural Variety: Gift to Catholic Schools," is published in monograph form, *The Non-Catholic in the Catholic School* (Washington, DC: National Catholic Educational Association, n.d.).

The effectiveness of Catholic schools is addressed in an extensive sociological study by Andrew M. Greeley, William C. McCready, and Kathleen McCourt, *Catholic Schools in a Declining Church* (Kansas City, MO: Sheed and Ward, 1976). McCready and McCourt cite evidence that 80 percent of the American Catholic population favors the continuation of parochial schools and that Catholic schools do in fact have an impact: Catholic education is second only to religiousness of the spouse in predicting religious behavior and correlates with a significant degree of racial tolerance. In regard to the "permeation theory," Greeley et al. conclude that "on the basis of our data there is no way religious instruction can return a greater payoff than Catholic schools, for the latter, however much they may cost, do accomplish something" (p. 310). Earlier research—including Greeley's earlier study with Peter Rossi *(The Education of Catholic Americans* [Chicago: Aldine, 1966])—is summarized in a nontechnical manner in Frances Forde Plude, *The Flickering Light* (New York: Sadlier, 1974). See also an earlier monograph by Michael O'Neill, *How Good Are Catholic Schools?* (Washington, DC: National Catholic Educational Association, 1968).

The literature on Catholic schooling is placed in context in the useful volume edited by James C. Carper and Thomas C. Hunt, *Religious Schooling in America* (Birmingham, AL: Religious Education Press, 1984); it also contains articles on Lutheran, Calvinist, Seventh-Day Adventist, Christian, and Jewish day schools. Likewise pertinent is James Coleman et al., *Public and Private Schools: A Report to the National Center for Educational Statistics Under Contract No. 300-78-0208* (Chicago: National Opinion Research Center, 1981).

Literature from Australia on Catholic schooling offers some valuable insights. See Marcellin Flynn, *Some Catholic Schools in Action* (Sydney: Catholic Education Office, 1975); Marisa Crawford and Graham M. Rossiter, *Teaching Religion in the Secondary School: Theory and Practice* (Sydney: Province Resource Group, Christian Brothers, 1985); and *Catholic Education in Victoria: Yesterday, Today and Tomorrow* (Catholic Education Office of Victoria, n.d.). See also the journal *Catholic School Studies*, Mount Saint Mary, 179 Albert Road, Strathfield, N.S.W. 2135. For a wider perspective see Michael Mason, ed., *Religion in Australian Life: A Bibliography of Social Research* (Bedford Park, S. Australia: The Australian Association for the Study of Religions and the National Catholic Research Council, 1982); and Edmund Campion, *Rockchoppers: Growing Up Catholic in Australia* (Ringwood, Victoria: Penguin, 1982). For a view of religious education in the United Kingdom, see the journal *New REview,* NCA 23 Kensington Square, London W85HN.

Literature on the "base communities" is rapidly developing. Especially useful is Sergio Torres and John Eagleson, eds., *The Challenge of Basic Christian Communities* (Maryknoll, NY: Orbis, 1981), which details theological perspectives. See also Alvaro Barreiro, *Basic Ecclesial Communities: The Evangelization of the Poor* (Maryknoll, NY: Orbis, 1982). Articles of note include Rosemary Radford Ruether, "'Basic Communities': Renewal at the Roots," *Christianity and Crisis* 41 (1981):234–37; Maurice L. Monette, "Basic Communities: Parish with a Difference," *PACE* 10 (1979):1–5 and idem., "Justice, Peace and the Pedagogy of Grass Roots Christian Community," in Padraic O'Hare, ed., *Education for Peace and Justice* (San Francisco: Harper & Row, 1983), 83–93. See also *Developing Basic Christian Communities: A Handbook* (Washington, DC: National Federation of Priests' Councils, 1979).

For a historical summary of this period, see Jay Dolan, *The American Catholic Experience: A History from Colonial Times to the Present* (Garden City, NY: Doubleday, Image Books, 1985), 421–54. For a perspective on the relation between liturgy and education in Catholicism, see Mary Kathryn Oosdyke, "The *Christ Life Series* in Religion (1934–1935): Liturgy and Experience as Formative Influences in Religious Education" (Ph.D. diss., Boston College, 1987).

Part Two

VISIONS

CHAPTER 7

Movements on the Horizon: Developments and Directions

A map is an essential guide for travelers, orienting them to the landscape charted by pioneers. Eventually, however, settlers have to proceed by their own sense of things. They will frequently consult the map, which will grow tattered and torn. But eventually settlers discover other paths and landmarks by which to make their way. To establish roots means in part to have greater confidence in one's perspective on certain territory, thereby to pay attention to one's own sense of direction.

So it is with thinking about religious education. Charting a map of the field in Part One was for me an exercise in orientation, a means of locating myself in a complex enterprise. Having found the process of mapmaking necessary to make sense of where I had landed, I now teach mapmaking to suggest to others ways of understanding their own journeys. Conversations with others in the field have heightened my realization that my map is but one way of analyzing religious education, and I have benefited greatly from other maps. Hence my desire that the mapping of Part One be a heuristic device, a stimulus for readers to develop their own layout of the territory. My confidence is less in the finality of my own map than in the validity of mapmaking as an educational experience. Only by trying to lay out the routes of previous theories will religious educators be able to progress in understanding what they are about.

When a friend recently reached the age of forty, she described her goal as wishing to "grow down." This is what I have tried to do in Part Two, where I have ventured into explanation of my own particular way of locating and settling. This section reveals one settler's views. To put it another way, my quest here is to speak of religious education in a way that is both *sufficiently inclusive*—to encompass the range of perspectives and activities mapped in Part One—and *appropriately particular* —to facilitate the development of specific ways of educating in faith. I shall keep the map alongside, but my own convictions and experience shall serve as guides as well. I shall utilize the map as a helper, often doubling back to retrace my steps before circling onwards.

With the map from Part One in hand, I propose in this chapter to venture into newer terrain. From this vantage point, I see an expanse of green shoots: an expanded understanding of knowledge; the contribution of different voices, particularly feminists', to rethinking certain foundational questions; the maturation of the social sciences; and the emergence of a new vision of the public responsibility of the church. I will describe each in turn, initially sketching the development in its broad dimensions and then filling in a more detailed account of the consequences for religious education. In the next chapter, I will deal explicitly with the meaning of these implications for conceptualizing the field.

WAYS OF KNOWING: DILATING OUR SENSE OF THE WORLD

The question of what it means to know, as I have argued from the outset, is fundamental to any theory of education. How we understand knowing is particularly significant today. Perhaps this is seen more vividly in its negative manifestation.

Since the Enlightenment Western society has tended to confuse technological advance with progress, information with knowledge, reason with wisdom, credentials with education, and teaching with technique. Consequently, it tends to prize that which is verifiable, measurable, and objective. It tends to exclude forms of knowledge that are not empirical and to assign precedence to fields dealing with quantitative realities. So engineering flourishes, while the budget for the fine arts is cut. When lower test scores come to public attention, slogans such as "back to the basics" often substitute for a more carefully articulated and creative approach to crises in the schools.

As a result, the West seems to have constricted its understanding of education. Historian Douglas Sloan indicts modern education for being rooted in a narrowly scientific epistemology that produces "a reason without rationality, an intellect without intelligence, a knowledge without understanding . . . an exquisitely stupid cleverness adept at taking the world apart with no grasp of what it is doing, nor apparent concern."[1] Similarly, Houston Smith, a scholar of comparative religions, says, "we have trimmed our epistemological sails too close to the scientific desiderata of objectivity, prediction, number, and control."[2]

Yet this is not the full story. Despite the prevalence of a mentality that treats knowledge reductionistically—what is true can be measured and objectified—evidence is accruing across the spectrum of the disciplines that such a truncated epistemology must be replaced by one that honors knowing as a complex process, mystery-laden and beyond our "ken." As scholars from diverse fields agree, human knowing transcends the verifiable and rational—a consensus significant for religious education.

No one way of describing the intricacies of knowing suffices. However, a recent volume, *Learning and Teaching the Ways of Knowing*, offers some useful distinctions. Of value, for instance, is Jerome Bruner's thesis that there are two irreducible modes of cognition, the "paradigmatic" (or logico-scientific) and the "narrative." Each provides a way of ordering experience, constructing reality, filtering perceptions, and organizing the memory. When well applied, the paradigmatic mode leads to good theory, tight analysis, logical proof, and empirical discovery guided by reasoned hypothesis. Complementing this way of knowing is the narrative mode, which, when artfully used, leads to good stories, gripping drama, and believable historical accounts. Both modes, of course, seek to express truth. But in the paradigmatic mode, truth is essentially a clear matter (one can subject the truth to verification by experiment); in the narrative mode, however, truth is more multifaceted and elusive. Thus one judges the truth value of the two modes differently. As Bruner sagely observes, "science 'progresses' in a way that storytelling and drama do not."[3] Parenthetically, Bruner's point is borne out by literary critic Northrop Frye's judgment that literature neither evolves nor improves. "We may have dramatists in the future who will write plays as good as *King Lear*, though they'll be very different ones, but drama as a whole will not get better than *King Lear*."[4]

Bruner's twofold classification notwithstanding, other dimensions of knowing may be named. Elliot Eisner argues for the importance of the aesthetic mode as corrective to the assumption that intelligence is the manipulation of abstract ideas.[5] Against those who advocate a return to the basics while excluding the fine arts, he argues:

The realization that the arts represent one of the ways through which humans construct and convey meaning and the creation of art forms requires the use of judgment, perceptivity, ingenuity, and purpose—in a word, intelligence—seems to have escaped most of those who have commented upon the state of education, not the least of whom are university professors sitting on admission committees and shaping admission policies for universities.[6]

Another way of knowing has been suggested by Ellen Berscheid: "interpersonal knowing," which includes both social intelligence (knowing other people and oneself) and social competence (the ability to produce the desired responses in interaction with others).[7] Others propose that we grant validity to "practical knowledge," procedural information that is useful in one's everyday life.[8] After all, in everyday situations, a person's thinking is "in the service of action."[9]

As scholars explicate the different modes of knowing, we may well feel that they are finally providing a theoretical base for what we have long sensed: there are many ways of knowing. And yet for all the wisdom of this conviction, most educational structures provide a quite narrow frame for knowing. As a case in point, consider those the culture in general regards as "intelligent." Typically, they are persons gifted with verbal or mathematical skills, as measured by standardized tests, including the "IQ" test. Not only are such tests marred by class, gender, and race biases, but the equation of certain skills with intelligence may lead people to ignore "the moral and ethical strengths of Dr. Martin Luther King, Jr. . . . the sensitivity to inner nuance that distinguishes the novels of Virginia Woolf or Henry James."[10]

It follows, then, that acknowledgment of diverse ways of knowing requires, among other factors, recognition of the complex character of human intelligence. Especially insightful in this regard is psychologist Howard Gardner's claim that intelligence is not a tangible, measurable entity, but rather a convenient way of labeling some phenomena. He suggests that we think of various intelligences that function as sets of "know-how." Specifically, Gardner proposes six distinct intelligences: linguistic, musical, logical, spatial, bodily-kinesthetic, and personal.[11] His theory of "multiple intelligences" brilliantly lays open the biases of much of Western education and provides a fascinating foundation for more imaginative curricula.

Moreover, as philosopher Maxine Greene notes, Gardner's work has political implications. Against the backdrop of the recent government report *A Nation at Risk*, with its rhetoric assailing the "rising tide of mediocrity" and promoting "excellence" in education, Greene concludes that Gardner gives us a warrant for thinking of excellence in a plural sense: ". . . as the development of particular capacities like critico-creative thinking, integrity, autonomy, fidelity, imaginativeness, adventurousness, self-reflectiveness, cooperativeness, moral sensitivity, and even strength of will or persistence or stubbornness."[12] Greene continues:

If stress is placed on a prescribed range of literacies, if human beings are thought of primarily as "resources" to promote the national interest, opportunities for differential growth and development may be severely limited in the name of relevance and efficiency. We need but think of those whose strengths and talents are not of the sort especially prized today: Henry David Thoreau, Margaret Fuller, James Baldwin, Gregory Bateson, Helen Caldicott, any number of others. We might think of persons peculiarly qualified to start storefront schools in inhospitable neighborhoods, those out to save the rivers, those who engage in civil disobedience to stop nuclear war.[13]

IMPLICATIONS FOR RELIGIOUS EDUCATION

The widened horizon of knowing proffered by the thinkers just named above permits a more expansive understanding of religious education. It calls attention to the transcendent and hence religious quality of all education—a theme central to the work of Parker Palmer and

Dwayne Huebner.[14] Moreover, it points to the need to incorporate a broadened concept of knowing in the field of religious education itself.

Here the work of Maria Harris is significant. Influenced particularly by philosopher Susanne Langer, as well as by Eisner, Harris has focused much of her teaching on the aesthetic quality of religious education. She recognizes the value of that empirical knowledge, "which makes arid land fertile, unlocks the secrets of obscure texts, or repairs damaged hearts." Nevertheless, Harris proposes that knowing is truncated unless it is completed by artistic knowing.[15] Art, she argues, is the "primordial form of knowing through our bodiliness. . . . A person speculating, thinking, knowing in the artistic mode does not think *about* objects: trees, rivers, clay, tone. A person knows *them,* thinks through *them,* in actual sensible, concrete engagement."[16] For Harris, artistic knowing is crucial to the educational process. She claims:

Perhaps the most valuable mental attitude of the educator, whether parent or pastor or preacher or pedagogue, is closer to the poetic, artistic intelligence than to discursive intelligence. For the subject matter of education is, as is the subject matter of theology, knowledge profoundly entered, knowledge in which one dwells. Guilt, forgiveness, death, reconciliation, resurrection, love, and faith are not primarily concepts. They are primarily human realities, best understood in immediacy and involvement.[17]

In theological terms, this knowing is the source of the sacramental imagination—that vision that sees all creation as mediating the divine. Religious educators who follow Harris's lead will necessarily be attentive to the revelatory character of art in all of its manifestations. Their pedagogical task comprises a sensitivity to metaphor; to shape, color, dimension, medium, texture; to movement and stillness; to sound and silence.

That such tasks are not peripheral to religious education is also the argument of James Michael Lee in the final volume of his trilogy, *The Content of Religious Instruction.* In this massive book (814 pages), Lee posits that the construct "religion" is constituted by nine contents: product and process, cognitive and affective, verbal and nonverbal, conscious and unconscious, and life-style. Among the numerous implications possible in Lee's detailed unfolding of this thesis are many that harmonize with Harris's, especially since both resist equating education in religion with instruction in theology. Extrapolating from Harris and Lee, I suggest the following obligations for all educators, but especially religious educators:

· To take great care with words and, in particular, to appreciate symbolic language. Teaching requires an awareness of the power of speech.
· To respect silence and draw upon nonverbal ways of communicating. Teaching has rhythms of sound and stillness, of action and reception. "For everything there is a season, and a time for every matter under heaven" (Eccles. 3:1).

· To take the body seriously and attend to the sensory character of learning. Teaching is grounded in sight, sound, touch, taste, and smell.
· To honor the "right brain." Teaching involves complementing the analytical, cognitive, and logical activities of the brain's left hemisphere with the more intuitive, affective, and nonverbal activities of the right hemisphere.
· To enter imaginatively into the subject. Teaching is a stretching, an awakening, a creative activity.

These are by no means the only possible connections between Harris and Lee, but they are, I believe, essential to a more vital religious education. I will return to them in the next chapter as I develop my own definition of the field.

One other significant dimension of an expanded epistemological basis for religious education deserves attention: the work of Thomas Groome in emphasizing that knowing encompasses *praxis*. That is, not only is knowing embodied (apropos Harris and Lee) but it also is necessarily "relational, experiential and active"—three adjectives Groome uses consistently to describe what he means by a praxis way of knowing. Furthermore, praxis denotes intentionally and reflectively chosen ethical action, so pedagogy drawing upon Groome's movements of "shared Christian *praxis*" necessarily invites participants to make decisions, to respond in faith to what is being taught.[18]

In certain respects, religious educators seem to have come full circle to an epistemology not unlike Jonathan Edwards's (see chapter 2). Though Harris, Lee, and Groome have considerably refined and extended the discussion, their interests foster a way of knowing strikingly similar to that "information of the understanding" of which Edwards spoke. For all three of them—albeit in varying ways—"spiritual knowledge," "wherein the mind not only *speculates* and *beholds,* but *relishes* and *feels,*" is central.[19] Like Edwards, they are convinced that the knowledge persons seek in matters religious should enable them to live differently.

In a phrase, what they—and I—advocate is an education that will "dilate" our sense of the world.[20] We need a theory of knowing that will complement our emphasis on autonomy, rationality, abstraction, and skill with attention to mutuality, emotion, particularity, and awe. This is the epistemology fundamental to any "religious" education.

PERSPECTIVES ON FOUNDATIONAL QUESTIONS: LISTENING TO FEMINIST VOICES

In suggesting that religious education needs to have an epistemological basis so that our outlook is enlarged, I have used the imagery of sight: dilating our sense of the world. As the great rabbi Abraham J. Heschel observed, we tend to see simply what we know, rather than know what we see.[21]

In this section I propose to amplify the visual image with an auditory one. In particular, I will draw upon a body of literature—feminist theory—that deals with the voice as a metaphor for intellectual and ethical growth.[22]

Feminist studies test the paradigms that have typically organized knowledge to exclude women or to make them marginal. By no means, however, is feminism articulated in one voice. Jean Bethke Elshtain observes: "under the broad umbrella of Women's Studies one finds a lively, at times contentious world of competing epistemologies, ideologies, narrative styles, and ethical and political commitments."[23] Nevertheless, I think it is possible to generalize that the following five fundamental activities are characteristic of feminist theory: questioning conventional wisdom—the concepts, conclusions, and principles deeply rooted in scholarship; reexamining sources; searching for information overlooked or previously inaccessible; attending to methodology; and stimulating new theories. Feminist theory is not so much about "raising" consciousness as it is about shattering or enlarging it. It is "perspective transforming," a matrix for an expanded understanding of reality.[24]

FEMINIST VOICES

Attentiveness to silence is the prelude to and prerequisite for feminist theory. Listening generates questions. Who has been excluded from this conversation? Why have the experiences of women not been sufficiently considered? Do the categories formulated by men take women's perspectives into account? For example, can one appropriately generalize about stages of development—whether in regard to moral reasoning, faith, or cognition—when the data have been drawn from male subjects? Can a theologian adequately reflect upon the human condition when only men serve as resources? Can the goals and processes of education serve society's needs when the thinking of only a relatively homogeneous group of men dominates the discussion?

Attentiveness to silence leads to suspicion: all knowing is partial and perspectival, all reason is "standpoint dependent."[25] What is suspect? Conclusions long taken for granted, methodologies apparently firmly established, and canons considered closed. What is especially suspect is that differences have been ignored and glossed over. Gender does matter—not simply as a natural consequence of sex difference, but as an analytic category within which humans think about and organize their social reality.[26] And because gender has not been taken into account, our views of the world are distorted.

Buried in the silence and suspicion are the seeds of transformation. Feminist theory ultimately is directed toward enlarging society's visions. This is the point I wish to underscore as I turn now to describe in brief some of the facets of feminist thinking in education and theology that I believe help us to reshape our understanding of religious education.

FEMINIST EDUCATIONAL THINKING

In recent years a number of feminist scholars have been scrutinizing conclusions drawn primarily from the experience of males. Carol Gilligan, for instance, in arguing that psychological theories either ignore or devalue the development of women, takes issue with the conclusions drawn by her late Harvard colleague Lawrence Kohlberg. Kohlberg maintained that the principles of moral reasoning were universal, developing through invariantly sequential, hierarchically structured stages. Yet his research was based entirely on interviews with males. Gilligan, on the basis of interviews with female subjects, proposes that women articulate their moral development "in a different voice." Whereas males tend to think formally, proceeding from theory to fact, and define the self and moral behavior autonomously, females tend to reason more contextually and inductively; moreover, they typically emphasize the interdependence of intimacy and care.[27] Theirs is an ethic of care rather than one of justice (as Kohlberg had concluded). Thus, the universal character of Kohlberg's claims is suspect.[28]

Gilligan's research, of course, is not the final word. Empirical studies do not fully support her claim that males and females differ in moral orientation.[29] In addition, Gilligan's research has focused only on the privileged classes and has thereby not taken social position into account. Joan Tronto suggests that the moral perspectives of minorities in the United States are much more likely to be characterized by an ethic of care than by an ethic of justice. Further, she criticizes Gilligan for insufficiently grounding her ethic in a larger context of moral and political theory.[30] Paul Philibert concludes that Gilligan falls prey to the same methodological weakness she has discovered in Kohlberg, namely, "a psychology of morality based upon individualistic, non-dialectical reflection."[31]

Such criticisms notwithstanding, Gilligan's work is important for the provocative questions it raises. Do men and women differ in their thinking? Do they differ in what they prize—autonomy and relationships, respectively? And if there are differences, are they grounded in socialization or biology? Is it possible to develop an ethical vision that honors both human relationships in their particularity and abstract principles in their universality?

If questions such as these are to receive a fair hearing, attention must be given to women's experience in education. One compelling study argues that women do indeed know and view the world from epistemological perspectives unlike men's. In their *Women's Ways of Knowing*, Mary Field Belenky and three coauthors describe how women's experience shapes the way they know. Based on extensive interviews with 135 women of varying ages, circumstances, and backgrounds,[32] the four authors postulate that women's ways of knowing might be described as follows:

- *Received* knowledge: "a perspective from which women conceive of themselves as capable of receiving, even reproducing, knowledge from the all-
  knowing external authorities but not capable of creating knowledge on their
  own."
- *Subjective* knowledge: "a perspective from which truth and knowledge are
  conceived of as personal, private, and subjectively known or intuited."
- *Procedural* knowledge: "a position in which women are invested in learning
  and applying objective procedures for obtaining and communicating knowledge."
- *Constructed* knowledge: "a position in which women view all knowledge as
  contextual, experience themselves as creators of knowledge, and value both
  subjective and objective strategies for knowing."[33]

The authors refuse to label these four perspectives "stages," in part
because they take issue with the predilection of psychologists to generalize about "universal developmental pathways" when their conclusions
are extrapolated from data drawn from one gender, class, or culture.[34]

One of the most transparent points in their work is the connection
between the interviewees' self-understanding and their way of knowing.
The authors point out that women in some circumstances are incapable
even of "received knowledge." These are women in a perspective the
authors designate "silence": women who understand themselves as
mindless and voiceless—persons deaf and mute, subject to the whims of
external authority. Ann, a battered woman, says:

I could never understand what they were talking about. My schooling was very
limited. I didn't learn anything. I would just sit there and let people ramble on
about something I didn't understand and would say, Yup, yup. I would be too
embarrassed to ask, What do you really mean. I had trouble talking. If I tried
to explain something and someone told me that it was wrong, I'd burst into tears
over it. I'd just fall apart.[35]

As one might suspect, these women were among the youngest interviewees and among the most deprived economically, socially and educationally. Because of their limited experience and lack of confidence,
they were only confirmed in their sense of ineptitude by schooling.

But, if a grace note might be discovered in the lives of women such
as Ann, it is that other experiences—most often giving birth and caring
for children—frequently initiated a revolution in thought. These women
discovered that they *can* learn. Perhaps for some, mothering nurtured
their own intellectual capacities, what Sara Ruddick terms "maternal
thinking":

I speak about a mother's *thought*—the intellectual capacities she develops, the
judgments she makes, the metaphysical attitudes she assumes, the values she
affirms. A mother engages in a discipline. That is, she asks certain questions
rather than others; she establishes criteria for the truth, adequacy, and relevance
of proposed answers; and she cares about the findings she makes and can act
on. Like any discipline, hers has *characteristic* errors, temptations, and goals. The

discipline of maternal thought consists in establishing criteria for determining failure and success, in setting the priorities, and in identifying the virtues and liabilities the criteria presume.[36]

Yet typically, women first finding their voice experience learning in a limited sense: receiving, retaining, and returning the words of authorities. Not unsurprisingly in the face of these "three Rs," women who are "received knowers" tend to be intolerant in the face of ambiguity, literal in their interpretations, and fond of predictability and clarity.

Life experience often leads to the position of "subjective knowledge" in which the woman becomes her own authority, finding truth within, and treasuring what she has learned by living. One such woman said: "There's a part of me that I didn't even realize I had until recently— instinct, intuition, whatever. It helps me and protects me. It's perceptive and astute. I just listen to the inside of me and I know what to do."[37] The authors conclude that women in this mode

distrust logic, analysis, abstraction, and even language itself. They see these methods as alien territory belonging to men. . . . It is not that these women have become familiar with logic and theory as tools for knowing and have chosen to reject them; they have only vague and untested prejudices against a mode of thought that they sense is unfeminine and inhuman and maybe detrimental to their capacity for feeling. This antirationalist attitude is primarily characteristic of women during the period of subjectivism in which they value intuition as a safer and more fruitful approach to truth.[38]

Consequently, as the authors observe, subjectivism, despite the increase of self-confidence it signals, is a way of knowing with "maladaptive consequences."[39] Significantly, for many women the period of subjectivism precedes the return to formal education.

It is formal education that, in large measure, contributes to "procedural" knowledge, the voice of reason and of more conscious, systematic analysis. The authors suggest that there are two forms of procedural knowledge. One form, "separate" knowledge or critical thinking, is the opposite of subjectivism and is essentially adversarial in character. The second form is "connected knowledge" or understanding and involves *receptive rationality*.[40] Connected knowing moves beyond procedure to empathy; the authors suggest it is related to procedural knowledge as a woman's conversation is to a male "bull session."[41] Women's conversation, to draw upon the distinction of Peter Elbow, is the "believing game" rather than the "doubting game"—a willingness to entertain the proposition rather than to criticize it.[42] For one student, this meant reading a poem as if she were eavesdropping on two people talking.

Typically, connected knowing involves collaboration; one sophomore described why she enjoyed class discussion of *Frankenstein* by Mary Shelley: "You can just read it on top for the story. Then you can get underneath into Mary Shelley's life and all the hidden parts, and some people see some parts more than others, and they can explain them to you and show them to you. And you don't have to agree, but it's there."[43]

Finally, the authors claim, some women understand knowing as "constructed." This mode begins with an attempt to integrate what one knows through intuition and experience with what one learns from others.

For constructivist women, simple questions are as rare as simple answers. Constructivists can take, and often insist upon taking, a position outside a particular context or frame of reference and look back on "who" is asking the question, "why" the question is asked at all, and "how" answers are arrived at. They no longer dutifully try to come up with answers when questions are asked. "You're asking the wrong question!" we often heard them say. "Your question is out of context."[44]

Women who know as constructivists can listen simultaneously to two inner voices: a voice for expressing emotion and a voice for sharing reasons.[45]

Women's Ways of Knowing stimulates considerable reflection about the way educators might be more sensitive to the effect of gender on knowing. One is suggested by the authors: "connected teaching." Imaged as midwifery, connected teaching involves students in the processes by which teachers have come to their conclusions. Teacher and student participate in a cycle of confirmation-evocation-confirmation. "Midwife-teachers help students deliver their words to the world, and they use their own knowledge to put the students into conversation with other voices—past and present—in the culture."[46]

As Belenky and her coauthors call our attention to the link between knowing and the categories of gender, race, and class, Jane Roland Martin raises our awareness of the question of gender in educational philosophy. In *Reclaiming a Conversation: The Ideal of the Educated Woman,* Martin proposes that society must educate both for its *productive* needs—citizenship and the workplace—and for its *reproductive* needs, which include not only conception and birth but also the rearing of children to maturity, caring for the sick, attending to family needs, and managing a household.[47] In her closely reasoned argument, Martin demonstrates how historians of educational thought have missed the concern for the reproductive processes of society evident in the work of Plato, Jean Jacques Rousseau, Mary Wollstonecraft, Catharine Beecher, and Charlotte Gilman. As a result, they have excluded from the educational realm the transmission of skills, beliefs, feelings, emotions, values, and worldviews that happens in child rearing (among other instances).

Such an omission, with its separation of reason from emotion and self from the other, has had tragic consequences:

Do the separations bequeathed to us by Plato matter? The great irony of the liberal education that comes down to us from Plato and still today is the mark of an educated man or woman is that it is neither tolerant nor generous. . . . There is no place in it for education of the body, and since most action involves bodily movement, this means there is little room in it for education of action. Nor is there room for education of other-regarded feelings and emotions. The liberally educated man or woman will be provided with knowledge about others but will not be taught to care about their welfare or to act kindly toward them. That person will be given some understanding of society, but will not be taught to feel its injustices or even to be concerned over its fate. The liberally educated person will be an ivory-tower person—one who can reason but has no desire to solve real problems in the real world—or a technical person—one who likes to solve real problems but does not care about the solutions' consequences for real people and for the earth itself.[48]

Martin proposes no panacea, but does call for a "gender-sensitive" education that would recognize—as Plato did not—that gender affects one's interests, expectations, behavior, and perceptions. Specifically, she proposes three steps in developing an education for the full range of society's needs:

1. Raise awareness of the hidden curriculum of schooling: its denigration of women and the tasks, traits, and functions our culture associates with them.
2. Integrate new scholarship on women into the curriculum.
3. Build nurturing capacities and an ethics of care into the curriculum itself.

Martin concludes that just as rationality and autonomy are posited as goals of particular subjects, and of the curriculum as a whole, so also nurturance and connection can become overarching educational goals as well as the goals of particular subjects.[49] She adds one warning, however: we must avoid replicating in the curriculum the dichotomy between society's productive and reproductive processes. If our education links "nurturing capacities and the 3 Cs [caring, concern and connection] only to subjects such as home economics that arise out of the reproductive processes," we will "lose sight of the *general* moral, social, and political significance of these traits."[50] And, if rationality and autonomous judgment are linked exclusively with society's productive processes, the reproductive processes will continue to be devalued.

When feminist scholars such as Belenky and her coauthors and Martin argue for the importance of a "gender sensitive" education, they hope to expand the horizons of education for men and women. As Martin remarks, "one of the unanticipated rewards of bringing women into the educational realm is that the study of the education of the 'other' half of the population enables us to see all of education differently."[51] In their insistence that we listen to the "different voice," these scholars stimulate us to converse about holistic educational goals, an understanding of knowing expanded by sensitivity to gender and class, a process-oriented pedagogy, an inclusive curriculum, and a vision of a society where men and women work in partnership. In short, they ask us to talk about those questions foundational to education.

FEMINIST THEOLOGICAL THINKING

In a similar way, feminist theologians have provoked rethinking of questions foundational to theology. Although, as Margaret Farley points out, *sustained* theological synthesis in the feminist mode is new on the horizon, a remarkable literature is burgeoning across the range of theological specializations.[52] It is my intention here to "listen in" on some of the discourse of feminist theology in order to articulate a more adequate foundation for religious education.

Feminist theologians, like their colleagues in education, recognize the epistemological grounding of their work; they consistently acknowledge the effect of standpoint, "challenging us to notice anew the angle of our vision, thereby examining *how* and *why* we see as we do, as well as examining *what* we see.[53]

Examination from the feminist angle of vision provides, in the first analysis, the specter of the distorted view of women in Christian history. Scrutiny of the tradition initially entails documenting its deformation of women. Farley aptly summarizes the results of this scrutiny:

And whether woman was thought consciously to be a threatening force in the dialectic of history, or a temptress of men throughout all history, or a symbol of what men feared within themselves, she appears throughout the centuries in Christian writings as a special agent of evil. It is almost unnecessary to cite in this regard the texts of Justin Martyr, Irenaeus, Tertullian, Origen, Augustine, Jerome, of Thomas Aquinas and Bonaventure, of Luther, John Knox and the Puritans.[54]

Similarly, feminists highlight women's invisibility in the story of the tradition, showing how the tellers of its tales—theologians and churchmen—have narrated only a part of the fuller text.

Precisely because the distortions and omissions in the tradition have resulted in the subordination and subjection of women, Elisabeth Schüssler Fiorenza argues that we must rethink our understanding of revelation. She cuts to the core of Christian self-understanding in her assertion that a theology that liberates men and women "cannot accord revelatory authority to any oppressive and destructive biblical text or tradition." We must, she argues, reject those texts and traditions that perpetuate "violence, alienation and patriarchal subordination" in God's name. Rather, we must recover those elements articulating the "liberating experiences and visions of the people of God."[55]

Thus the work of feminist theology is ultimately constructive. Indeed, one of its most singular contributions is the integration of imagination and reason in alternative renderings in areas such as Bible, systematics, and spirituality. For example, Phyllis Trible uses feminism as a "hermeneutical clue" in her sensitive reading of the creation stories of Genesis, permitting her to highlight female metaphors for God and thus "allowing scripture to interpret scripture for new occasions."[56] Likewise, Schüssler Fiorenza, conscious of women's invisibility,[57] refuses to accept the argument from silence; that is, just because women are not explicitly mentioned in a passage does not mean only men were involved. Instead, she uses the silences about women's historical and theological experience as a clue to the "egalitarian reality" of the early Christian movement. She supplements historical-critical method—the biblical scholar's tool—with an imaginative reconstruction of historical reality: "rather than understand the text as an adequate reflection of the reality about which it speaks, we must search for clues and allusions that indicate the reality about which the text is silent."[58]

In a similar vein, Rosemary Radford Ruether has gathered a collection of texts to serve as a resource for feminist theology. Her anthology goes beyond the bounds of the Bible to include classical texts from the ancient Near East and from marginalized communities at the edges of Judaism and Christianity (e.g., Gnostic texts). In addition, she incorporates parables and poetry and myths. Ruether terms her collection a "working handbook of those stories from our enlarged memory of our experience"; its purpose is to stimulate discussion so that its readers can "start the work of our own theological reflection."[59] Ruether maintains that such a collection helps us to read canonical, patriarchal texts in a new light. Accordingly, those texts lose their normative status, and readers are stimulated to engage in the process of forming a new canon—the old one is insufficient for feminist theology—so that women can define themselves rather than be defined by others.[60]

Clearly, the authority of divinely revealed texts is a crucial question for both Schüssler Fiorenza and Ruether. In fact, it is a characteristic concern of feminist theologians and the focus for lively debate among them—not all agree with Schüssler Fiorenza and Ruether.[61] By no means are feminist theologians of a single mind.

The meaning of revelation (admittedly, a larger question than the authority of Scripture, but inextricably linked to it in Christian theology) has preoccupied twentieth-century thinkers. Feminist theologians have moved the debate ahead in their insistence that women's historical experience be taken seriously in any formulation of what is normative. In part, this reflects their rejection of theological abstraction as an end in itself. The centrality of revelation's authoritative claim comes also from the importance feminists place on relationship; as Jean Lambert observes, "scripture's authority is inseparable from its function of inviting persons into relation."[62]

The concept of relation is key throughout feminist theory and is particularly evident in the field of spirituality. Re-imaging God is fundamental; the image of God as father served so long as a dominant metaphor in Christian life that it came to legitimize domination, whether the divine right of kings or the lordship of men over women.[63] Feminists have written extensively on the feminine image of God—most notably Phyllis Trible—and suggested new images, such as God as "friend."[64] Of course, as Elizabeth Johnson astutely notes, calling into question an exclusively male idea of God does not therefore suggest that male imagery for God is inappropriate, since "what has been destroyed as an idol can return as an icon."[65] Nor should using female imagery for God introduce a distraction from belief in the one God of the Judeo-Christian tradition, because "the use of startling metaphors opens up the possibility of new religious experience of the one Holy Mystery."[66]

So important is relationship that it lies at the heart of feminist definitions of spirituality. Anne Carr speaks of spirituality as our deepest self in relation to God, and to the whole of life, embracing our relations with others, politics, society, and the world.[67] Joann Wolski Conn equates spirituality with the capacity to be self-transcending, that is, to be relational and freely committed. She posits that the central issues of the women's movement are also key issues in the development of spirituality in Christian life. For instance, "an empirical approach to spiritual direction" [presumably, one that takes experience seriously] "maintains that growth in prayer involves the ability to heighten awareness of what one *really wants* in life and how one *really feels* in God's presence."[68]

Similarly, Carol Ochs advances the thesis that women's experience allows new insight into relationship with reality and thereby fosters a spirituality of *this* world. She uses mothering as a central image, defining it as a way of love, a "de-centering" of the ego with two fundamental rhythms: holding on and letting go. Like Conn, she speaks of spirituality as the culmination of the natural process of maturation. A woman contributes a vital perspective to spirituality, since men's definitions of maturity have traditionally stressed independence or individuation. In contrast, women tend to think of maturity in terms of growth in the ability to relate with others. Women offer a way of viewing the ordinary as the ground of the holy.[69]

IMPLICATIONS FOR RELIGIOUS EDUCATION

The range and richness of feminist voices is breathtaking, especially in view of the relatively brief period in which they have spoken. Their voices have a distinctive timbre. At times susceptible to the judgment that preoccupation with victimization has produced "one-note criticism,"[70] they nevertheless provide stimulating conversation partners for religious educators. Let us consider feminist educators and theologians as interlocutors as we examine two interrelated dimensions of religious education, curriculum and teaching.

If curriculum is broadly understood as the "accumulating wisdom of the Christian community," then we need to be aware of the complex, dynamic character of the tradition.[71] Our sources for understanding Christianity originated in the finiteness of historical situations. Too often we have looked away from their incompleteness (women and other minorities invisible) and distortions (women as subordinate). The sources we have generally relied on are excessively narrow in scope and point of view, since most texts are authored by white, Western males. In more recent years, we may have attempted to compensate by supplementing bibliographies and by adding a session on "women in the Bible" or "Luther's view of women." But such additive approaches to the curriculum are inadequate. What is needed is an integration of feminist voices into the discipline itself, so that gender becomes a category for analysis of sources. What is needed, in short, is nothing less than a rethinking of the entire curriculum. Margaret Anderson writes:

Since women have been excluded from the creation of formalized knowledge, to include women means more than just adding women into existing knowledge or making them new objects of knowledge. . . . Including women refers to the complex process of redefining knowledge by making women's experiences a primary subject for knowledge, conceptualizing women as active agents in the creation of knowledge, including women's perspectives on knowledge, looking at gender as fundamental to the articulation of knowledge in Western thought, and seeing women's and men's experiences in relation to the sex/gender system.[72]

The feminist voice needs to stay with us as a nagging suspicion that the way things have been presented is not the full picture. Not only is the vision we have all inherited partial, but its objectivity is suspect— perspective has gone unrecognized. Despite their claim of objectivity, men have not described the world as it is, but as they perceive it. Adrienne Rich provocatively observes that "men in general think badly: in disjuncture from their personal lives, claiming objectivity where the most irrational passions seethe, losing, as Virginia Woolf observed, their senses in the pursuit of professionalism."[73] The feminist voice is necessary in the first instance to harmonize "objective" and "subjective." Feminist theory is the insistent reminder that rationality, although important, is not an end in itself. Moreover, feminist voices are speaking with a more resonant tone as they develop; their self-critique deepens— witness the lively conversation around Gilligan's *In a Different Voice*—and their creativity is evident.

Feminist theory also reflects concern for process. In conversing with theologians, religious educators contribute an interest in pedagogy that is intrinsic to the feminist commitment to process and collaboration. Theologians operating in more traditional modes have typically relegated teaching to the periphery of scholarship, regarding it as mere technique. I believe that one of the most important litmus tests of feminist theology will be how seriously it takes teaching.[74] It is in the act of teaching that many of the ideals feminists propound are actualized.

Teaching reveals the contours of one's commitment to process. How we structure classes, workshops, and presentations reveals our conviction about relationships, both to the subject at hand and to others. It tests our understanding of authority, our reading of sources, the value we place on imagination, and the priority we assign to dialogue.

I will develop some of these themes in chapter 8. But for now I will continue my survey of the new terrain by looking at the maturing social sciences.

"HOLINESS IS WHOLENESS": THE PERSPECTIVES OF THE SOCIAL SCIENCES

In this third section, I propose to outline how the social sciences enhance religious education. As in each of the other three topics of this chapter, such a subject is deserving of a volume in itself. In fact, the current state of scholarship about the social sciences gives one pause; the complexity of issues means that any survey will necessarily be selective. The social sciences have been described as an "ambitious concept," embracing a "set of disciplines of scholarship which deal with aspects of human society."[75] There exists no unanimity in a definition of social science or of its divisions and methodologies. The extent to which the fields encompassed by the social sciences are "scientific" is heatedly debated. Also at issue is the extent to which they are or should be empirical. Moreover, though psychology is generally omitted from the various typologies offered by social science theorists, common parlance seems to categorize it among the activities of social science—an inclusion I will follow.

The perils indicate the importance of proceeding cautiously; they need not obscure the ways the social sciences are reshaping religious education. Insofar as the social sciences study humankind in its unity,[76] they permit some fascinating angles on the theme "holiness is wholeness." In face of the vast array of insights, I will limit my report to how sociology and psychology affect religious education.

SOCIOLOGY

I see at least three sociological streams influencing the field of religious education. One, empirical research, establishes a data base, identifying and classifying viewpoints and behaviors. Here scientific methods are prized; research design—often described at length in an appendix—is key to validating a study. Sociology in this mode examines the influence of factors such as class, ethnicity, schooling, and income on religious groups; it studies life in cults, the experience of adolescent crises of faith, and the adherence of church members to doctrinal statements.

One need only survey journals such as the *Review of Religious Research* or *Journal for the Scientific Study of Religion* to gain a sense of the careful methodologies and range of topics. Issues such as the effects of church schools,[77] the phenomenon of church dropouts,[78] and the dynamics of life in a congregation[79] are also analyzed. The descriptive studies proffered by such sociologists challenge religious educators to be cognizant of the complex variables at play in any given situation.

The second stream of sociological study, more attentive to historical, philosophical, and theological literature, is exemplified in the work of scholars such as Peter Berger, Gregory Baum, Robert Bellah and his associates (most notably in *Habits of the Heart*), and John Coleman. I will take up the work of Bellah and Coleman in particular in my concluding section on the church's new awareness of its public responsibilities.

The third stream, bearing relation to the above, is best categorized as "sociology of knowledge." This enterprise, associated originally with Max Scheler and Karl Mannheim, studies the way a person's social life influences his or her knowledge, thought, and culture.[80] More recently, "critical theory"—used to end critique innocent of its own presuppositions[81]—has entered the vocabulary of influential religious educators and thus given prominence to sociology of knowledge.

It is most evident in the work of Thomas Groome, who, originally influenced by Paulo Freire's work (see chapter 6), found that critical theory permitted a deeper grasp of human praxis as a way of understanding. Groome's sources include Georg Hegel (on the unity of *theoria* and *praxis*) and Karl Marx (authentic knowing should be a transformative activity directed toward human freedom and emancipation). He has also drawn upon Jürgen Habermas to broaden Marx's narrow meaning of praxis and to illuminate the "objectivist illusion"—the mistaken notion that a person can be free of presuppositions and interests. Sociology of knowledge forms a foundation of Groome's second movement of "shared Christian praxis," since, following Habermas, he stresses the primacy of the knowing subject and questions the spectrum of interests, symbols, attitudes, assumptions, technologies, and interests that distort communication and repress dialogue.

Shared praxis attempts to bring people to name their own constitutive knowing (that is, the knowing which arises from their own engagement in the world), and to critically reflect on that knowing in order to uncover its source and consequence (their "interests").[82]

Sociology of knowledge similarly influences William Bean Kennedy in his argument that religious educators need a greater ideological consciousness. In a recent article, Kennedy uses Douglas Kellner's distinction between "ideology-as-ism" (the power to give birth to a new view of the world and to motivate its advocates to political action) and "hegemonic ideology" (the acceptance of the way things are and thus an acceptance and legitimation of the status quo). Concerned lest religious educators represent instruments of hegemonic ideology, Kennedy makes six recommendations for pedagogical action. The first is a general statement that religious educators must be attentive to the content of the curriculum in which educational knowledge is "framed" in relationships between student and teacher:

As we shape our courses and develop our syllabi, we are involved in that ideological activity [in which the educational system controls knowledge and perpetuates the control of the present, hegemonic ideology]. We can all too easily give up resisting and trying to make radical breakthroughs, and even forget that in sharing course goals, resources, and teaching-learning processes with students we have much free space in which to subvert or counter the larger structural controls.... As teachers in practical fields we have considerable freedom to experiment, to challenge the prevailing modes of curriculum design and course organization.[83]

The other five flow from this. Kennedy recommends that religious educators make greater use of aesthetic and creative modes of learning so as to overcome "technical rationality." Furthermore, they should pay particular attention to the knowledge and experiences of oppressed groups, engage in "problem-posing" education (following Freire), utilize conflict as a tool of reflection and analysis, and operate with a "hermeneutic of suspicion"—identifying and analyzing society's contradictions. Kennedy concludes, "When things are not as they should be, religious education is called to keep a vision fresh among us, against which we can judge the personal and political decisions we must make."[84]

In sum, if empirical studies make transparent the factors that shape the thoughts and behaviors of individuals and groups, then sociology of knowledge provides a lens through which patterns of domination can be identified. Sociology offers a tool for disciplining oneself to be more attentive to the world as it is. It is indispensable to religious education.

PSYCHOLOGY

Whereas sociology, particularly sociology of knowledge, has yet to influence religious education dramatically, modern psychology exercises an enormous effect on the field. Often it seems that one preparing to become a professional religious educator studies but two areas, theology and psychology. Indeed, since the days of George Albert Coe, who initiated his long career with an empirical study of the psychological dynamics of conversion in 1900, psychology has increasingly dominated the educational enterprise, with developmental psychology preeminent. Even a document heavily indebted to theological categories, *Sharing the Light of Faith,* the catechetical directory for Catholics in the United States, gives prominence to stages of human development.[85]

Of course, developmental psychology is not theology's only conversation partner. Psychoanalytic approaches indebted to Freud and Jung have long provoked discussion and debate, though with less obvious influence on religious education than on pastoral care. However, a development within psychoanalytic thought, "object relations theory," is currently stimulating considerable interest, especially through Ana-Maria Rizzuto's pioneering work, *The Birth of the Living God.*[86] Educational psychology, with its insights into teaching-learning processes, and social psychology, with its insights into the dynamics of groups and the socialization process, have also influenced the practice of religious education.

Nevertheless, developmental psychology eclipses other perspectives. Because, among various developmental theories, James Fowler's theory of faith development is a particularly stimulating conversation partner for religious education, I will assign it primacy in this section.[87] Furthermore, I am selecting this theory as a paradigm of the maturation of the social sciences—a new stage of development characterized by creative exchange among scholars and by the attempt to engage public policy makers. Accordingly, I will lay out the essential elements of faith development theory, describe the general contours of the scholarly commentary the theory is engendering, and utilize its inclusion of public concerns as the transition to the fourth section of this chapter.

Fowler's identification of three sets of underlying questions faith developmentalists are pursuing establishes the intent of his theory. First, he maintains, is the inquiry about how persons become aware of and begin to form (and be formed in) attitudes of trust and loyalty, of belief and commitment that sustain them throughout their lives. Here he and his colleagues at the Center for the Study of Faith Development at Candler School of Theology at Emory University are probing for differences in the styles of knowing and valuing that constitute faith. They cast their second question in a developmentalist's terms. Are there predictable stages or revolutions in the course of a person's attempts to make meaning? Do patterns recognizable in the cognitive, psychosocial, and moral spheres have a correlate in the realm of faith? Their third question asks whether a deep and abiding trust in, and loyalty to, a cause or causes greater than oneself is necessary to become fully adult and fully human.[88] Sharon Parks notes that the central insight of faith development theory is that

the composing of meaning at the level of ultimacy undergoes predictable patterns of development in the direction of an enlarged capacity to embrace and discern complexity—and thus to compose a more adequate faith (a more adequate and trustworthy perception of a fitting composition of self, world and "God").[89]

What are these "predictable patterns"? Fowler, in the tradition of structural-developmental thinkers such as Jean Piaget and Lawrence Kohlberg, posits the existence of seven hierarchical, sequential, and invariant stages of faith. A stage ("an integrated set of prerational structures that constitute the thought processes of a person at a given time") names a transition critical to the maturation of one's faith.[90] Stage theory offers what Dwayne Huebner has termed a "scaffolding of understanding."[91]

Fowler's stages have not only been ably explicated in his own works but are also well summarized in a number of sources.[92] Since they defy simple listing, I merely give a succinct outline for the sake of the reader's recall (or initiation). My intent lies less in analysis of Fowler than in reflection on his contribution to religious education.

The stages begin with the infant's *primal faith* developed in interaction with the primary care givers and move to the young child's *intuitive-projective faith*. In this second stage, the child's expanding horizon means that he or she can call upon symbols and stories that will form long-lasting images. The school-age child's reliance on stories, rules, and values marks the *mythic-literal* stage; this stage should eventually give way in adolescence to that synthesis of the strands of identity formed out of conventional beliefs and values that Fowler terms *synthetic-conventional faith*. Adulthood is characterized by a more explicit sense of self, *individuative-reflective faith;* when it leads to an appreciation of paradox and appropriation of a "second naiveté" (a reclaiming of symbols after critical scrutiny), adulthood may foster *conjunctive faith*. Finally, Fowler asserts that some adults may be so transformed that they are closely identified with the love of the Creator for creatures; they have reached the juncture of *universalizing faith*.

These stages, and the theoretical construct in which they are embedded, have served as a catalyst of intense discussion. Some scholars offer a refinement of the stage theory. Sharon Parks, for instance, proposes that the movement from stages three to four really embraces two transitions: the young adult's "probing commitment" and "fragile inner dependence"; and the mature adult's "tested commitment" and "confident inner dependence."[93] Some, such as Walter Conn, critically assess stage theory in order to illumine the dynamics of conversion; for Conn, development is the middle term between conscience and conversion: "at key points, then, development requires conversion, and conversion always occurs within a developmental process."[94] Still others, such as Gabriel Moran, whom I will cite below, are more generally skeptical toward stage theory and question some of Fowler's basic premises.

Of note in this regard is the controversy over Fowler's conviction that faith is a "human universal." He understands faith as the activity of making meaning, of shaping an "ultimate environment," of "construing, interpreting and responding to the factors of contingency, finitude and ultimacy in our lives."[95] Because all persons—whether believers or nonbelievers—have faith, his theory transcends the boundaries of any particular religious stance.

Such an assumption avoids parochialism and situates faith in a broad context, but it is not without its critics. Gabriel Moran claims that by distinguishing faith's structure from its content (belief), Fowler has constructed a dichotomy that robs faith of its complexity.[96] Fowler, who takes his critics seriously, counters that the description of a person's or a group's faith is incomplete without attentiveness to the stories, beliefs, symbols, and practices that constitute the content or grammar of that faith.[97] Fowler utilizes the final three chapters of *Becoming Adult, Becoming Christian* to detail his understanding of the way the "Christian story" shapes its members; he uses the thematic of covenant and vocation to reflect on how the narrative of the Christian life calls one to maturity.

Fowler's critics seem not to be entirely persuaded by his response. John McDargh, cognizant that Fowler has indeed made his presentation of faith more nuanced, questions whether the clarifications and modifications can compensate for a more fundamental problem: the structural-developmental model itself. McDargh, who finds contemporary psychoanalytic theory a more sympathetic interlocutor with religion, argues that structural-developmental thinking needs to be integrated with psychoanalytic theory.[98] His reservations are echoed by Carl Schneider, who claims that Fowler lacks the "chastening of the hermeneutics of suspicion exercised by the psychodynamic approach."[99] Consequently, argues Schneider, Fowler overvalues words to the neglect of affect and behavior, neglects the significance of early childhood, and has an inadequate doctrine of evil and sin.[100] The critics' comments suggest at least one reason why cognitive-developmental theories have exercised more impact on religious education than on pastoral care.[101]

I call attention to the criticisms lest religious educators accept faith development theory—or any schema—prematurely and simplistically. But my reading of the burgeoning literature on faith development has persuaded me that an extraordinary network of scholarship is emerging. Crossing the boundaries of the disciplines, this literature provides an important horizon for religious educators because the questions are foundational. What is faith? Conversion? How does social science enhance theology? What are the limitations of social science?[102] What does theology have to say to the social sciences?[103]

Before leaving faith development theory, I wish to point out another component: its turn toward society. This turn has two aspects. One is a receptivity to critical theory. For example, Sharon Parks, following Dwayne Huebner, notes the danger of the metaphor of development, an image rooted in biological maturation that may also absorb a disguised imperialism (e.g., "underdeveloped" nations); she suggests that the metaphor of transformation may be preferable.[104]

The other aspect is an interest in the education of "public" Christians. In Fowler's reading of the American experience, covenant was once a "root metaphor" that drew together a diverse yet harmonious human society. With the disestablishment of religion and the embrace of secularism, neither schools nor other social institutions could reinforce moral teaching as they had in colonial days. Consequently, education has become increasingly divorced from its ethical moorings.

What is needed, Fowler proposes, is attentiveness to the moral dimension of development. This includes a critical appraisal of current root metaphors such as power, "mechanism" (a machinelike predictability to relations), relationship, and systems. Moreover, these metaphors ought to be governed by covenantal commitment so that citizens can build a society in partnership with one another, nature, and their Creator. If this were the case, then four implications for public policy would follow. First, the state should provide assistance for families in nurturing children rather than fostering competition. Second, school curricula ought to reflect prevalent root metaphors and the stages of faith development. Third, the state should assume leadership in monitoring and guiding television programming along relational and covenantal lines. Fourth, this nation ought to find ways to teach and give public expression to its theocentric and biblical grounding.[105]

Fowler's interest in widening the circle of conversation leads directly to a consideration of the public responsibility of the church.

BOTH DISCIPLES AND CITIZENS: THE PUBLIC RESPONSIBILITY OF THE CHURCH

James Fowler's advocacy of the power of biblical metaphors to serve as a centripetal force in a fragmented society highlights a topic being probed by a loose network of scholars working in the area of religion and society.

Sociologist John Coleman, for instance, argues that although three different traditions—republican theory, biblical religion, and Enlightenment liberalism— have contributed to the public self-understanding of the United States, the "tradition of biblical religion seems the most potent symbolic resource we possess to address the sense of drift in American identity and purpose."[106] Similarly, Robert Bellah and his associates, authors of *Habits of the Heart,* cite Martin Luther King, Jr.'s usage of biblical and republican themes as a model of how American individualism might be transformed.[107]

Nevertheless, the mere appropriation of biblical language does not in itself lead to civic commitments, as each of these authors is keenly aware. Alan Peshkin has documented this in his educational analysis of a fundamentalist Christian school. Despite his respect and admiration for the integrity of the faculty, administration, and students of Bethel Baptist Academy (the fictitious name assigned to the school), where Peshkin spent four semesters as an observer, Peshkin concludes that such a school is ultimately divisive. He writes, "when one's beliefs admit of no uncertainty, one thereby bars debate, bargaining, and compromise."[108]

Because the school communicated facts and feelings that led students to look negatively on Americans of differing beliefs, Peshkin argues, "from the perspective of the pluralist America that I value I see that the more successful the Bethanys of America are, the less successful will be the ideal of pluralism which assures their survival."[109]

Like Peshkin, historian Martin Marty laments the decrease of faith in civility in recent times. He lampoons the current situation in which "civility yields to uncivil bumper-sticker warfare, where non-sequiturs posing as premises turn out to be conclusions."[110] Marty argues that the church needs to accept the call to help people combine their inward journey with their vocation as citizens. In contrast to the narrow dogmatism of the ecclesiology chronicled by Peshkin, Marty stresses the inclusive character of the "public church": "a family of apostolic churches with Jesus Christ at the center, churches which are especially sensitive to the res publica, the public order that surrounds and includes people of faith."[111] Its special task is correlating the evangelistic impulse with an ecumenical viewpoint.

The public church may never be a majority, at least in the present order where the simple answers of more authoritarian traditions of faith dominate. Yet its members have a vital vocation: to bring humanity to a new stage of faith in which "the God of prey is left behind and people can affirm what they believe without pouncing on others."[112]

Educating people for membership in the "public church" is one of the most important tasks religious educators confront in the late twentieth century. It is a demanding task, raising many questions and posing new challenges. For example, how is it possible in a pluralistic society to educate people in the traditions of their own community of faith while simultaneously preparing them to participate in the shaping of the *res publica*? How does one teach passionate loyalty to God while also teaching tolerance for people who do not share that commitment? How does one develop the ability to be steeped both in the language of faith and in the language of secular culture?

Questions such as these are not quickly answered. But simply to ask them leads to new directions. Further, three topics that constitute a basis for initial wrestling with the questions are the mission of the church, the relation of religion and politics, and the obligations of citizenship in enhancing the practice of Christian life. Each of these topics contains implications for religious education.

MISSION OF THE CHURCH

One of the tasks incumbent upon Christians is the obligation to understand how the church relates to the world. As H. Richard Niebuhr's study *Christ and Culture* demonstrates, Christians have assumed radically different perspectives. Moreover, even within a particular denominational heritage, diverse viewpoints may coexist or new ones emerge. As the survey of Catholic educational philosophy in chapter 5 has shown, twentieth-century Catholicism has moved from its nineteenth-century defensive, intransigent position relative to the world to a more affirming, open stance. This is reflected in Vatican II's *Pastoral Constitution on the Church in the Modern World* and boldly articulated in this key statement from the 1971 Synod document "Justice in the World":

Action on behalf of justice and participation in the transformation of the world fully appear to us as a constitutive dimension of the preaching of the Gospel, or, in other words, of the Church's mission for the redemption of the human race and its liberation from every oppressive situation.[113]

But what concepts undergird such a notion of ecclesial mission? Roger D. Haight's argument is persuasive: mission, a constitutive symbol of the church, is most broadly conceived as humanization. Haight proposes two analogies: the church *(communio)* is related to its mission *(missio)* as existence is to the purpose of existence; and the church is related to the modern world as the missionary church is to the non-Christian world.[114] By nature, the church is turned outward toward the world. The "whole being of the church is a being-for-the-world."[115] Its mission is to be a vital sign of Christ among all peoples and cultures. And just as the missionary church inculturates itself in order to bear witness to the Christ, so too should the church *critically* and *consciously* adapt to the modern world if it hopes to be an adequate sign. Inculturation makes new demands: "If the church is to be really immersed in a culture because it grows out of the lived experience of Christ in that culture, then there must be doctrine in new languages, sacramental symbols with new meanings and nuances, church polity with different styles of organization."[116] Only an inculturated church can bear witness to Christ adequately.

What does the inculturated church have to say in the modern world? What has become clearer in our time is that evangelization must enfold humanization. Both, as Haight puts it, are "equally essential dimensions of one outward symbolic thrust of the church."[117] He cites Philippine theologian Catalino G. Aravelo: "Wherever the church sees grace overcoming sin, it must put its force and energy. Its whole direction is toward forwarding the purposes of grace in the world."[118] The church has a responsibility to *name God's activity in the world,* to be a *prophetic critic of society,* and to be a *mediating agency,* supporting whatever seems to be the manifestation of God's gracious activity in the world.

THE CHURCH AND POLITICS: SOME HELPFUL DISTINCTIONS

To talk, however, of the church's commitment to the public order inevitably seems to result in an emotional debate about the propriety of ecclesial participation in politics. Almost always the problem lies, at least initially, in the conflation of the term "politics" with "partisan politics."

And yet the political order embraces a much broader spectrum of activities, such as the formulation of policy, debate over laws, advocacy of certain programs, and the exercise of the powers of elected office. Some distinctions are needed.

Madonna Kolbenschlag suggests a tri-level taxonomy of the political order. The first level, partisan activity, represents the narrowest use of the term; its aim is gaining and exercising political power in government. The second level is more properly nonpartisan: activity directed toward influencing the exercise of power, public policy, or the electoral process outside constituted political structures. She suggests that strikes, demonstrations, lobbying, and testimony before a legislature exemplify this level. Groups such as political action committees, ecumenical and interfaith organizations, women's groups, labor unions, episcopal conferences, and neighborhood action committees participate in politics primarily at this level.

At the third level is activity directed toward the presentation of a general philosophy of socio-political life or of a moral vision. Church teaching (e.g., the recent letters of the U.S. Catholic bishops and of the Methodist bishops on peace) exemplifies this level, as do groups such as the League of Women Voters, Common Cause, "think tanks," and research institutes.[119]

Richard McBrien has suggested a more refined differentiation in his identification of eight levels of political activity: (1) participation in public debate over an issue; (2) personal association with officeholders in order to influence their behavior; (3) public action intended to highlight deficiencies in the political system; (4) leadership of organized religious-political movements that have a broad social and political agenda; (5) active support of, or opposition to, candidates for public office by means of voter registration, fund-raising, direct mailing, and endorsements; (6) indirect support of, or opposition to, candidates for public office by means of public statements and appearances; (7) acceptance and exercise of appointed public office; (8) active candidacy for, and service in, elected political office.[120]

The usefulness of both the Kolbenschlag and McBrien taxonomies is that they give clarity to politics, a term carelessly used in everyday speech. Those who claim, for instance, that the "church ought to stay out of politics," need to refine their assertion, to specify at what level ecclesial participation is misguided and to provide warrants for their judgment. Politics embraces a wide spectrum of activities. It has to do "with the public forum and with the process of decision making that occurs there."[121] The public church, therefore, is necessarily engaged in the political order, although not all its adherents will come to consensus about the appropriateness of participating on all levels.

A further note: the lack of clarity regarding the term "politics" is a serious problem for the church today. Especially in denominations whose leaders are actively engaged in articulating a moral vision (e.g., in the episcopal letters on peace), educators have an obligation to help members in making distinctions. Clarification is necessary so that members may understand not simply the goals of their leaders but also grasp their own obligation to contribute to the political order.

CITIZENSHIP AND DISCIPLESHIP

In *The Church in the Education of the Public*, the authors claim that communities of faith are the only intentional agencies that bear a primary responsiblity for the religious. "For the church *to restrict its educational ministry to itself* ignores this crucial public responsibility" [emphasis added].[122] It is the task of the church to reclaim the religious (i.e., the sacred dimensions of reality) in education. Accordingly, the authors challenge educators in the church to develop ways for people to make meaning out of the interplay between religious experience and daily life. Fundamental to their challenge is shaping the "sacramental imagination"—seeing all of reality in light of God's incarnate presence in the world—so that the stories, images, and rituals of the church might "infuse the whole of our common life with a religious dimension."[123] Church members bring to the public order a sense of compassion honed by the images and stories of their tradition.[124]

There can be little doubt that the heritage of Christians offers them a profound formation in the inextricable linkage of love of God and love of neighbor (see Mark 12:29–31). Whether it is the passionate outcry of the prophet Isaiah against empty rituals (see Isa. 1:1–17) or Luke's parable of the so-called good Samaritan (see Luke 10:29–37) or the powerful rhetoric of interpreters such as Martin Luther King, Jr., educators have an extraordinarily rich tradition of stories and images from which to draw.[125] What the church has to contribute to the political order is, in the phrase of Walter Brueggemann, the language of "transformative imagination."[126] It is the educator's task to teach the church's communal language so that this imagination is formed for the good of the world.

But educators in the church also have something to gain from the public sphere precisely because the demands of citizenship enhance discipleship. John Coleman argues that the obligations of citizenship add three dimensions to Christian discipleship. First, citizenship widens the scope of one's love of neighbor; "the duties of citizenship protect the church from narrow parochial introspection."[127] To be conscious of one's obligation in the public sphere forces the person of faith to look beyond his or her own needs and to widen the horizon of concerns. It demands praying with one's eyes wide open, as it were, taking notice of the world's suffering.

In the second place, citizenship offers the opportunity for humbler service, for sharing in the day-to-day *ascesis* of giving form to a vision, for laboring in the "often intractable day-to-day reality of politics."[128] To participate in the public forum involves learning to speak in the language of secular warrants, rather than simply in the familiar terminology of faith. It asks the church to ground its proclamations in activity in the daily interactions of society; it demands the church become knowledgeable about the resolution of conflict, about economics, about food and transportation systems, and other issues so vital in the global village. Third, Coleman terms citizenship a demanding test of reality that provides an "experiential proving ground . . . for Christians to put flesh on their hopes for a transformed future based on the already achieved and transforming power of Christ in history."[129] Disciples who are citizens cannot merely proclaim "Lord, Lord" but must show how their hope that Christ has conquered death and sin makes a difference in *this* world.

If Coleman's argument is taken seriously, educators *must* look to the public responsibilities of the church as an essential dimension of their curriculum. Several implications follow.

IMPLICATIONS FOR RELIGIOUS EDUCATION

A decade ago Gabriel Moran suggested that religious educators needed to be bilingual. They needed, he claimed, to be able to speak both the language of their ecclesiastical tradition and of the educational realm.[130] Today we might say that this bilinguality extends to the responsibility of religious educators to engage in the pedagogies of both citizenship and discipleship. Educators must give access to the traditions of the church and to the understandings and skills prerequisite for participation in the common life. Otherwise, the educator has constricted the meaning of the church's mission. It is the responsibility of the religious educator, among others, to evangelize in such a manner as to engage civic concerns. John Coleman has said that "churches must regain a sense of their public role as corporate citizens. They can uniquely create forums for a moral culture of politics and economic life. They can provide shared 'neutral space' where politics can be pursued beyond mere naked interest."[131]

The obligation to form people for a dual commitment gives even more importance to the dynamics of teaching. To teach another the communal language of one's religious heritage implies immersing her or him in the great symbols, stories, and rituals that transform the imagination. To teach another the obligations of citizenship suggests practice in "translating" religious meanings into secular terminology. Religious education requires the artistry of the sacramental imagination and the pragmatics of public service.

To engage in these two pedagogies, religious educators themselves need to participate in the political realm at some level. This implies a commitment to study issues and to discuss them both within and beyond the boundaries of one's religious heritage. Religious educators also should consider linking with other agencies in the community with which they share a common agenda.[132]

Consider, for example, those agencies that, like the church, are committed to fostering brotherhood and sisterhood and eradicating racial hatred. Religious congregations can form their members in the "transformative imagination" by evoking, for example, the root metaphor of *covenant:* those bound to God in covenant are bonded to their brothers and sisters as well. Thus, in Boston about a decade ago, Jewish and Christian leaders concerned about the atmosphere of racial intolerance asked their congregants to sign a covenant pledging commitment to "justice, equity and harmony."[133] But not all people speak (or are persuaded by) the language of covenant. Other agencies beyond the confines of church and synagogue need to draw upon alternative languages, such as those that express the ideals of American life (e.g., the Bill of Rights), and to argue their cases in secular terms.

An excellent example is the recent work of the New England regional office of the National Conference of Christians and Jews (NCCJ) in sponsoring three programs to counter racism. A videotape of dramatic vignettes, "Minorities in the Mainstream," focused on issues of discrimination in the corporate world. A workshop for real estate professionals explored issues involved with fair housing. A curriculum on conflict resolution for elementary school students enabled young people to develop skills to confront prejudice.

Programs by agencies like the NCCJ deserve the support of church educators because they complement the symbols, stories, and rituals of particular religious traditions with others from this nation's heritage. To this end, every ministerial and educational group in the church (e.g., the directors of religious education in a diocese) ought to designate a liaison with agencies such as the NCCJ, Bread for the World, and neighborhood associations. If, as Moran has suggested, religious education is "the attempt to keep education open to the undreamt possiblities of the human race," its practitioners in the churches must find ways of embodying that vision in the world.[134] Only when religious educators in the church move beyond ecclesial boundaries will they become leaven.

NOTES

1. Douglas Sloan, *Insight-Imagination: The Emancipation of Thought and the Modern World* (Westport, CT: Greenwood, 1983), 201.
2. Houston Smith, *Beyond the Post-Modern Mind* (New York: Crossroad, 1982), p. 84.
3. Jerome Bruner, "Narrative and Paradigmatic Modes of Thought," in Elliot Eisner, ed., *Learning and Teaching the Ways of Knowing* (Chicago: University of Chicago Press, 1982), 99. Bruner's distinction roughly parallels that of Rudolf Arnheim, "The Double-edged Mind: Intuition and Intellect," in Eisner, ed., *Learning and Teaching the Ways of Knowing*, 77–96.

4. Northrop Frye, *The Educated Imagination* (Bloomington, IN: Indiana University Press, 1964), 24–25.

5. Elliot Eisner, "Aesthetic Modes of Knowing," in Eisner, ed., *Learning and Teaching the Ways of Knowing*, 23–36.

6. Elliot Eisner, *Cognition and Curriculum: A Basis for Deciding What To Teach* (New York and London: Longman, 1982), 74.

7. Ellen Berscheid, "Interpersonal Modes of Knowing," in Eisner, ed., *Learning and Teaching the Ways of Knowing*, 60–76.

8. Robert J. Sternberg and David R. Caruso, "Practical Modes of Knowing," in Eisner, ed., *Learning and Teaching the Ways of Knowing*, 133–58.

9. Barbara Rogoff and Jean Lave, eds., "Introduction," in *Everyday Cognition: Its Development in Social Context* (Cambridge, MA: Harvard University Press, 1984), 7.

10. "Rethinking the Value of Intelligence Tests," *New York Times* (9 November 1986), Section 12, p. 23.

11. Howard Gardner, *Frames of Mind: The Theory of Multiple Intelligences* (New York: Basic Books, 1985).

12. Maxine Greene, "'Excellence,' Meanings, and Multiplicity," *Teachers College Record* 86 (Winter 1984): 288. Cf. National Commission on Excellence in Education, *A Nation at Risk: The Imperative for Educational Reform* (Washington, DC: Government Printing Office, 1983).

13. Greene, "'Excellence,' Meanings, and Multiplicity," 287–88.

14. See especially Parker Palmer, *To Know as We Are Known: A Spirituality of Education* (San Francisco: Harper & Row, 1983); Dwayne Huebner, "Spirituality and Knowing," in Eisner, ed., *Learning and Teaching the Ways of Knowing*, 159–73.

15. Maria Harris, "Completion and Faith Development," in Craig Dykstra and Sharon Parks, eds., *Faith Development and Fowler* (Birmingham, AL: Religious Education Press, 1986), 117.

16. Ibid., 120.

17. Ibid., 118.

18. Thomas Groome, *Christian Religious Education: Sharing Our Story and Vision* (San Francisco: Harper & Row, 1980).

19. Jonathan Edwards, *The Works of President Edwards*, 10 vols. (New York: Burt Franklin, 1968), 4:168.

20. I borrow the phrase from Smith, *Beyond the Post-Modern Mind*, 87.

21. "What impairs our sight are habits of seeing as well as the mental concomitants of seeing. Our sight is suffused with knowing, instead of feeling painfully the lack of knowing what we see. The principle to be kept in mind is to know what we see rather than to see what we know." Abraham J. Heschel, in *The Prophets*, 2 vols. (New York: Harper & Row, Torchbooks, 1962), 1:xi.

22. See Mary Field Belenky, Blythe McVicker Clinchy, Nancy Rule Goldberger, and Jill Mattuck Tarule, *Women's Ways of Knowing: The Development of Self, Voice, and Mind* (New York: Basic Books, 1986), 18–19.

23. Jean Bethke Elshtain, "The New Feminist Scholarship," *Salmagundi* 70–71 (1986):4.

24. See my "Women as Leaven: Theological Education in the United States and Canada," in Elisabeth Schüssler Fiorenza and Mary Collins, eds., *Concilium* No.182 (Edinburgh: Clark, 1985), 114.

25. This is a phrase from Ronald Green (*Religious Reason* [New York: Oxford University Press, 1978]) used by Elizabeth Dodson Gray, *Patriarchy as a Conceptual Trap* (Wellesley, MA: Roundtable Press, 1982), 46.

26. Sandra Harding, *The Science Question in Feminism* (Ithaca, NY: Cornell University Press, 1986), 17.

27. Carol Gilligan, *In a Different Voice: Psychological Theory and Women's Development* (Cambridge, MA: Harvard University Press, 1977).

28. For a succinct contrast of Gilligan and Kohlberg, see Mary Brabeck, "Moral Judgment: Theory and Research on Differences between Males and Females," *Developmental Review* 3 (1983):275–91.

29. Ibid., 286.
30. Joan Tronto, "Beyond Gender Difference to a Theory of Care," *Signs* 12 (1987): 644–63.
31. Paul Philibert, "Relation, Consensus and Commitment as Foundations of Moral Growth," *New Studies in Psychology* 5/2 (1987):183–95.
32. Of their 135 subjects, 90 were at six schools (including a New York City public school serving "at risk" minority students and Wellesley College). The other 45 included women seeking assistance with parenting, mothers of children in a rural health program, teenage mothers, and women working to overcome a history of child abuse and family violence.
33. Belenky et al., *Women's Ways of Knowing*, 15.
34. Specifically, Belenky et al. are critical of William Perry, *Forms of Intellectual and Ethical Development in the College Years* (New York: Holt, Rinehart and Winston, 1970). Perry concludes, based on interviews with college students—mostly male—that all students give meaning to their educational experiences through a sequence of nine positions from dualism to commitment. See *Women's Ways of Knowing*, 9, 14–17 for their assessment of his methodology.
35. Belenky et al., *Women's Ways of Knowing*, 23.
36. Sara Ruddick, "Maternal Thinking," in Joyce Treblicot, ed., *Mothering: Essays in Feminist Theory* (Totowa, NJ: Rowman and Allanheld, 1983), 214.
37. Belenky et al., *Women's Ways of Knowing*, 69.
38. Ibid., 71.
39. Ibid., 83.
40. This phrase is from Nel Noddings, *Caring: A Feminine Approach to Ethics and Moral Education* (Berkeley: University of California Press, 1984), p. 1.
41. Belenky et al., *Women's Ways of Knowing*, 114.
42. Cited in Ibid., 113.
43. Ibid., 119.
44. Ibid., 139.
45. Ibid., 182.
46. Ibid., 217.
47. Jane Roland Martin, *Reclaiming a Conversation: The Ideal of the Educated Woman* (New Haven, CT, and London: Yale University Press, 1985), 6–7.
48. Ibid., 190.
49. Ibid., 196.
50. Ibid.
51. Ibid., 198–99.
52. Margaret Farley, "Feminist Theology and Bioethics," in Barbara Hilkert Andolsen, Christine E. Gudorf, and Mary D. Pellauer, eds., *Women's Consciousness, Women's Conscience* (Minneapolis, MN: Winston, 1985).
53. June O'Connor, "On Doing Religious Ethics," in Andolsen et al., eds., *Women's Consciousness, Women's Conscience*, 266.
54. Margaret Farley, "Sources of Sexual Inequality in the History of Christian Thought," *Journal of Religion* 56 (1976):165.
55. Elisabeth Schüssler Fiorenza, *In Memory of Her: A Feminist Theological Reconstruction of Christian Origins* (New York: Seabury, Harper & Row, 1983), 32–33. See also her *Bread Not Stone: The Challenge of Feminist Biblical Interpretation* (Boston: Beacon, 1984), 39–40.
56. Phyllis Trible, *God and the Rhetoric of Sexuality* (Philadelphia: Fortress, 1978), 69.
57. Elisabeth Schüssler Fiorenza, "Breaking the Silence—Becoming Visible," in Schüssler Fiorenza and Collins, eds., *Concilium* no. 182, 3–16.
58. Schüssler Fiorenza, *In Memory of Her*, 41.
59. Rosemary Radford Ruether, *Womanguides: Readings Toward a Feminist Theology* (Boston: Beacon, 1985), xii.
60. Ibid., xi.
61. See Schüssler Fiorenza, *In Memory of Her*, 16–21.

62. Jean Lambert, "An 'F Factor'? The New Testament in Some White, Feminist, Christian Theological Construction," *Journal of Feminist Studies in Religion* 1 (1985):113.

63. See, however, Carolyn Walker Bynum, *Jesus as Mother: Studies in the Spirituality of the High Middle Ages* (Berkeley: University of California Press, 1982), esp. 110–69.

64. Sallie McFague, *Metaphorical Theology* (Philadelphia: Fortress, 1982), 145–92.

65. Elizabeth Johnson, "The Incomprehensibility of God and the Image of God Male and Female," in Joann Wolski Conn, ed., *Women's Spirituality: Resources for Christian Development* (New York: Paulist, 1986), 257.

66. Ibid.

67. Anne Carr, "On Feminist Spirituality," in Conn, ed., *Women's Spirituality*, 96–97.

68. Joann Wolski Conn, "Women's Spirituality: Restriction and Reconstruction," in Conn, ed., *Women's Spirituality*, 9–10.

69. Carol Ochs, *Women and Spirituality* (Totowa, NJ: Rowman and Allanheld, 1983).

70. Patricia Meyer Spacks, "The Difference It Makes," in Elizabeth Langland and Walter Grove, eds., *A Feminist Perspective in the Academy* (Chicago: University of Chicago Press, 1983), 13.

71. See Mary Elizabeth Moore, *Education for Continuity and Change* (Nashville, TN: Abingdon, 1983), 176–77.

72. Margaret Anderson, "Changing the Curriculum in Higher Education," *Signs* 12 (1987):224. See Marilyn Schuster and Susan Van Dyne, eds., *Women's Place in the Academy: Transforming the Liberal Arts Curriculum* (Totowa, NJ: Rowman and Allanheld, 1985).

73. Adrienne Rich, *On Lies, Secrets, and Silence: Selected Prose 1966–1978* (New York: Norton, 1979), 245.

74. See my "Women's Role in Theological Research, Reflection and Communication," in Luke Salm, ed., *Proceedings of the Thirty-Seventh Annual Convention* 38 (Bronx, NY: The Catholic Theology Society of America), 58–62.

75. Ralf Dahrendorf, "Social Sciences," in Adam Kuper and Jessica Kuper, eds., *The Social Science Encyclopedia* (London: Routledge and Kegan Paul, 1985), 784.

76. See Maurice Duverger, *An Introduction to the Social Sciences* (New York: Praeger, 1964), 11–23.

77. See, for example, Andrew Greeley, William C. McCready, and Kathleen McCourt, *Catholic Schools in a Declining Church* (Kansas City, MO: Sheed and Ward, 1976).

78. See, for example, Dean R. Hoge et al., *Converts, Dropouts, Returnees: A Study of Religious Change Among Catholics* (Washington, DC, and New York: United States Catholic Conference and Pilgrim, 1981). Also, Dean R. Hoge and David A. Roozen, *Understanding Church Growth and Decline* (New York: Pilgrim, 1979).

79. See, for example, David Roozen, William McKinney, and Jackson W. Carroll, *Varieties of Religious Presence: Mission in Public Life* (New York: Pilgrim, 1984).

80. See Werner Stark, "Sociology of Knowledge," in Paul Edwards, ed., *The Encyclopedia of Philosophy*, 8 vols. (New York: Macmillan, 1967), 7:474–78.

81. Matthew Lamb, "The Challenge of Critical Theory," in Gregory Baum, ed., *Sociology and Human Destiny* (New York: Seabury, 1980), 185.

82. Groome, *Christian Religious Education*, 174. This second movement is also influenced by Groome's attention to "knowing" as used in the Scriptures.

83. William Bean Kennedy, "Ideology and Education: A Fresh Approach for Religious Education," *Religious Education* 80 (1985):337.

84. Ibid., 343.

85. *Sharing the Light of Faith: National Catechetical Directory for Catholics of the United States* (Washington, DC: United States Catholic Conference, 1979), esp. #s 174–176, 177–180, 182–184.

86. Ana-Maria Rizzuto, *The Birth of the Living God* (Chicago: University of Chicago Press, 1979). "Object relations" is a psychoanalytic theory that emphasizes the formative character of personal relationships in the development of the human psyche.

87. See Craig Dykstra, "Faith Development and Religious Education," in Dykstra and Parks, eds., *Faith Development and Fowler,* 256.

88. James W. Fowler, *Becoming Adult, Becoming Christian* (San Francisco: Harper & Row, 1984), 51–52.

89. Sharon Parks, "Imagination and Spirit in Faith Development," in Dykstra and Parks, eds., *Faith Development and Fowler,* 140.

90. James W. Fowler, *Stages of Faith* (San Francisco: Harper & Row, 1981), 49. In his earlier writings, Fowler spoke of six stages; now he includes the infant's "primal stage."

91. Cited in Dykstra and Parks, eds., *Faith Development and Fowler,* 261. Cf. Fowler, "Dialogue Toward a Future in Faith Development Studies," (Dykstra and Parks, eds., *Faith Development and Fowler,* 295), who quotes Huebner as speaking of a "scaffolding of remembering."

92. See also Fowler's chart on pp. 244–45 of *Stages of Faith,* as well as that of Walter Conn, *Christian Conversion: A Developmental Interpretation of Autonomy and Self-Surrender* (New York: Paulist, 1986), 37. For an especially articulate explication of Fowler, see Sharon Parks, *The Critical Years: The Young Adult Search for a Faith to Live By* (San Francisco: Harper & Row, 1986), esp. 9–72. Groome gives a brief account, *Christian Religious Education,* 66–73.

93. Sharon Parks, "Young Adult Faith Development: Teaching in the Context of Theological Education," *Religious Education* 77 (1982): 657–72; *The Critical Years,* 73–106.

94. Conn, *Christian Conversion,* 157.

95. Fowler, *Becoming Adult, Becoming Christian,* 52. See also *Stages of Faith,* xiii.

96. Gabriel Moran, *Religious Education Development: Images for the Future* (Minneapolis, MN: Winston, 1983), 12–126. Cf. Craig Dykstra, "What Is Faith? An Experiment in the Hypothetical Mode," in Dykstra and Parks, eds., *Faith Development and Fowler,* 45–64.

97. Fowler, "Dialogue Toward a Future in Faith Development Studies," 285.

98. John McDargh, "Faith Development Theory at Ten Years," *Religious Studies Review* 10 (1984): 341–42.

99. Carl Schneider, "Faith Development and Pastoral Diagnosis," in Dykstra and Parks, eds., *Faith Development and Fowler,* 241.

100. Ibid., 241–48.

101. See K. Brynolf Lyon and Don S. Browning, "Faith Development and the Requirements of Care," in Dykstra and Parks, eds., *Faith Development and Fowler,* 209.

102. See John McDargh, "Theological Uses of Psychology: Retrospective and Prospective," *Horizons* 12 (1985):247–64.

103. See Don S. Browning, *Religious Thought and the Modern Psychologies: A Critical Conversation in the Theology of Culture* (Philadelphia: Fortress, 1987).

104. Sharon Parks, "Imagination and Spirit in Faith Development," in Dykstra and Parks, eds., *Faith Development and Fowler,* 156, n. 28.

105. James Fowler, "Pluralism, Particularity, and Paideia," *Journal of Law and Religion* 2 (1984):263–307.

106. John Coleman,"A Possible Role for Biblical Religion in Public Life," *Theological Studies* 40 (1979):706.

107. Robert Bellah, Richard Madsen, William M. Sullivan, Ann Swidler, and Steven M. Tipton, *Habits of the Heart* (Berkeley: University of California Press, 1985).

108. Alan Peshkin, *God's Choice: The Total World of a Fundamentalist Christian School* (Chicago: University of Chicago Press, 1986), 295.

109. Ibid.

110. Martin Marty, *The Public Church* (New York: Crossroad, 1981), 103.

111. Ibid., 3.

112. Ibid., 136–37.

113. In Joseph Gremillion, ed., *The Gospel of Peace and Justice: Catholic Social Teaching Since Pope John* (Maryknoll, NY: Orbis, 1976), 514.

114. Roger D. Haight, "The 'Established' Church as Mission: The Relation of the Church to the Modern World," *The Jurist* 39 (1979):11–19.
115. Ibid., 11.
116. Ibid., 24.
117. Ibid., 26.
118. Ibid., 38.
119. Madonna Kolbenschlag, "Introduction: The American Experience," in Madonna Kolbenschlag, ed., *Between God and Caesar: Priests, Sisters and Political Office in the United States* (New York: Paulist, 1985), 6–7.
120. Richard P. McBrien, *Caesar's Coin: Religion and Politics in America* (New York: Macmillan, 1987), 47–49.
121. Ibid., 20.
122. Jack L. Seymour, Robert T. O'Gorman, and Charles R. Foster, *The Church in the Education of the Public* (Nashville, TN: Abingdon, 1984), 21.
123. Ibid., 145.
124. See Karen Lebacqz, "Paul Revere and the Holiday Inn," in Nelle Slater, ed., *Tensions Between Citizenship and Discipleship: A Case Study* (New York: Pilgrim, forthcoming).
125. See James M. Washington, ed., *A Testament of Hope: The Essential Writings of Martin Luther King, Jr.* (San Francisco: Harper & Row, 1986).
126. Walter Brueggemann, "2 Kings 18–19: The Legitimacy of a Sectarian Hermeneutic," in Mary C. Boys, ed., *Education for Citizenship and Discipleship* (New York: Pilgrim, forthcoming).
127. John Coleman, "The Two Pedagogies: Discipleship and Citizenship," in Boys, ed., *Education for Citizenship and Discipleship.*
128. Ibid.
129. Ibid.
130. Gabriel Moran, "Two Languages of Religious Education," *The Living Light* 14 (1977):7–15.
131. John Coleman, "Beginning the Civic Conversation" (paper given to the National Faculty Seminar, Christian Theological Seminary, Indianapolis, IN, 6 February 1987), 8.
132. See Seymour et al., *The Church in the Education of the Public,* 151.
133. "The Covenant for Justice, Equity and Harmony" reads:
Because as People of Faith we believe we are both brothers and sisters and the creatures of one God:
Because as Americans we are committed to the fundamental constitutional principle that all people are created equal and are endowed with certain inalienable rights to life, liberty, and the pursuit of happiness;
Because we know that Freedom for everyone is the only climate conducive to full development of the human spirit;
And because we have witnessed in our society and in our city enough of conflict and violence so as to threaten the very fabric of our freedoms and diminish the dignity of all: Be it here resolved:
(1) That we seize the moment for a new day of peace and harmony in our common existence;
(2) That in our deeper reverence for the God who commands us and for the nobility of humankind that impels us, we denounce every form of violence in every neighborhood, we lay aside the weapons and words of political conflict, the taunts and jibes of insidious disrespect;
(3) That we reject outright any and all special interest groups and leaderships that serve only to deepen our divisions and entrench us, angered, into separate camps.
(4) That we perceive the legitimate struggles for equal justice and rights for everyone not as a cause that divides us, but as the imperative that unites us;
(5) That we [not] only respect but even celebrate the richness of our varied cultures, manners and traditions as they each, and together, contribute to the unique tapestry of our city.

(6) That in prayer, in attitudes, we foster a new mood of healing and forgiveness so that we transcend not only our differences but even our grievances.

(7) That here and now, at this time and in this city, we stand committed to bring fulfillment to a dream that must compel us all: "When all God's children, black people and white people, Jews and Gentiles, Catholics, Protestants, and Muslims will be able to join hands and sing . . . 'Free at least. Free at last. Thank God Almighty we are free at last!!!

Free! right here in Boston. Free! from violence.

Free! from hatred. Free! from fear of one another.

Free! to live together. Free! to learn together.

Free! to build together. Free! to celebrate together.

Free! to pray to God together.'"

May God the Merciful witness our covenant, and out of the harmony of our differences may He grant us unison, in will and wisdom, to keep it (in Timothy W. Sweet, ed., *Boston Catholic Directory* 39 [1987], 264).

134. Gabriel Moran, *Interplay: A Theory of Religion and Education* (Winona, MN: Saint Mary's Press, 1981), 62.

Bibliographic Essay

Movements on the Horizon: Developments and Directions

This chapter itself provides an overview of the new developments I find particularly important for religious education today and includes many bibliographic references that I consider vital to the contemporary discussion. Thus in the following essay I will restrict my references to works not cited in chapter 7 and works that are so foundational to my own thinking that they bear repeating.

WAYS OF KNOWING

In the current work on ways of knowing, Susanne Langer's book, *Philosophy in a New Key: A Study in the Symbolism of Reason, Rite, and Art* (Cambridge, MA: Harvard University Press, 1957), contributes to the discussion of aesthetic education and the role of imagination. See also Elliot Eisner, *The Educational Imagination* (2d rev. ed, New York: Macmillan, 1985) and *Cognition and Curriculum* (New York: Longman, 1982). Jerome Bruner situates his work in his *In Search of Mind: Essays in Autobiography* (New York: Harper & Row, 1983).

The exhaustive treatment of "religious instruction" by James Michael Lee in his trilogy, *The Shape of Religious Instruction* (Dayton, OH: Pflaum, 1971); *The Flow of Religious Instruction* (Dayton, OH: Pflaum, 1973); and *The Content of Religious Instruction* (Birmingham, AL: Religious Education Press, 1985) makes the social science approach central to the epistemology of religious education.

In a work in progress (tentatively titled *Shared Praxis;* forthcoming publication by Harper & Row), Thomas H. Groome is attempting to reclaim from classical Western philosophy a notion of knowing that is grounded in practice and essentially connected to values—with rich implications for religious education. For a fine anthology of writings on the affective character of religious commitment, see Roger Lundin and Mark A. Noll, eds., *Voices from the Heart: Four Centuries of American Piety* (Grand Rapids, MI: Eerdmans, 1987). Forthcoming is Nathan O. Hatch and Harry S. Stout, *Jonathan Edwards and the American Experience* (New York: Oxford University Press, 1988).

FEMINIST VOICES

There is a burgeoning literature across the disciplines. I recommend as foundational Gerda Lerner, *The Creation of Patriarchy*, Women and History Series, vol. 1 (New York: Oxford University Press, 1986). Works that survey the meaning of the feminist perspective include M. Vetterling-Braggin, F. A. Elliston, and J. English, eds., *Feminisim and Philosophy* (Totowa, NJ: Littlefield, Adams, 1978); J. A. Sherman and E. Torton Beck, eds., *The Prism of Sex: Essays in the Sociology of Knowledge* (Madison, WI: University of Wisconsin Press, 1979); and Sandra Harding and M. B. Hintakka, eds., *Discovering Reality* (Dordrecht and Boston:

Reidel, 1983). Gloria Bowles and Rente Duelli Klein, eds., *Theories of Women's Studies* (London: Routledge and Kegan Paul, 1983) has appended a fine annotated bibliography. Also, Josephine Donovan, *Feminist Theory: The Intellectual Traditions of American Feminism* (New York: Ungar, 1985) and Marilyn Boxer, "For and About Women: The Theory and Practice of Women's Studies in the United States," *Signs* 7 (1982): 661–95.

Among works specifically on education, see especially Marilyn R. Schuster and Susan R. Van Dyne, *Women's Place in the Academy: Transforming the Liberal Arts Curriculum* (Totowa, NJ: Rowman and Allanheld, 1985). Also pertinent is Sharon Lee Rich and Ariel Phillips, eds., *Women's Experience and Education*, Harvard Educational Review Reprint Series #17 (Cambridge, MA: Harvard University Press, 1985). The "conversational partners" cited by Jane Roland Martin in *Reclaiming a Conversation: The Ideal of the Educated Woman* (New Haven, CT, and London: Yale University Press, 1985) are: *Plato's Republic*, trans. G. M. A. Grube (Indianapolis, IN: Hackett, 1974); Jean Jacques Rousseau, *Emile*, trans. Allan Bloom (New York: Basic Books, 1979); Mary Wollstonecraft, *A Vindication of the Rights of Woman*, ed. Charles W. Hagelman, Jr. (New York: Norton, 1967); Catharine Beecher, *A Treatise on Domestic Economy* (New York: Schocken, 1977); and Charlotte Perkins Gilman, *Herland* (New York: Pantheon, 1979).

See also Kathleen Weiler, *Women Teaching for Change: Gender, Class & Power* (South Hadley, MA: Bergin & Garvey, 1988); and Madeleine R. Grumet, *Bitter Milk: Women and Teaching* (Amherst, MA: The University of Massachusetts Press, 1988).

Works that complement Mary Belenky et al., *Women's Ways of Knowing: The Development of Self, Voice, and Mind* (New York: Basic Books, 1986) are Jean Baker Miller, *Toward a New Psychology of Women* (Boston: Beacon, 1976) and Ruthellen Josselson, *Finding Herself: Pathways to Identity Development in Women* (San Francisco: Jossey-Bass, 1987). *The Journal of Moral Education* devotes an entire issue (16/3 [1987]) to "Feminist Perspectives on Moral Education and Development."

In terms of theological and religious education, see The Cornwall Collective, *Your Daughters Shall Prophesy: Feminist Alternatives in Theological Education* (New York: Pilgrim, 1980); The Mud Flower Collective, *God's Fierce Whimsy: Christian Feminism and Theological Education* (New York: Pilgrim, 1985); and Fern M. Giltner, ed., *Women's Issues in Religious Education* (Birmingham, AL: Religious Education Press, 1985).

Though I have cited many works by feminist theorists in this chapter, I call attention to the inclusion of feminist perspectives in earlier chapters. For instance, I have sought to integrate the work of feminist historians in my account of the classic expressions. I refer readers especially to the authors cited in the bibliographic essay accompanying chapter 2 (e.g., the Ruether-Skinner documentary histories, James, Epstein et al.).

A number of new journals are already making their mark. Among the most important are *Journal of Feminist Studies in Religion*, Membership Services, P.O. Box 1608, Decatur, GA 30031-1608; *Signs: Journal of Women in Culture and Society*, The University of Chicago Press, Journals Division, P.O. Box 37005, Chicago, IL 60637; and *Gender and Society* (official publication of Sociologists for Women in Society), Sage Publications, Inc., 275 South Beverly Drive, Beverly Hills, CA 90212.

In this bibliographic essay I have chosen also to integrate feminist perspectives on knowing, the social sciences, and the public church under those categories. In the bibliographic essay accompanying chapter 8, I cite feminist sources on teaching.

THE PERSPECTIVES OF THE SOCIAL SCIENCES

The work of Peter Berger illustrates what I have called the "second stream of sociological study," concerned with history, philosophy, and theology. See especially his *The Social Construction of Reality: A Treatise in the Sociology of Knowledge* (with Thomas Luckmann [New York: Irvington, 1966]) and *The Heretical Imperative: Contemporary Possibilities of Religious Affirmation* (Garden City, NY: Doubleday, Anchor Press, 1979).

For a fascinating perspective on Carol Gilligan, see Paul J. Philibert, "Addressing the Crisis in Moral Theory: Clues from Aquinas and Gilligan," *Theology Digest* 34/2 (1987): 103–13. On faith development theory, the article by John McDargh cited in this chapter, "Faith Development Theory at Ten Years" (*Religious Studies Review* 10 [1984]:341–42) is a helpful survey of the current literature. See also Diane Jonte-Pace, "Object Relations Theory, Mothering and Religion," *Horizons* 14 (1987): 310–27. Craig Dykstra and Sharon Parks, eds., *Faith Development and Fowler* (Birmingham, AL: Religious Education Press, 1986) is a more recent collection of essays by Fowler and others on the present state of faith development theory and new possibilities for its future. Sharon Parks's book *The Critical Years: The Young Adult Search for a Faith To Live By* (San Francisco: Harper & Row, 1986) is the subject of a "Review Symposium," in *Horizons* 14 (1987): 343–63.

Social science references for definitions and divisions of the field include: Adam Kuper and Jessica Kuper, eds., *The Social Science Encyclopedia* (London: Routledge and Kegan Paul, 1985); and *International Encyclopedia of Social Science*, ed. David L. Sills (New York: Macmillan and Free Press, 1968). For a critique of social science methodology, see Shulamit Reinharz, *On Becoming a Social Scientist: From Survey Research and Participant Observation to Experiential Analysis* (San Francisco: Jossey-Bass, 1979) and Helen Roberts, ed., *Doing Feminist Research* (London: Routledge and Kegan Paul, 1981).

THE PUBLIC CHURCH

My work on this topic has been influenced by my membership on the National Faculty Seminar, whose members have two volumes in press: Mary C. Boys, ed., *Education for Citizenship and Discipleship* (New York: Pilgrim) and Nelle Slater, ed., *Tensions Between Citizenship and Discipleship: A Case Study* (New York: Pilgrim).

In the Catholic tradition, much of this discussion is shaped by John Courtney Murray. See *We Hold These Truths: Catholic Reflections on the American Proposition* (New York: Sheed and Ward, 1960; reprint 1985); also his articles "The Problem of Religious Freedom," *Theological Studies* 25 (1964):503–75, and "The Issue of Church and State at Vatican II," *Theological Studies* 27 (1966):580–606.

Valuable are A. James Reichley, *Religion in American Public Life* (Washington, DC: The Brookings Institution, 1985); Mary Douglas and Steven M. Tipton, eds., *Religion and America* (Boston: Beacon, 1983); Robert N. Bellah and Frederick E. Greenspahn, eds., *Uncivil Religion: Interreligious Hostility in America* (New York: Crossroad, 1987); Martin E. Marty, *Religion and Republic: The American*

Circumstance (Boston: Beacon, 1987); and Max L. Stackhouse, *Public Theology and Poltical Economy* (Grand Rapids, MI: Eerdmans, 1987).

The entire May 1987 issue of *Educational Leadership* is devoted to articles on religion and public schools.

CHAPTER 8

Marking Out the Boundaries: A Way of Thinking About Religious Education

The other thing I wish to say here is that maps lie. Even the best of maps, those in the Kitab of al-Idrisi, are liars, and they cannot help being liars. That is because everything shown on a map appears measurable by the same standards, and that is a delusion. For one instance, suppose your journey must take you over a mountain. The map can warn you of that mountain before you get to it, and even indicate more or less how high and wide and long it is, but the map cannot tell you what will be the conditions of terrain and weather when you get there—or what condition *you* will be in. A mountain that can be easily scaled on a good day in high summer by a young man [woman] in prime health may be a mountain considerably more forbidding in the cold and gales of winter, to a man [woman] enfeebled by age or illness and wearied by all the country he [she] has already traversed. Because the limited representations of a map are thus deceptive, it may take a journeyer longer to travel the last little fingerbreadth of distance across a map than it took him [her] to travel all the many handspans previous.[1]

Having sustained the metaphor of a map throughout this book, I offer this reprise, gleaned from a delightful novel. What I have written in the first six chapters is a "lie." It's *my* rendering of what traversing the mountain entailed. Each reader needs to make his or her annotations.

In the previous chapter and now in this one, my aim is to lay out as clearly as possible my own vision of the territory. By offering my emendations, I hope to stimulate readers to articulate their own. In this final chapter, therefore, I will articulate my view of religious education. As will be immediately apparent, it is a vision shaped by my standpoints as a Western, white, middle-class, feminist, Catholic woman. I am acutely conscious it is not the whole picture. As the novelist says, "The overland journeyer knows the same sensation that a man [woman] feels when he [she] is stark naked—a fine sense of unfettered freedom, but also a sense of being vulnerable, unprotected and, compared to the world about him [her], very small."[2]

My way of proceeding is straightforward: I will offer a definition of the field, explicate its basic elements, and link them to the foundational questions outlined in the initial chapter.

RELIGIOUS EDUCATION: A DEFINITION

Religious education is the making accessible of the traditions of the religious community and the making manifest of the intrinsic connection between traditions and transformation.

My definition has four fundamental elements: tradition and transformation, and the activities of "making accessible" and "making manifest." I shall take each in turn.

TRADITIONS

For many, the term "tradition" is problematic, since it seems to imply a fixation with the past and a resting place in the status quo. Such a judgment, however, fails to acknowledge how essential the past is to the present. Perhaps the disregard for tradition results from a confusion identified by historian Jaroslav Pelikan: "Tradition is the living faith of the dead; traditionalism is the dead faith of the living" and "it is traditionalism that gives tradition such a bad name."[3]

Thinking of tradition as the "living faith of the dead" highlights its grounding in human experience. Sociologist Edward Shils claims that what constitutes tradition at its most basic is the handing on from one generation to the next that which human actions have created:

Tradition—that which is handed down—includes material objects, beliefs about all sorts of things, images of persons and events, practices and institutions. It includes buildings, monuments, landscapes, sculptures, paintings, books, tools, machines. It includes all that a society of a given time possesses and which already existed when its present possessors came upon it and which is not solely the product of physical process in the external world or exclusively the result of ecological and physiological necessity.[4]

Thus, tradition is a "reservoir of community experience"; it is a "saga of experiences and their interpretation."[5] When a sacred text (e.g., Scripture, the U.S. Constitution) is passed on, for instance, each generation receives not only that text, but the body of interpretations that also constitute a tradition. And these interpretative traditions may conflict. Witness, for example, the debate over so-called loose and strict readings of the Constitution or the controversy spawned in biblical study by the application of a newer tradition, historiography, to what had been largely regarded as a "timeless text." Of course, even within a single stream of interpretations, variants exist. As Shils observes, "Within the 'same' tradition there are not only levels of differentiation and specificity in possession, but also substantively different interpretations and emphases."[6]

Another helpful distinction is that between *content*—that which is handed on—and the *process* of handing on. There is both a *traditium*, the material being transmitted, and a *traditio*, the process of passing material from one generation to the next. Through this process of transmission, the community of the present connects with people in other times and places. In Edward Burke's phrase, tradition reflects a "partnership not only between those who are living, but between those who are living, those who are dead, and those who are to be born."[7]

Furthermore, tradition is both conserving and liberating. On the one hand, it refers to that which a person or group desires to have preserved; on the other, it applies to the situation in which an "artifact" is freed from its moorage in the past in order to be applied in a new context.[8] Tradition is the past preserved and reactualized. James Barr observes that although the Bible seems on the first level to narrate the past, on a deeper level it speaks of the future and for the future.[9] So too tradition.

In fact, the process of composing the Bible is a prime model of the dynamics of traditioning. At various junctures in their history, Israel and the early church preserved interpretation-laden memories about constitutive events, such as the Exodus and the death and resurrection of Jesus. These traditions served as building materials for each community to recreate itself in changed circumstances. Second Isaiah (Isaiah 40–55) reappropriated Exodus imagery to console the exiles in Babylon in the sixth century B.C.E. Even though the Exodus had been Israel's "root experience,"[10] the "mother memory," Isaiah dared to put the image to new use: an even greater thing would be done by the God who had freed the exiles' ancestors in Egypt over seven hundred years earlier (Isa. 43: 18–19):

> Remember not the former things,
>   nor consider the things of old.
> Behold, I am doing a new thing;
>   now it springs forth, do you not perceive it?
> I will make a way in the wilderness
>   and rivers in the desert.

And because Ezekiel remembered his people's origins, how the Creator breathed life into the dirt and fashioned it into a living being, he can console Israel that its dry bones will rise (Ezek. 37:11b–14):

"Behold, they say, 'Our bones are dried up, and our hope is lost; we are clean cut off.' Therefore prophesy, and say to them, Thus says the Lord God: Behold, I will open your graves, and raise you from your graves, O my people; and I will bring you home into the land of Israel. And you shall know that I am the

Lord, when I open your graves, and raise you from your graves, O my people. And I will put my Spirit within you and you shall live, and I will place you in your own land; then you shall know that I, the Lord, have spoken, and I have done it, says the Lord."

And because the disciples of Jesus knew these traditions, they understood Jesus as the one who, like God, makes all things new. The Fourth Gospel tells of the risen Jesus returning to the upper room, greeting his disciples with peace, and then breathing upon them—the genesis of the recreated community (John 20:22). Mark and Matthew preserve a saying, "new wine is for fresh skins" (Mark 2:22; Matt. 9:17). In the new Jerusalem of the book of Revelation, Jesus says, "Behold, I make all things new" (21:5).

Because the members of the early church were so steeped in tradition, their image for a faith-filled future was that of the new creation. Paul reminded the Corinthians: "Therefore, if any one is in Christ, he [she] is a new creation; the old has passed away, behold, the new has come" (2 Cor. 5:17). To the Galatians, preoccupied by past strictures, he wrote: "For neither circumcision counts for anything, nor uncircumcision, but a new creation" (6:15). In the same letter he quoted a baptismal confession that served as the key theological self-understanding of the Christian missionary movement: "There is neither Jew nor Greek, there is neither slave nor free, there is neither male nor female; for you are all one in Christ Jesus" (3:28). In the community of the new creation, whatever distinctions still exist are insignificant; a new kinship has been formed that obliterates distinctions with regard to nationality, political status, and sex and gender roles. All the baptized are equal.

This vision, of course, was not sustained, in part because it stood at such tension with societal norms. The institutions of slavery and patriarchy were so entrenched that the symbol of the new creation could not penetrate the rigid boundaries of time-bound customs. Elisabeth Schüssler Fiorenza observes that conversion and baptism into Christ *for men* "implied a much more radical break with their former social and religious self-understanding—especially for those who were also wealthy slave owners—than it did for women and slaves."[11] Thus the tradition of radical newness was lost. It remains a tradition to be reclaimed nearly two millennia later.

Biblical scholar Paul Achtemeier summarizes the process of handing on traditions:

As new situations arise they are understood in the framework of traditions that grew out of past situations, but these in turn are then reinterpreted for the present. . . . Hence, although the past informs and thus shapes the future, the past is also open to the *dynamic* process of growth and interpretive change. As a result, each successive new generation has an enlarged traditional base from which to draw its own understanding of itself and its new situation [emphasis added].[12]

Achtemeier's identification of the dynamic process of utilizing the past is critical for a proper grasp of why I consider tradition so essential to religious education. Traditions constitute a storehouse from which a community shapes its self-understanding. It selects traditions as sources for survival and growth amidst new realities. Always the changed context stimulates rethinking of the past. What happened before thus lies open to numerous possible understandings. The past is always open, never finished.

Precisely because the past is both determinative yet unfinished, feminist writers scrutinize history, questioning its categories, assumptions, and canons. They search for hitherto overlooked sources and seek to uncover clues that point to alternative traditions. Convinced that "our heritage is our power," feminists know that the way the story of the past is told shapes the present order.[13] For example, Bernadette Brooten argues that reconstructing the cultural context of early Christian women necessitates a shift of emphasis so that women are in the center of the frame. Accordingly, the categories formulated to understand the history of man may no longer be adequate, nor the traditional historical periods and canons of literature may not provide an appropriate framework for writing women's history. New types of questions need to be asked, and new sources sought: ". . . it is absolutely necessary that we cast the net as widely as possible drawing upon hitherto overlooked sources, such as nonliterary documents (inscriptions, papyri), monumental remains, art, funerary remains, the few literary fragments and works composed by women, as well as women's oral traditions quoted in literary sources."[14] Feminists know that, indeed, the past is always open, never finished.

In sum, tradition is both *traditium* and *traditio,* both the past preserved and the past reactualized. It is, as Wilfred Cantwell Smith observes, the "historical construct in continuous and continuing construction, of those who participate in it.[15] For Smith, tradition and faith ("the act one makes, oneself, naked before God") are the two fundamental realities of the religious life of humankind. Faith is deeply personal—the individual's stance. Tradition expresses a community's embodiments of faith over time in particular historical situations; it is cumulative and multidimensional.

TRADITION AND REVELATION, BELIEF AND THEOLOGY

I am aware that the importance I accord tradition flows in part from my Catholic roots. Let me describe briefly—since a full treatment would demand a book on each topic—how tradition affects my understanding of revelation, belief and faith, and the role of theology. By so doing, I am making transparent the basics of these questions so foundational to religious education.

For all the words written about revelation, which has virtually preoccupied theologians of the twentieth century, it remains an elusive reality.

I propose, however, two starting points: the past has power in giving meaning to the present and direction to the future; and coming to faith is not a solipsistic encounter with the Divine but an irrevocably historical and communal activity. Revelation means that certain events from the past are constitutive; in the Jewish and Christian traditions, it points to the Creator's involvement in creation. God is present—but elusively so. So the revelatory moments are always cloaked in symbolic language and the events never described at the level of mere fact. We can never grasp entirely "what really happened," never penetrate the mysterious encounter of those who have "met" God, yet we rely on the testimony of our ancestors in faith as pointing us to God's "will."

Revelation is scandalously particular. Jews and Christians talk about God's being made manifest in strange forms—a burning bush, a still small voice—and of appropriating an ancient treaty form, the covenant, to make a pledge of mutual fidelity. They understand that revelation makes demands, first Jews, then also Christians understanding their responsibility to be a "light to the nations" (see Isa. 60:3; Acts 13:47).

To continue with the image of light: Christians "see" the God who dwells in inaccessible light through the face of Jesus, whom God has "transfigured" in the resurrection. In turn, Christians, through the Spirit's power, are being transfigured into his likeness (see 2 Cor. 3:18) and are called to discipleship. This is a summons to conversion: "Do not be conformed to this world but be transformed by the renewal of your mind, that you may prove what is the will of God, what is good and acceptable and perfect" (Rom. 12:2).

And though God's radiance has been revealed in its full intensity in Jesus of Nazareth, the light continues to be diffused through the witness of faithful human beings through the ages. The revelatory process continues through the Spirit's presence in the world. And it is this same Spirit who illumines the church's "reading" of revelatory events so that its members can live in the light of truth.

The classic text of the divine-human encounter—sacred Scripture—is inextricably linked with the community's reading of it, so one can never equate the revelatory process with an unmediated encounter with the text alone. Moreover, not all interpretations, whether from a scholar's vantage point or from "lived experience," are equally valid readings—hence the need for a norming body, some way of determining authority.

In Catholicism, this norming body is a "magisterium," the teaching office that ultimately arbitrates between conflicting traditions. It is not the source of revelation, but rather the arbiter of a community's assessment of which traditions are constitutive.

What is misleading is that narrow conception of the magisterium that equates the teaching office with the papacy and episcopacy. This understanding differs from that of the apostolic era, in which teachers had authority by virtue of their knowledge rather than simply by office.[16]

Nor does it reflect the more differentiated view of the Middle Ages, when the magisterium included the authority of the pope, the bishops' collective authority, the consensus of theologians, and the consensus of the faithful. Nor does Thomas Aquinas's distinction between the "magisterium of the pastoral or episcopal chair" and the "magisterium of the teaching chair" prevail today.

But a number of contemporary theologians suggest reclaiming such earlier views. Avery Dulles has utilized Thomas's distinction to propose that Catholics might appropriately look to two complementary and mutually corrective magisteria: pastors and theologians.[17] Although during the past ten years it has seemed that Dulles's proposal and similar arguments have been rejected in Vatican circles, I think the more differentiated understandings of the magisterium will eventually have their day.

Moreover, as a feminist, I find Dulles's mandate a *sine qua non* for a more catholic understanding of authority. With too few exceptions, magisterial formulations have been articulated by men, especially by white, European clerics. Such a relatively homogeneous group simply cannot reflect the diverse range of human experience, so its articulation of what is normative rests upon an insufficient foundation. As a consequence, significant traditions that provide other perspectives on doctrinal concerns have been overlooked or suppressed. Until women and people of color participate fully in both the pastoral and theological magisteria, the assessment of normative traditions will be faulty.

Looked at from another angle, one of the persistent problems of Catholicism is that, in Rosemary Haughton's terms, "Mother Church" has been allowed too often to dominate "Sophia." Haughton says that "the Catholic thing" is expressed in the interplay of the twin figures of "Mother Church" and "Sophia." Mother Church, though a dedicated person, deeply concerned about her children, patient, and imperturbable, even unshockable,

is extremely inclined to feel that her will and God's are identical. In her eyes there can be no better, no other, way than hers. . . . She is hugely self-satisfied, and her judgement, while experienced, is often insensitive and therefore cruel. She is suspicious of eccentricity and new ideas, since her own are so clearly effective, and non-conformists get a rough time, though after they are dead she often feels differently about them.

This is Mother Church, a crude, dominating, violent, loving, deceitful, compassionate old lady, a person to whom one cannot be indifferent, whom one may love much and yet fight against, whom one may hate and yet respect.[18]

Sophia, on the other hand, plays freely and charismatically, resists conformity, and refuses to be bound by institutional sclerosis. Most importantly, Sophia is immortal, whereas Mother Church is mortal. Sophia will prevail![19]

Though I take issue with the way the magisterium presently functions in Catholicism, I nevertheless regard it as important. There needs to be, I believe, some way that a church body can identify which traditions are constitutive for its life and which traditions need either to be reclaimed or rejected as no longer appropriate. Traditions that served the church in one era may be destructive in another. Not all the past is equally "usable"—but it cannot be ignored. Anne Carr's description of her work as a feminist theologian describes the methodology necessary to judge traditions:

In my work on feminist theology some form of "critical correlation" is implicitly or explicitly at work. As a *Christian* theologian, I am committed to reflection on the central symbols, doctrines, history, and practice of Christian faith. . . . As a *feminist* theologian, I am committed to the women's movement and its tradition of praxis and scholarship. In working at the juncture of two movements or traditions, I draw on both Christian and feminist sources to suggest connections, correspondences, contradictions in the relationships between Christianity and the situation of women in the churches and in society. And since official Christianity and feminism are frequently at odds, "critical correlation" better express-es the character of the Christian feminist theological task today. Both traditions call for a mutually critical analysis and assessment that leads to theological inter-pretation that is both feminist and Christian.[20]

It follows that I, like Carr, assign significance to assent to creeds.[21] A church that places emphasis on defining normative traditions obviously grants "pride of place" to carefully crafted formulations of the community's beliefs. It rejects the assertion that it doesn't matter what people believe as long as they are sincere—the community's faith cannot be interpreted arbitrarily in any way. But what an understanding of tradi-tion contributes to this is a proper contextualizing of beliefs. Every credo arose in time; every formula of faith was fashioned in response to a particular crisis. Every statement must be read in its literary and histor-ical context.[22] Creeds, moreover, properly belong in a context of wor-ship. As the axiom of Prosper of Aquitaine (d. 460) says, *"Lex orandi, lex credendi,"* "the law of praying is the law of believing." And every creedal statement must be examined in terms of what fruits it bears in daily life. Orthodoxy and orthopraxis are integrally related.

Furthermore, assent to dogma—formally defined doctrines—and oth-er teachings of the church ought never to be confused with faith, that primordial response to God's love that lies beyond words. Beliefs are *formulations* of the community's understandings. Faith involves, in Paul Tillich's terminology, its *"ultimate concerns."*[23] To identify one's beliefs is relatively easy. Probing one's faith is more difficult because it involves asking questions such as, "What gives meaning to my life?" "In whom do I place my trust?" From the Christian perspective, Sallie McFague says, faith "affirms the underlying direction of the universe to be on the side of life and its fulfillment. . . . Faith in the God of the Judeo-

Christian tradition is faith in the ultimate trustworthiness of things."[24] In addition, one's life of faith demands asking about the congruence between one's convictions and one's behaviors: "Am I living in faithful obedience to the God who is worthy of my trust?" "How does my faith show itself in my daily activities?"

Faith, of course, has a cognitive dimension—it stimulates thinking. Faith sustains and energizes searching and inquiry. Thus, although faith is also not to be confused with theology, it certainly relates to it. As Richard McBrien points out, "faith exists always and only in some theological form."[25] Theology is an enterprise of the second order, a systematic reflection on faith. A "faith that does justice" must be a knowing faith, one that embraces analytic and strategic elements. Though the simplicity and openness of the child is the model *par excellence* of the human before the divine, maturity in faith necessarily mandates outgrowing childish understandings of God and the world. And it is theology that offers so much possibility for deepening in one's life of faith. In contrast to Gabriel Moran, I believe that theology makes more than a "modest contribution" to religious education.[26] Yet, in agreement with Moran and James Michael Lee, I agree—albeit for somewhat different reasons—that theology may be overemphasized in religious education.[27] A word of explanation is in order.

First, why is theology significant for religious education? Theological reflection provides a way of constructing analytical categories to examine past and present movements, events, theorists, and programs. There is, for instance, David Tracy's system of a "mutually critical correlation" between culture and theology.[28] Theology offers methodologies, such as historical criticism, necessary for penetrating ancient texts; no one can adequately teach the Bible in the twentieth century without a well-honed historical consciousness and literary sensitivity. Theology provides knowledge prerequisite for an in-depth perspective on the community's identity in relation to the One whom it worships. It takes up in systematic fashion the meaning of terms that, in their very familiarity to the church, may have lost their power of disclosure (e.g., "redemption," "salvation," "sin").

Theology is without doubt elemental to religious education. Especially in Catholicism, where the life of the mind is prized and enthusiasm suspect, theology is vital. Yet theological erudition is an insufficient foundation for a religious educator precisely because the community's traditions transcend theological discourse. They embrace the wider realm: that of the religious. They encompass both verbal and nonverbal expression: *sacred places* (e.g., temples, churches, shrines), *journeys* (e.g., pilgrimages), and *times* (e.g., liturgical seasons and feasts); *scriptures, commentaries,* and *theological systems; legal* and *moral* codes; *polity, customs,* and *ways of service; rituals;* and *myths, legends, art, devotional manuals,* and *stories of holy people.* Theology, however important, never exhausts the traditions. Its role, as Sandra Schneiders suggests, is analogous to literary criticism: it renders judgments on the adequacy of particular traditions and challenges partial or one-sided approaches. But it is always in the "service of Christian experience."[29]

Theology constitutes just one of Joseph Cahill's five categories of religious traditions: a body of literature; visual art forms; aural art forms; historical formulations and monuments; and theological formulations. These categories imply a curriculum for the preparation of religious educators. One needs to be steeped in the community's texts, its Scripture and foundational writings (e.g., early Christian writers, conciliar documents). A religious educator also needs a sense of popular religion (e.g., as manifested in devotional manuals) to be able to recognize how the tradition was handed on—and the theological astuteness to evaluate it. Historical consciousness is another *sine qua non;* everyone who teaches needs to be able to situate events and expressions of faith in their context. But educators must also encounter classic artifacts in painting, sculpture, architecture, and music. They need, moreover, to respect the power of holy times and places—to have "spiritual knowledge" of the *mysterium tremendum.* As Peruvian theologian Gustavo Gutiérrez points out, authentic theological reflection is grounded in contemplation and practice. "Talk about God (theo-logy) comes after the silence of prayer and after commitment."[30] Theological discourse sinks its roots into a faith lived in ecclesial communion.

An extended example will make my point clearer. In recent years, I have asked students in one of my courses to articulate their understanding of four interrelated questions. (1) What does it mean to be a Christian in the _____ tradition (e.g., Catholic, Presbyterian, Episcopalian, etc.)? (2) What does it mean to educate in faith? (3) What are the appropriate objectives or goals for educating in faith in the _____ tradition? (4) What content and experiences should be included in the curriculum so as to meet these objectives?

I use this exercise (adapted from *Stone House Conversations*)[31] to challenge course participants to create educational experiences consistent with the identity and mission of their respective communities of faith. I describe below the way one group answered the fourth question about the content and experiences that should be included in a curriculum for adults inquiring into Catholicism.

Their suggestions, oriented primarily to adults and suggestive rather than exhaustive, are as follows:

Take learners through some evangelizing event (e.g., a parish mission, a cursillo, a preached retreat, Marriage Encounter, a Life in the Spirit Seminar).

Lavish the learners with stories.

The core stories, of course, are from the Scriptures, especially the Gospels: the parables of Jesus, the stories of healing, the Passion story. One should find a rich variety of ways to hand them on: learners telling them in their own words;

acting them out; imaginatively experiencing them (i.e., Ignatian contemplation); seeing classic paintings; seeing stained glass windows; exploring the findings of Scripture scholars.

Explore the lives of the saints; take on a "patron" saint.

Chart out the local story. Have members of the local community tell their own story of conversion and faith. Have an elderly member tell the story of the parish.

Lavish the learners with ritual, official and unofficial: Eucharists, liturgies of the Word, vespers, penance services. Make full use of "sacramentals," whether ashes or anointings, lighted candles or pilgrimages. Let them experience the rituals first; only afterward reflect on the cluster of meanings.

Find sponsors with whom learners can share, whom they can befriend, from whom they can seek guidance, and whom they can imitate.

Have them do some work of charity, preferably on an ongoing basis. Invite them to volunteer in a soup kitchen or a nursing home.

Have them do some work of social justice: help in community organizing, join in a peace march, write a congressman or congresswoman.

Help them discover our commonalities with other Christians by studying their church buildings, their self-descriptions, attending a service or by speaking with their priest or minister.

Choose to analyze some systematic theologian as a way to integrate the different elements of the faith (e.g., Augustine, Aquinas, Rahner). Or perhaps study a popular equivalent (e.g., *The Dutch Catechism* or Richard McBrien's *Catholicism*).

Pray. Learn forms of prayer, such as the "Jesus prayer" or the rosary. Find a spiritual director. Read one of the classics of Western spirituality, such as *The Cloud of Unknowing* or St. Teresa of Avila.

Explore the artifacts of the Catholic imagination: Gregorian chant, medieval cathedrals, Dante's poetry, Michelangelo's paintings and sculptures.

Study major events in the tradition with an eye to seeing how the Church finds its way to its teaching, e.g., Vatican II, the Council of Nicea. See the historical circumstances and doctrinal debates that occurred before, during, and after. Perhaps bring it alive by recreating the debates.

Learn the international face of Catholicism. Become a sister parish with a parish in Africa or Asia. Explore Oriental prayer forms or the Latin *communidad de base*.

Accompany some minister through the rounds of his or her work, e.g., a eucharistic minister visiting shut-ins, a deacon in the process of preparing a sermon.

Study a tradition of spirituality as it is concretely embodied, e.g., visit a monastery or a Catholic hospital.

Invite the local bishop for a catechetical session. Follow up the concerns of the National Conference of Catholic Bishops.

Do case studies on moral questions. Discuss first, then explore biblical, systematic, and magisterial contributions to questions. Explore what "prudence" is in the concrete case.

Tap the rich life experience of the local community to see the variety of ways that Christian life is concretely lived: the experience of the elderly, the parents of a large family, the health professional, a local politician.

Engage in an exercise in dreaming. Try to visualize how one's city might look if the Kingdom of God were actualized.

Engage in an exercise in reading the signs of the times. Take a newspaper and focus on a current story, investigate, discuss with an eye to what resources faith has to bring to it.[32]

This list could well become the framework for an entire curriculum in the "Catholic thing."[33] It illustrates what it means to make *traditions*—including theology, but not restricted to it—accessible to the religious community. Lest I narrow my examples to Catholicism, let me provide another, this time from a Hasidic Jewish group in which a male child is introduced to the Torah.

In this particular community (in Brooklyn, New York), a boy has his first haircut at three years of age with the Rov (an ordained Rabbi). The Rov slips a *talis katan*—a white cotton vest with four fringed corners—on the child's shoulders and places a yarmulkah on his head. Then he lifts the child, places him in his father's arms, and wraps them both in the talis. The father kisses the son and gently gives him back to the Rov.

The Rov places the child in his lap. An alphabet primer appears on the desk with a small cup of honey. The Rov opens the primer to the first page, dips his finger into the honey, touches the first letter of the alphabet, and offers the honeyed finger to the child, who licks at it tentatively "to sweeten his taste for learning Torah." The Rov then begins what is to be the child's first official instruction. He points to the first letter and asks the child what it is. . . .

The recital ends as the Rov pronounces the child fit for learning. He expresses the hope that this generation will grow up in the tradition of Hasidus and Torah, and to see the coming of the Messiah. Parents and relatives crowd the child. Cake and whiskey are passed around, and the traditional toast "L'chaim" (to life) is extended to all.[34]

TRANSFORMATION

However important, the community's traditions are not ends in themselves: they are to lead to its renewal. A community draws upon its traditions not merely for maintenance, but for transformation. Traditions should offer the pattern that enables the community to recognize God's involvement with creation. Consequently, they summon their adherents into the process of ongoing conversion. Without conversion as their end, traditions become idols. Hence, my belief, in my definition of religious education, that there is an "intrinsic connection between traditions and transformation."

Accordingly, I believe that all education in faith ultimately is oriented to conversion. A religious educator serves as a catalyst of transformation. But what is transformation or conversion? I will explicate my own view, connecting it with foundational questions on the use of the social sciences and on the relationship of faith and culture.

As I see it, conversion is a profoundly personal journey with serious ramifications both for the religious community and for society as a whole. Following Bernard Lonergan, the late Jesuit theologian, I think of conversion as a radical transformation of a person at every level of his or her being. Lonergan recognizes that conversion involves the entirety of one's conscious and intentional operations: it directs a person's gaze, pervades the imagination, releases symbols that penetrate the depths of the psyche, enriches understanding, guides judgment, and reinforces decisions.[35] Thus, he says, conversion may happen at the intellectual, the moral, and the religious levels; each level is sublated—preserved and carried forward to a fuller realization with a richer context—and interrelated.

But it is one of Lonergan's students, Walter Conn, to whom I am most indebted for opening up his mentor's categories and relating them to the work of the developmentalists. I will use Conn as my primary guide in exploring the dimensions of conversion.[36]

Conn grounds his views in a definition of self-transcendence as moving beyond oneself at the cognitive, moral, and affective levels. He distinguishes this from popular notions of both self-fulfillment (a naive individualism) and self-sacrifice (a denial of the right to self-assertion).[37] Because the self-transcending person is freed from the illusion of "quantitative fulfillment," he or she senses the "peace of authentic realization in the very activity of realistic knowing, responsible choosing and genuine loving."[38] Conversion, then, is the "radical drive of the personal subject for self-transcendence—and it is more; mature, truly adult conscience is the self-transcending drive of the morally converted personal subject."[39]

What does Conn mean by the "morally converted" person? Here, like Lonergan, he means a shift in the criterion of the person's decisions and choices from what merely satisfies to what one truly values. It is the movement from being a "drifter" to acting as an "open-eyed, deliberate subject." A person has undergone a "critical moral conversion" when he or she can recognize and accept the responsibility of discovering and establishing his or her own values in dialogue with the community.[40] Implicit in this level of conversion is a level of maturity consonant with what Lawrence Kohlberg has described as "principled reasoning." Thus, it would not occur at least before young adulthood.

Conversion is not brought about by argument alone; it also happens at the level of cognition. Here one surrenders the pursuit of certainty, recognizing that truth is not self-evident. A cognitive conversion involves the *pursuit* of understanding, even to the point of entry into our lives of genuine mystery.[41]

Moreover, persons experience the conversion of their affections: a direction of their passion and commitments. They reorient their passionate desires so that they are transformed from an obsession with the needs of the self to a concern for the needs of others.

These three interrelated levels of conversion are encompassed by religious conversion—what Lonergan used to speak of simply as "otherworldly falling in love."[42] As Conn says, it is only at the intersection of absolute contingency and infinite actuality that a person can meet the real God and not an idol of one's choosing.[43] For a Christian, conversion "not only sets us in a direction marked by the prints of Jesus' sandals, but calls us to respond to the demands of the journey with the same radical openness to divine mystery which characterized Jesus' response to his Father."[44]

Conn, informed by Paulo Freire's work, also points out that each element of conversion has a social dimension. Moral conversion, for example, necessarily extends to the sphere of action. Cognitive conversion bears similarities to Freire's notion of conscientization, and affective conversion "reorients one's desires from an instinctive obsession with self-needs to a reflectively guided personal concern for the needs of others."[45] And, in Conn's last chapter, he shows how the social dimension is intrinsic to a genuine religious conversion, illustrating this in an analysis of Thomas Merton.

TRANSFORMATION, THE ROLE OF THE SOCIAL SCIENCES, AND THE RELATION OF FAITH AND CULTURE

Throughout his book, theologian Conn engages the developmentalists. His reasons are twofold: conversion requires previous development (e.g., critical moral conversion cannot happen before young adulthood); and conversion requires subsequent development. Though not uncritical of the developmentalists, he takes them with seriousness because, as he concludes: "development requires conversion, and conversion always occurs within a developmental process."[46]

Conn thereby illuminates not only the dimensions of conversion, but also serves as a model of how modern theological work is indebted to, but not exhausted by, the social sciences. His specific focus—the relation between developmental theories and conversion—invites speculation on the larger question. Let me comment briefly.

As I have observed many religious educators in recent years, I have seen a tendency toward uncritical acceptance of the theories of social scientists, particularly psychologists. This is understandable, because psychology has an inherent fascination for moderns. For teachers, it seems to offer, if not answers, at least clues for dealing with the complexities of their profession. Psychology may well seem more "practical" than theology or philosophy of education, more applicable to the daily round of human interactions. The structural developmentalists seem to offer a schema by which one can readily identify the linear progression of moral reasoning and the life of faith.

But this enthusiasm engenders three concerns. One is the tendency to focus on a specific methodology (e.g., structural developmentalism) to the exclusion of another (e.g., psychoanalytic perspectives). "A little learning is a dangerous thing," says the old maxim—and religious educators have perhaps too quickly "landed" on a theory without taking a long look at either its assumptions or at alternative theories. A second is potentially more serious: the preoccupation with one of the social sciences (e.g., psychology) and subsequent inattention to others (e.g., sociology, anthropology). This has grave consequences in a society where individualism runs rampant.

I have a third concern: that the theological dimensions not be obscured in the turn toward the social sciences. I am not alone in this judgment. Paul Vitz and William Kirk Kilpatrick have written at length of theology's co-option by psychology.[47] I do not share either their theological perspective or their conclusions; but even in what I regard as their oversimplified analysis and excessive polemics, I think they serve a useful task by raising the question. Rather, I find myself more persuaded by Don Browning's thesis that "significant portions of the modern psychologies, and especially the clinical psychologies, are actually instances of religio-ethical thinking."[48] Theological analysis, therefore, is both appropriate and useful. And, although not every religious educator will have the erudition of a Conn or a Browning in sorting out the theological grounding of a given psychological school, all can commit themselves to casting a discerning eye on each psychological theory, lest it be mindlessly or prematurely accepted. In fact, such a commitment may well be an aspect of the cognitive conversion to which all persons—most especially educators—are called.

The relative importance one assigns to the social sciences or theology seems to be rooted, at least implicitly, in the way one understands the relationship of faith to culture. Obviously, the two extremities make for a simple hierarchy. In the "Christ against culture" stance, the social sciences are assessed negatively. William Kirk Kilpatrick's indictment of humanistic psychology in religious textbooks illustrates this,[49] as do the recent suits in Tennessee (*Mozert et al. v. Hawkins County Public Schools et al.*) and Alabama (*Smith et al. v. Board of School Commissioners of Mobile County*) over school textbooks infected by "secular humanism."[50] In the "Christ in culture" type, the social sciences are the dominant partner, and the distinctiveness of theology is lost. While I perceive less evidence of this type in religious education circles, perhaps its traces are evident in the passionate interest in "futurology." I think of James Connor's tongue-in-cheek observation that "futurists have replaced mystics. The Christian contemplative was slow. She watched trees and stars; she lived in silence. The futurist is fast. He doesn't look for essences but for trends. He keeps his eyes on what may be. He speaks at conventions."[51]

Clearly, my sympathies lie somewhere in the middle range of H. Richard Niebuhr's typology. As a Catholic, I identify in part with the synthesists, for whom God's rule is established in the nature of things. Yet as a modern informed by social analysis, in which one looks systematically at the *structures* of evil, I increasingly see the need for the conversion of culture—both within and outside the boundaries of the church.

In sum, what I have attempted to show in this section is that reflection on the meaning of conversion leads logically to a consideration of the role of the social sciences and to the larger question of the relationship of faith and culture. The foundational questions are closely linked.

MAKING ACCESSIBLE AND MAKING MANIFEST

Schooled to write with lively verbs, I confess to discomfort with the awkwardness of the gerunds "making accessible" and "making manifest." But if the phrases are not eloquent, I find them, nevertheless, eminently descriptive of my understanding of teaching and indeed of the larger educational enterprise. In particular, "making accessible" suggests the artistry of teaching. "Making manifest" highlights the teacher's responsibility to make transparent the link between traditions and transformation. A word about each activity.

TEACHING AS "MAKING ACCESSIBLE"

Teaching, as A. Bartlett Giamatti writes, is "an instinctual art, mindful of potential, craving of realizations, a pausing, a seamless process, where one rehearses constantly while acting, sits as a spectator at a play one directs, engages every part in order to keep the choices open and the shape alive for the student."[52] It is, accordingly, more adequately imaged than defined and more properly conceptualized in artistic images than in scientific terminology.

Looked at from one standpoint, the core of artistry is disciplined imagination. Talent alone is insufficient; skills must be practiced. Every artist worthy of the name possesses a repertoire of carefully honed skills—*"know-how"*—and *knowledge* of his or her endeavor and of the self. A cellist, for instance, must know how to read music, how to hold the bow, and how to position the fingers. And the cellist must also know the range of the cello and the body of cello literature. He or she must know others' rendering of a piece of music. Long hours of practice and taxing lessons before the critical eyes and ears of mentors are the prerequisites of every performance. Only with self-knowledge can the musician benefit from such scrutiny. After the performance follows analysis, reflection, and a new cycle of rehearsals.

Teaching, like musical performance, depends upon painstaking preparation, reflective practice, judicious analysis, and systematic evaluation. Talent and discipline, inspiration and deliberateness combine. Both know-how and knowledge are required.

The knowledge incumbent upon the religious educator is fundamentally knowledge of the traditions. Obviously, this entails a commitment to study, to developing one's critical faculties—in short, to cognitive conversion. But more than clear-minded thinking is needed. The religious educator needs also to cultivate contemplation and empathy, as Monika Hellwig has identified.[53] Why contemplation? Hellwig associates contemplation with one's "habit of vision," one's experience of reality:

The essence of a contemplative attitude seems to be vulnerability—allowing persons, things, and events to be, to happen, allowing them their full resonance in one's own experience, looking at them without blinking, touching them and allowing them to touch us without flinching. It is a matter of engaging reality in action, allowing it to talk back to us and listening to what is said. It is a constant willingness to be taken by surprise. It is a deep existential grasp of the truth that all our theory is a critique of our praxis and that evasion of experience means distortion or alienation in our theory.[54]

Yet contemplation is insufficient if it does not spill over into empathy. It is this quality that enables us to enter into the realm of mystery, to engage the "more subtle logic of story and iconography, of symbol and ritual."[55] In addition, empathy plays another crucial role:

The personal experience of the theologian is a very small, and all too often a very shrivelled, part of human experience. It is always important and at present also very urgent that we should enter into the human questions of those whose voices do not ordinarily reach us—the destitute, the vast masses of the starving, the despised, the forgotten, the vast masses of oppressed people, the whole populations of uprooted refugees, the races and classes who "do not count," who are written off by the human makers of public history as waste, future generations threatened with overwhelming ecological and nuclear disaster, the elderly and handicapped, and otherwise "useless" people of our society. Without entering by empathy into such dimensions of human experience, human suffering and human hope, we are simply not dealing with the reality of the human situation—the reality of creation, sin and redemption, the real issue of human freedom and accountability. Unless the experience we draw upon has this kind of breadth and depth by virtue of a costly compassion, the theology we do is nothing but a passing cerebral aberration.[56]

Knowledge of the traditions, then, involves reason, contemplation, and empathy. But what is the religious educator's *know-how*? Here I think the word "access" is key.

Teaching is a complex activity that demands its practitioners play many roles, among them listener, convener, explorer, lecturer, analyst, inquirer, mediator, facilitator, advocate, and evaluator. Yet as varied as the activities of teaching are, one particular concept orders all the others: teaching is a way of giving people *access* to the community's traditions.

Access is given in numerous ways. To provide access means to erect bridges, to make metaphors, to build highways, to provide introductions and commentaries, to translate foreign terms, to remove barriers, to make maps, to demolish blockages, to demonstrate effects, to energize and sustain participation, and to be hospitable.[57] All of these have their analogues in religious education. Without such activities, the traditions will remain impenetrable.

Implicit in my advocacy of "giving access" as an appropriate description of teaching is this prerequisite for the religious educator: because the tradition, not the teacher, is the focal point, the teacher needs to have sufficient ego strength to "get out of the way," not to impose his or her own needs for recognition. Conn terms this "self-transcending subjectivity."[58] The "readiness for teaching" I am suggesting rests in part upon the practice of the spiritual disciplines insofar as *ascesis* helps us to decenter the ego.[59]

Giving access also requires the discipline of practice, of crafting one's skills. Over the years I have frequently recommended the work of Bruce Joyce and Marsha Weil,[60] because I believe their painstaking analysis of various models of teaching establishes a fundamental mind-set: one needs a repertoire of strategies to honor the complexity of knowledge and of human beings—no single method suffices. Rather, the religious educator needs to know a range of models, and to know how and when to adapt them. Sara Little's book shows this with clarity.[61]

Furthermore, the work of Joyce and Weil testifies to the centrality of *practicing* one's strategy. One learns to teach by teaching reflectively. Discussing one's philosophy of teaching is necessary, but demonstrating it and participating in critique are vital. It is easy, for instance, to claim that one rejects the teacher-as-banker approach (depositing information in one's students), but one's rejection of the teacher-banker will be evident only in the demonstration of an alternative. To know how to do "problem posing" (Freire) or "shared praxis" (Groome) or any other strategies (e.g., role playing, concept formation) requires rehearsing specific moves. To "think from the other end" (Russell), one must lay out a systematic way of proceeding. Teachers must have both breadth—a range of models—and depth—rigorous practice of each. Josiah Royce said, "when you teach, you must know when to forget formulas; but you must have learned them in order to be able to forget them."[62]

Research has been unable to prove that any single way of teaching is inherently better than any other. No one "right" way of teaching exists. Nor is there some model of the "perfect" teacher. There are only people who believe so much in the power of the traditions that they are willing to risk learning to teach. Learning to teach is the task of a lifetime.

Teaching deserves to be taken more seriously than it is when theology or psychology reigns supreme. Teaching demands that its practitioners pay close attention to the richly textured ways people learn. The teacher's task involves amplifying and challenging the narrowness of personal experience and the limits of a single perspective. It makes different demands according to the nature of the tradition and the context in which it is being taught and thus requires know-how and knowledge. It calls for the imagination and discipline of the artist, the humility and commitment of the religious person, and the practice and perseverance of the performer.

TEACHING AS MAKING MANIFEST: THE GOAL AND POLITICAL CHARACTER OF EDUCATION

Because the community's traditions are for the sake of transformation, educators must seek to make this relationship transparent. It is their responsibility to make the traditions luminous and to enhance the community's thinking about them. It is not their responsibility to indoctrinate the community, that is, to stress the *transmission* of beliefs to the exclusion of showing how one *thinks* about beliefs.[63] Nor is it the religious educator's role to monitor an individual's conversion. Teaching has a transcendent quality. Each person needs to be respected; the educator necessarily stands in awe before the mystery of God at work in the community.

How, then, might it be possible to think about the goal of education? It seems to me that all education must necessarily have a transformative purpose. One articulation of this belief is that the most fundamental goal of education is human liberation. James Macdonald and David Purpel comment accordingly:

Negatively, liberation means being free from unnecessary constraints and barriers to human dignity and potential such as those that come from being poor, frightened, misguided, ignorant and unaffirmed—in a word, controlled. Human liberation in a positive sense refers to the capacity for full consciousness, fulfillment, joy, integration—in a word, freedom.[64]

Transformative education has a political goal: changing society to make it more just. I also find Jane Roland Martin's work relevant in thinking about the directions in which education should lead society. Her thesis that education should not only enhance society's productive processes, but also its reproductive needs (rearing of children, care for the sick and disabled, needs of families and management of households) is one I find persuasive.[65] If Martin's "3 Cs" of *caring, concern,* and *connection* were to be infused into curricula as rationality and autonomy are now, the "educated person" would have a different face.

That care should be at the center of education is also the thesis of Dwayne Huebner, who thinks of education as "care for the finite transcendence of men [women], for the forms a life takes between birth and death, for the emerging biography of others."[66] It may well be that religious educators have a distinct contribution to make in developing ways of educating that respect both reason and emotion. For instance, I think that the debate in the United States about prayer in schools hides a real possibility. The pluralism we represent as a nation and the priority we assign to the rights of the individual make it inappropriate to initiate worship in the classroom of the public school. But what if the dynamic of prayer were probed further, so that its linkage of reason and emotion were seen? Might not it be possible for teachers to find other modes of thinking caringly about the world?

In this regard, I have found the description of conversion in Lonergan and Conn pertinent, as well as theologian John Macquarrie's fourfold description of prayer as passionate, compassionate, responsible, and thankful thinking. Prayer, says Macquarrie, is "passionate thinking":

If there is a thinking that is content to analyse and measure and compare the phenomena of the world, there is also a thinking that enters feelingly into the world and knows itself deeply involved in all that goes on there. Such a thinking is not content to learn what is, but considers what ought to be. It searches for values among the facts, for ideals among the phenomena. Such a thinking is sometimes intermingled with painful longing and desire as it catches the vision of what might be and longs for its realization; sometimes it is suffused with joy and thankfulness as it recognizes great achievement or great horizons of hope and possibility; sometimes it is tinged with shame as we acknowledge that so much of the world's grief and pain has come about "through my fault, through my own fault, through my own most grievous fault."[67]

Prayer is also "compassionate thinking," because prayer involves turning outward toward the other; it is a "dwelling with reality in the sense of compassionate confrontation in thought with human beings in their actual situations."[68] Moreover, prayer entails "responsible thinking" because it means answering or responding to that which lies beyond us; it is "thankful thinking" because it acknowledges those moments of undeserved graciousness.

Macquarrie's identification of the inextricable link between reason and emotion in prayer invites educators to design curricula and practice pedagogical strategies that similarly involve the whole person. Philosopher Nel Noddings proposes that schools ought to employ three major means, *dialogue, practice,* and *confirmation,* to nurture students in the ethical ideal of caring. Dialogue implies a sense of relatedness between teacher and student, teacher and parent; it also entails a willingness to confront controversial issues. For instance, Noddings suggests that the teacher ought to expose students not only to information about religions, but also to the "affective accompaniments," such as religious writings, art, and music. She writes accordingly:

[Students] should have opportunities to feel what the other is feeling as a result of deeply held beliefs. They should be touched by the beauty, faith, and devotion manifested in the religious practices of others. Through such experiences—feeling with the other in spiritual responsiveness—they may be reconnected to each other in caring. The mother's hope is, of course, that this caring will be held above all particular religious beliefs and that young people devoted to each other will refuse to bayonet, shoot, and bomb each other. Will young people educated in this fashion "lose" their religions? Perhaps. If a particular set of beliefs is so fragile that it cannot stand intellectual examination, or so uncharitable that it cannot tolerate caring relations, then indeed it should be lost.[69]

Schools, Noddings adds, ought to provide students with ways of practicing caring by participating in regular service activities. This practice in caring should extend to cooperative learning ventures, so that students learn to relate with others. Her third means, confirmation, depends upon and is connected to dialogue and practice. Confirmation means more than having high expectations of students, because that is just "another form of product control."[70] It means encouraging and enhancing the manifestations of caring, valuing the students' ethical and intellectual lives, and pointing them to their best possible selves.

The skillful, generous teacher receives ordinary questions and, through her [his] sensitive reception and faithful interpretation, confers special significance and dignity on them.

Nothing is more important in nurturing the ethical ideal than attribution and explication of the best possible motive. . . . Thus the child is led to explore his [her] ethical self with wonder and appreciation.[71]

Social scientists may also contribute to an ethics of care. Research on "pro-social behavior" or altruism has demonstrated that *empathy* is the precursor of altruism. The curricula of schools and families need to be examined for ways in which they might encourage the development of altruism.[72]

Religious education ought to be directed particularly toward instilling an ethics of care into its curriculum. As Burton Cohen and Joseph Lukinsky observe, "the intent in religious settings is always to affect individuals, to confront them and force them to relate seriously to the material studied, to be present to it, and to make it their own."[73]

It is the work of religious education to lead people outside the confines of their narrow experience, to broaden their horizons and deepen their capacities to feel and act. To do so, however, the explicit curriculum needs to be transformed so that the experience of men *and* women can be taken into account. And to be "Catholic" it must become more "catholic"—more inclusive of cross-cultural perspectives. The "null" curriculum—what religious educators have taught about women, people of color, and other "marginal" voices by ignoring or misrepresenting their contribution—needs to be brought to the fore. The "implicit" curriculum—that which teaches by virtue of implicitly assigning value—needs to be examined for the biases it has assumed. One thinks, for instance, of a contradiction in Catholicism: leaders talk about the importance of family life, especially the nurturance of children and care for the disabled and elderly, but are themselves seldom involved in it.

And if religious educators are to enhance both the productive and reproductive processes of society, they need to think comprehensively about curriculum. Here I recognize the contribution of educational historian Lawrence Cremin, who writes persuasively about an "ecology" of education.[74] Cremin recognizes that many institutions educate: family life, classrooms, museums, factories, camps, churches, television, film, day-care centers, newspapers, and self-help groups. The educational theorist needs to recognize the distinctive curriculum of each and then to think relationally about the total pattern.

To illustrate this again with reference to the Catholic vision, education happens through the mediation of a wide variety of agencies. Foremost is the church's worship. Though education is not the primary purpose of liturgy, there can be little doubt that liturgy is one of the most powerful educative tools in the church.[75] One needs only to recall Aidan Kavanagh's point that the liturgy teaches "nondiscursively, richly, ambiguously, elementally."[76] Certainly, education happens in formal pedagogical situations in classrooms, lecture halls, and church basements. But other forms of Catholic communal life also play an important educative function.

A specific example illustrates my point. Consider, for example, one of the pressing issues today: how to educate for peace and justice. A comprehensive educational analysis may begin with a study of the liturgy. How do the symbols, texts, and homilies shape participants? In what ways does the church's liturgical life form people in ways of acting justly? In what ways does it contribute to oppression?[77] Necessarily, the analysis incorporates the curriculum of the schools and of parish and diocesan educational programs (e.g., the "Renew" program) across the range of generations. But a thorough analysis will also consider the role of organizations such as Pax Christi, Network, and the Center of Concern—agencies that typically produce newsletters and curricular materials and often include some sort of internships or advocacy work. Other, older forms of Catholic communal life require scrutiny as well (e.g., the Knights of Columbus, the National Council of Catholic Women, the St. Vincent de Paul Society), as well as movements such as Marriage Encounter, cursillos, and charismatic prayer groups. Moreover, an educational analysis must weigh the contributions of the media, especially the materials available through Catholic journals of opinion. In short, one who would offer leadership in the Catholic community on issues of peace and justice needs to think across varied situations and institutions, and to think relationally in order to allocate financial and human resources.[78]

In this chapter I have suggested a definition of religious education that is broad enough to encompass more than a Christian understanding of the field. At the same time, I have explicated my definition with reference to the Catholic community, so that the implications can be seen in terms of how the definition "fits" a particular body. I make no pretense to having done much more than open up the foundational questions. Each is deserving of a chapter—or even a book—in its own right.

I am aware that I have passed through some dense territory, and that my own thinking is still maturing. But my goal is not so much the presentation of a finished product. Rather, mine is the pioneer's project—to pass on what I have seen in my forays and to invite readers to frontiers of their own. I hope I have cleared some pathways and stimulated a worthwhile conversation for the journey.

Figure 6

Religious Education as "Making Accessible the Traditions of the Religious Community and Making Manifest the Intrinsic Connection Between Traditions and Transformation" (*M. C. Boys*)

FOUNDATIONAL QUESTIONS	*RELIGIOUS EDUCATION*
REVELATION	· Revelatory moments always cloaked in symbolic language. · Past has power in giving meaning to present, direction to future. · God's radiance revealed in its full intensity in Jesus and continues through Spirit's presence in world. · Scripture the "classic" text of divine-human encounter; community's reading needs a norming body.
CONVERSION	· A radical transformation of the person at every level of his or her being. · Self-transcendence. · Has a social dimension. · Traditions summon believers to ongoing conversion. · Conversion the goal for education in faith.
FAITH & BELIEF	· Faith: a primordial response to God's love; coming to faith historical and communal. · Beliefs: formulations of the community's understandings of God. · Creeds significant and need to be understood in context. · Faith demands congruence between one's convictions and action. · Faith exists in a theological form.

FOUNDATIONAL QUESTIONS	*RELIGIOUS EDUCATION*
THEOLOGY	· A systematic reflection on faith. · Provides religious education with analytical categories, methodologies, and knowledge. · A vital but insufficient foundation for religious education: community's traditions transcend theological discourse.
FAITH & CULTURE	· Structures of evil necessitate a conversion of culture– "Christ transforming culture."
GOAL OF EDUCATION	· Lead people outside confines of narrowness, broaden their horizons, deepen capacities to feel and act–a conversion. · Liberation from ignorance and for full consciousness, joy, integration. · Transformation of society.
KNOWLEDGE	· Essential to link "caring, concern, and connection" with rationality and autonomy. · Reason and emotion necessary for "thinking caringly about the world."
SOCIAL SCIENCES	· Important to religious education, but need to be carefully appropriated. · Need to look at range of social sciences, not merely developmental psychology. · Theological dimensions should be examined.
CURRICULUM & TEACHING	· Teaching makes the traditions accessible. · Teaching demands knowledge (reason, contemplation and empathy) and know-how (disciplined practice). · Need to think comprehensively about the curriculum. · Curricula need to be more inclusive. · Teaching needs to foster an "ethics of care."
EDUCATION AS POLITICAL	· Transformative education seeks to make a more just society. · More inclusive curricula will incorporate gender, race, and class analysis, and cross cultural perspectives.

NOTES

1. Gary Jennings, *The Journeyer* (New York: Avon, 1984), 170.
2. Ibid.
3. Jaroslav Pelikan, *The Vindication of Tradition* (New Haven, CT: Yale University Press, 1984), 65.
4. Edward Shils, *Tradition* (Chicago: University of Chicago Press, 1981), 12.
5. Mary Elizabeth Moore, *Education for Continuity and Change* (Nashville, TN: Abingdon, 1983), 129, 127.

6. Shils, *Tradition*, 27.
7. Cited in Pelikan, *A Vindication of Tradition*, 20.
8. See Douglas A. Knight, *Rediscovering the Traditions of Israel*, rev. ed., SBL Dissertation Series #9 (Missoula, MT: Society of Biblical Literature and Scholars Press, 1975), 5–20.
9. James Barr, *The Scope and Authority of the Bible* (Philadelphia: Westminster, 1980), 60.
10. The phrase is from Emil Fackenheim, *God's Presence in History* (New York: Harper & Row, Torchbooks, 1970), 8–14.
11. Elisabeth Schüssler Fiorenza, *In Memory of Her: A Feminist Theological Reconstruction of Christian Origins* (New York: Seabury, Crossroad, 1983), 217.
12. Paul Achtemeier, *The Inspiration of Scripture* (Philadelphia: Westminster, 1980), 130.
13. Judy Chicago, *The Dinner Party: A Symbol of Our Heritage* (New York: Doubleday, Anchor Books, 1979), 249.
14. Bernadette Brooten, "Early Christian Women and their Cultural Context: Issues of Method in Historical Reconstruction," in Adela Yarbro Collins, ed., *Feminist Perspectives on Biblical Scholarship* (Chico, CA: Scholars Press, 1985), 67.
15. Wilfred Cantwell Smith, *The Meaning and End of Religion* (San Francisco: Harper & Row, 1978), 165.
16. See Bernard Cooke, *Ministry to Word and Sacraments* (Philadelphia: Fortress, 1976), 61–63, 210.
17. Avery Dulles, "The Theologian and the Magisterium," *Catholic Mind* 75 (1977):6-16. Thomas Aquinas's distinction may be found in "Quaestiones quodlibetales" (3:4,1-2) in Roberto Busa, ed., *S.Thomae Aquinatis Opera omnia* 3 (Stuttgart-Bad Cannstatt: Frommann-Holzboog, 1980), 450.
18. Rosemary Haughton, *The Catholic Thing* (Springfield, IL: Templegate, 1979), 9.
19. Ibid.
20. Carol Christ, Ellen Umansky, and Anne Carr, "Roundtable Discussion: What Are the Sources of My Theology?" *Journal of Feminist Studies in Religion* 1 (1985):127. Cf. Carr's comments with those of Carol Christ, who writes, "When I do theology, or rather thea-logy, reflection on the meaning of Goddess, I do not turn to the Christian tradition as source or norm. My thealogy is rooted rather in my own experience and that of other women" (120). Umansky's essay parallels Carr's rather than Christ's (see 123–24).
21. See Berard L. Marthaler, *The Creed* (Mystic, CT: Twenty-Third Publications, 1987).
22. See Avery Dulles, *The Survival of Dogma* (Garden City, NY: Doubleday, 1971), especially chap. 11, "The Hermeneutics of Dogmatic Statements," 171–84.
23. Paul Tillich, *The Dynamics of Faith* (New York: Harper & Row, 1957).
24. Sallie McFague, *Models of God* (Philadelphia: Fortress, 1987), 29.
25. Richard McBrien, *Catholicism*, 2 vols. (Minneapolis, MN: Winston, 1980), 1:26.
26. See Gabriel Moran, "From Obstacle to Modest Contributor," in Norma H. Thompson, ed., *Religious Education and Theology* (Birmingham, AL: Religious Education Press, 1982), 42–70.
27. See James Michael Lee, "The Authentic Source of Religious Instruction," in Thompson, ed., *Religious Education and Theology*, 100–197.
28. See David Tracy, *Blessed Rage for Order* (New York: Seabury, 1975), 45–46.
29. Sandra M. Schneiders, "Theology and Spirituality: Strangers, Rivals, or Partners?" *Horizons* 13 (1986):272–74.
30. Gustavo Gutiérrez, *We Drink from Our Own Wells: The Spiritual Journey of a People* (Maryknoll, NY: Orbis, 1984), 136.
31. See Chapter 6, subsection "Religious Education in the Unitarian Tradition."
32. J. William Harmless, Bruce Pontbriand, and Thomas Royce, "Educating in Faith in the Catholic Tradition," a paper submitted for the course "Traditions of Religion and Education," April 1987. I have made minor edits for clarity and parallel structure.
33. See Haughton, *The Catholic Thing*, 15–16.
34. Robert Mark Kamen, *Growing Up Hasidic: Education and Socialization in the Bobover Hasidic Community* (New York: AMS Press, 1985), 40–41.

35. Bernard Lonergan, *Method in Theology* (New York: Herder and Herder, 1972), 130–31.
36. See Walter Conn, *Christian Conversion: A Developmental Interpretation of Autonomy and Self-Surrender* (New York: Paulist, 1986). Also see his edited collection, *Conversion: Perspectives on Personal and Social Transformation* (New York: Alba House, 1978).
37. Rosemary Radford Ruether remarks that conversion has typically been an ambivalent experience for women. "Although women have been taught to internalize the demand for obedience to patriarchal authority as the expression of their obedience to God, for many women conversion experiences actually functioned to free them from repressive social authority by transferring their exclusive obedience to God or Christ." See her *Womanguides: Readings Toward a Feminist Theology* (Boston: Beacon, 1985), 136.
38. Conn, *Christian Conversion*, 22. Those familiar with Lonergan recognize his transcendental precepts: "Be attentive, Be intelligent, Be reasonable, Be responsible" (*Method in Theology*, 20).
39. Conn, *Christian Conversion*, 133.
40. Ibid., 112–25. See also Walter E. Conn, *Conscience: Development and Self-Transcendence* (Birmingham, AL: Religious Education Press, 1981).
41. Ibid., 125.
42. Lonergan, *Method in Theology*, 240.
43. Conn, *Christian Conversion*, 237.
44. Ibid., 213.
45. Ibid., 156.
46. Ibid., 157. James Fowler also discusses the relation of development and conversion. See his *Becoming Adult, Becoming Christian* (San Francisco: Harper & Row, 1984), 138–41.
47. See Paul Vitz, *Psychology as Religion: The Cult of Self-Worship* (Grand Rapids, MI: Eerdmans, 1977) and William Kirk Kilpatrick, *Identity and Intimacy* (New York: Dell, 1975) and *Psychological Seduction: The Failure of Modern Psychology* (Nashville, TN: Nelson, 1983).
48. Don Browning, *Religious Thought and the Modern Psychologies* (Philadelphia: Fortress, 1987), 8.
49. Janice D'Avignon and William Kirk Kilpatrick, "On Serving Two Masters," *Catholicism in Crisis* 2 (August 1984):7–12.
50. See Donna Hulsizer, "Public Education on Trial," *Educational Leadership* 45 (May 1987):12–16. For a helpful summary of cases in regard to religion and schooling, see Richard P. McBrien, *Caesar's Coin: Religion and Politics in America* (New York: Macmillan, 1987), 169–80.
51. James Connor, "America's Culture of Speed," *New Catholic World* 230 (May–June 1987):119.
52. A. Bartlett Giamatti, "The American Teacher," *Harper's* 261 (July 1980):24.
53. Monika Hellwig, "Theology as a Fine Art," in Jane Kopas, ed., *Interpreting Tradition: The Art of Theological Reflection*, College Theology Society no. 29 (Chico, CA: Scholars Press, 1984), 6.
54. Ibid.
55. Ibid., 7.
56. Ibid., 8.
57. See my "Religious Education: Access to Traditions and Transformation," in Padraic O'Hare, ed., *Tradition and Transformation* (Birmingham, AL: Religious Education Press, 1979), 9–34.
58. See Conn, *Conscience: Development and Self-Transcendence*, 26–31.
59. See my "The Grace of Teaching," *Momentum* 17 (December 1986):8–9.
60. See Bruce Joyce and Marsha Weil, *Information Processing Models of Teaching* (Englewood Cliffs, NJ: Prentice-Hall, 1978); *Social Models of Teaching* (Englewood Cliffs, NJ: Prentice-Hall, 1978); and with Bridget Kluwin, *Personal Models of Teaching* (Englewood Cliffs, NJ: Prentice-Hall, 1978).

61. Sara Little, *To Set One's Heart: Belief and Teaching in the Church* (Atlanta, GA: John Knox, 1983).
62. Josiah Royce, "Is There a Science of Education?" in Merle L. Borrowman, ed., *Teacher Education in America: A Documentary History* (New York: Teachers College Press, 1965), 113.
63. See Thomas F. Green, *The Activities of Teaching* (New York: McGraw-Hill, 1971), 30–31.
64. James Macdonald and David Purpel, "Curriculum and Planning: Visions and Metaphors," *Journal of Curriculum and Supervision* 2 (1987):187. I am indebted to Prof. Sara Lee for this reference.
65. See chapter 7, subsection "Feminist Educational Thinking."
66. Dwayne Huebner, "Education in the Church," *Andover Newton Quarterly* 12 (1972):126.
67. John Macquarrie, *Paths in Spirituality* (New York: Harper & Row, 1972), 26.
68. Ibid., 27.
69. Nel Noddings, *Caring: A Feminine Approach to Ethics and Moral Education* (Berkeley: University of California Press, 1984), 185.
70. Ibid., 196.
71. Ibid., 123.
72. See M. Hoffman, "Altruistic Behavior and the Parent-Child Relationship," *Journal of Personality and Social Psychology* 31 (1975):937–43.
73. Burton Cohen and Joseph Lukinsky, "Religious Institutions as Educators," in Mario D. Fantini and Robert L. Sinclair, eds., *Education in School and Nonschool Settings*, Eighty-fourth Yearbook of the National Society for the Study of Education, part 1 (Chicago: National Society for the Study of Education, 1985), 144.
74. See Lawrence Cremin, *Public Education* (New York: Basic Books, 1976).
75. See Thomas H. Groome, "'And the Word Was Made Flesh': An Educational Perspective on Ministries of the Word," in Gerard F. Baumbach, ed., *Dimensions of the Word: Exploring a Ministry* (New York: Sadlier, 1984), 47–50.
76. Aidan Kavanagh, "Teaching Through the Liturgy," *Notre Dame Journal of Education* 5 (1974):41.
77. See Virgil Michel, "Liturgical Religious Education: Answers to Separation of Dogma from Life," *Orate Fratres* 11 (1937):267–69; John Egan, "Liturgy and Justice: An Unfinished Agenda," *Origins* 13 (1983): 246–53; Mark Searle, "The Pedagogical Function of the Liturgy," *Worship* 55 (1981):333–59.
78. See Cremin, *Public Education*, 57–58.

Bibliographic Essay

Marking Out the Boundaries: A Way of Thinking About Religious Education

As in the previous bibliographic essay, I mention only those sources that complement those cited in the notes to this chapter or are so foundational as to merit a special recognition.

Much of my thinking on the role of tradition has been shaped by biblical studies. In particular, I note Rudolf Bultmann, *The History of the Synoptic Tradition*, trans. John Marsh (New York: Harper & Row, 1963); Klaus Koch, *The Growth of the Biblical Tradition: The Form-Critical Method* (New York: Scribner, 1969); Gerhard von Rad, *Old Testament Theology*, 2 vols., *Volume 1: The Theology of Israel's Historical Traditions* (New York: Harper & Row, 1962); and *Volume 2: The Theology of Israel's Prophetic Traditions* (New York: Harper & Row, 1965). Edward Shils's *Tradition* (Chicago: University of Chicago, 1981) offers a superb amplification from a sociologist's viewpoint.

For a thorough review of the literature on revelation, see Avery Dulles, *Models of Revelation* (Garden City, NY: Doubleday, 1983). On the topic of faith, see another work by Dulles, "The Meaning of Faith Considered in Relationship to Justice," in John Haughey, ed., *The Faith That Does Justice* (New York: Paulist, 1977), 10–46. Also: Edward Schillebeeckx, *The Understanding of Faith: Interpretation and Criticism* (New York: Seabury, 1974); Lucy Bregman, *Through the Landscape of Faith: Christian Life Maps* (Philadelphia: Westminster, 1986); and Richard R. Niebuhr, *Experiential Religion* (New York: Harper & Row, 1972).

Useful in understanding Catholicism are Avery Dulles, *The Catholicity of the Church* (Oxford: Clarendon, 1985); Stephen Happel and David Tracy, *A Catholic Vision* (Philadelphia: Fortress, 1984); Edward Braxton, *The Wisdom Community* (New York: Paulist, 1980); and Mary Jo Weaver, "'Overcoming the Divisiveness of Babel': The Languages of Catholicity," *Horizons* 14 (1987):328–42. For fuller discussion on the magisterium, see Francis A. Sullivan, *Magisterium: Teaching Office in the Catholic Church* (New York: Paulist, 1983); see also his article s.v. "Magisterium" in Joseph A. Komonchak, Mary Collins, and Dermot A. Lane, eds., *The New Dictionary of Theology* (Wilmington, DE: 1987): 617–23; Avery Dulles, *A Church To Believe In: Discipleship and the Dynamics of Freedom* (New York: Crossroad, 1982), esp. 103–32 and 149–69; and an issue of *Chicago Studies* 17 (1978):149–307, which is entirely devoted to the topic. See also William M. Thompson, "Authority and Magisterium in Recent Catholic Thought," *Chicago Studies* 16 (1977):278–98.

A valuable historical perspective on theology is given by Edward Farley, *Theologia: The Fragmentation and Unity of Theological Education* (Philadelphia: Fortress, 1983). In "The Role of Theology in Religious Education," *Horizons* 11 (1984):61–85, I develop in detail my thinking about the place of theology. I also deal with the relation of theology to religious studies.

For perspectives on religious traditions, see Edith Turner and Victor Turner, *Image and Pilgrimage in Christian Culture: Anthropological Perspectives* (New York: Columbia University Press, 1978); Peter Brown, *The Cult of the Saints* (Chicago: University of Chicago Press, 1981); and David N. Power, *Unsearchable Riches: The Symbolic Nature of Liturgy* (New York: Pueblo, 1984).

Helpful in developing the implications of Bernard Lonergan's understanding of conversion is Tad Dunne, *Lonergan and Spirituality: Towards a Spiritual Integration* (Chicago: Loyola University Press, 1985).

On the relation between public and religious education, see Theodore R. Sizer, ed., *Religion and Public Education* (Boston: Houghton Mifflin, 1967); and David E. Engle, ed., *Religion in Public Education* (New York: Paulist, 1974). Fascinating is the volume by James Turner Johnson, ed., *The Bible in American Law, Politics, and Political Rhetoric* (Philadelphia: Fortress; Chico, CA: Scholars Press, 1985).

My thinking on "making accessible" first appeared in my essay, "Access to Traditions and Transformation," in Padraic O'Hare, ed., *Tradition and Transformation in Religious Education* (Birmingham, AL: Religious Education Press, 1979), 9–34. I have reviewed the literature in my "Teaching: The Heart of Religious Education," *Religious Education* 79 (1984):252–72.

Marsha Weil and Bruce Joyce, *Information Processing Models of Teaching; Social Models of Teaching;* and with Bridget Kluwin, *Personal Models of Teaching* (Englewood Cliffs, NJ: Prentice-Hall, 1978) offer the most thorough presentation of the praxis of teaching. The authors work from the premise that professional competence is developed by utilizing a repertoire of approaches (the models). Each model is presented in four components: description, demonstration transcript, planning, and adaptation. The language is, at times, somewhat marred by jargon, but this does not detract from the superb analytical work of Weil et al.

Margo Culley and Catherine Portuges, *Gendered Subjects: The Dynamics of Feminist Teaching* (Boston: Routledge and Kegan Paul, 1985) is a fascinating collection of essays using feminist theory as a lens through which to assess classroom practice. The authors deal as well with the effects of ethnic and racial differences. Less sophisticated but with potential is the journal *Feminist Teacher* (442 Ballantine Hall, Indiana University, Bloomington, IN 47405).

Michael J. Dunkin and Bruce J. Biddle, *The Study of Teaching* (New York: Holt, Rinehart and Winston, 1974) reviews hundreds of research studies of teaching and a discussion of their methods and issues. Readers eager to gain prescriptive knowledge will be disappointed; perhaps the chief value of this compendium lies in its "debunking" quality. In a similar vein, James Michael Lee, *The Flow of Religious Instruction* (Birmingham, AL: Religious Education Press, 1973) summarizes learning and teaching theory and lays out some key findings about learning. Though I think he overvalues the research, his chapters are well worth reading. Likewise is his *The Content of Religious Instruction* (Birmingham, AL: Religious Education Press, 1985), a compendium of information with many valuable references and leads on a variety of topics crucial for teachers.

Elliot W. Eisner, *The Educational Imagination: On the Design and Evaluation of School Programs* (New York: Macmillan, 1979 [2d ed., 1985]) draws upon the author's interest in the visual arts to develop the metaphor of educational connoisseurship and to undergird a complementary notion: educational criticism.

Related are Maxine Green, *Teacher as Stranger: Educational Philosophy for the Modern Age* (Belmont, CA: Wadsworth, 1973) and V.A. Howard, *Artistry: The Work of Artists* (Indianapolis, IN: Hackett, 1982). See also Linda Verlee Williams, *Teaching for the Two-Sided Mind: A Guide to Right Brain/Left Brain Education* (Englewood Cliffs, NJ: Prentice-Hall, 1983).

Other relevant studies of teaching include Paul D. Eggen, Donald P. Kauchak, and Robert J. Harder, *Strategies for Teachers: Information Processing Models in the Classroom* (Englewood Cliffs, NJ: Prentice-Hall, 1979); Stanford C. Ericksen, *The Essence of Good Teaching: Helping Students Learn and Remember What They Learn* (San Francisco: Jossey-Bass, 1984); Nancy T. Foltz, ed., *Handbook of Adult Religious Education* (Birmingham, AL: Religious Education Press, 1986). Paulo Freire, *Pedagogy of the Oppressed* (New York: Herder and Herder, 1970) is essential reading. Those who work in college and university settings will also benefit from Kenneth E. Eble, *The Craft of Teaching* (San Francisco: Jossey-Bass, 1976).

Compare Thomas Green, *The Activities of Teaching* (New York: McGraw-Hill, 1971), 49-55, on indoctrination with Barry Chazan, "'Indoctrination' and Religious Education," *Religious Education* 58 (1972):243–52.

Hope Jensen Leichter, in "The Concept of Educative Style," *Teachers College Record* 75 (1973):239–50, writes a fascinating and suggestive essay on the human differences that affect and shape the styles of learning. Ira Shor, *Critical Teaching and Everyday Life* (Boston: South End Press, 1980) proposes a "radical pedagogy" for open-admissions students in a university or community college setting that brings together (albeit a bit glibly) Dewey and Freire.

William Ayers writes a gem of an essay on teaching as midwifery, "Thinking About Teachers and the Curriculum," *Harvard Educational Review* 56 (1986):49–51.

General Index